THE STUDENT ACTOR PREPARES

THE STUDENT ACTOR PREPARES
ACTING FOR LIFE

GAI JONES

intellect Bristol, UK / Chicago, USA

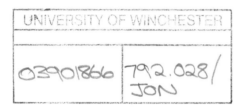
First published in the UK in 2014 by
Intellect, The Mill, Parnall Road, Fishponds, Bristol, BS16 3JG, UK

First published in the USA in 2014 by
Intellect, The University of Chicago Press, 1427 E. 60th Street,
Chicago, IL 60637, USA

Series: Theatre in Education
Series ISSN: 2049-3878
Cover designer: Holly Rose
Copy-editor: MPS Technologies
Production manager: Jessica Mitchell
Typesetting: Holly Rose

Print ISBN: 9781783201907
ePDF ISBN: 9781783202591
ePUB ISBN: 9781783202607

Printed and bound by Hobbs, UK

CONTENTS

PREFACE TO TEACHERS: USING THIS BOOK TO INSTRUCT STUDENTS

Education is not preparation for life. Education is life itself.
John Dewey, educational reformer

This Preface is dedicated to teachers who will guide students through *The Student Actor Prepares: Acting for Life.* As a Theatre education professional, I have one of the best jobs, working with creative, emotional, passionate, talented students and other Theatre experts every day. I trust the transformative empowerment of Theatre education and acting in particular. Studying acting engages students in learning and prepares them with skills for work success. Sometimes being in Theatre is the reason students come to school and stay in school. Often, involvement in Theatre education transforms students' lives, and sometimes it saves their lives.

I admire Theatre educators, who inspire students through the art form of Theatre. I believe in sequential standards-based Theatre education taught by credentialed Theatre teachers. I believe in working with Theatre arts providers who help the classroom Theatre educator, by supplementing existing Theatre programs. I believe in awards and scholarship recognitions for Theatre educators and students. I believe in teaching students about careers, twenty-first century life skills, and national standards. I believe in a network of Theatre educators, professionals, and students who share ideas for creativity, critical thinking, collaboration, and communication in Theatre education.

A teacher is an actor. To desire to teach, a person must have been enthralled by an idea or an experience of some kind himself and must desire that others have the opportunity to know about and be inspired by that same event or material in some way. To be able to transfer ideas, he must develop, in addition to the knowledge he accumulates, the ability to communicate that knowledge. This ability to communicate is an art or skill also known as teaching. . .
A *Teacher Is Many Things,* Earl v. Pullias and James D. Young

The Student Actor Prepares: Acting for Life is designed for use in middle school and high school Theatre classes with your guidance as the Theatre educator. It can be used by some high school, college and university Theatre students as an instruction book for individual learning. Either way, its content can be enhanced with your guidance. The book's tools and tips can be implemented for practical application as well as creative input. As a teacher, you can help each student learn how to reflect on his/her ideas and communicate the creative process. The involved student will construct meanings and will value their creative thinking. Your students will benefit from your inclusion in their learning processes. Your inviting student opinions, thoughts, and feelings encourages participation, stimulates discussion, and maintains a positive atmosphere for continuous creative and reflective work. The book is written for sequential learning with building blocks toward your students' life-long journeys. Each chapter or unit is a complete study in itself. Whether you as the educator are teaching with electronic media or old-school paper and pencil, the book's content is formatted for the student's success by posing achievable, continuing goals and objectives.

The acting practice is creative and reflective in nature so it seems natural for this book to introduce imaginative and thoughtful review methods. This book provides ongoing inquiries for the student's input. Creative inquiry asks for imaginative investigation and response. Reflective inquiry asks that the student think about the content of the book or remember something from his/her life to answer the questions. Sometimes the questions require that the student refer back to previous chapters to ascertain the answers. Referring to the text is an integral part of an actor's work. This book provides opportunities for the emerging actor's original and insightful inquiry.

The material is constructed for continuous study and the revisiting of topics, so as the student's learning matures, he/she can give additional insights. I hope that you will devise more questions to stimulate student thinking, and you will take time to allow the student to field any questions for further study. This book is an opportunity for the student's ongoing exploration.

The information presented in this book supports many of the anchor standards and principles of the present educational trends and movements. The standards define what students should understand and be able to do by the end of each acting unit. Big ideas with Enduring Understandings, Essential Questions, Twenty-first Century Skills of creative and critical thinking, along with assessments of the students' work are inherent in this book, which is meant to be a projects-based experience. At the beginning of each learning unit, intellectual stimulations direct the students to imagine, investigate, construct, and reflect with clear goals and objectives. Each instructional unit identifies the enduring understandings and essential questions.

The Enduring Understandings are defined as statements that summarize important ideas central to the subject matter and have lasting value. They synthesize what the actor should understand. The Essential Questions are queries that help the student figure out what he/she knows about the subject. The question may have multiple answers. Some sample questions prompted by this book might include: What happens when I (the student actor) use my imagination and engage in a creative, brainstorming exploration? Why do my choices change when I am creating? What do I learn by studying acting that might help me in my life?

The National Standards and Core Content Objectives include improvisation, particularly in regard to scriptwriting that is based on personal experiences, developing sustaining characters, interpreting dramatic texts, determining the various methods of physical relaxation and exploring acting techniques. Some of the Core Content Objectives involve the student actors making informed choices about character development, creating good storytelling through the use of voice and facial expressions, analyzing dialogue, locating motivating character desires, and assessing the student's rehearsal and performance.

By being in Theatre activities, your students are succeeding in mastering objectives. Because they take part in Theatre activities, they are able to do the following tasks based on Bloom's *Taxonomy of Educational Objectives*. The actors involved in Theatre activities have experience in the following categories:

Knowledge-Students can:

~ Observe bodily gestures of a variety of people to recall for performance.
~ Repeat speeches, lines, movements during the rehearsal process.
~ Label tools, genres of plays, etc.
~ Gather all the things needed to begin a scene or rehearsal.
~ List items needed for a scene or performance.
~ Record blocking and staging.
~ Match terms to the items.

- ~ Memorize lines for a role.
- ~ Recall lines, blocking, and stage business.
- ~ Recount stories, improvisations.
- ~ Define stage terms and acting vocabulary.

Comprehension-Students can:

- ~ Recognize elements of dramatic analysis.
- ~ Locate areas of the stage.
- ~ Identify stage terminology.
- ~ Restate the playwright's ideas.
- ~ Paraphrase language to gain a contemporary understanding.
- ~ Show an audience what a character is thinking through acting the part.
- ~ Describe the mood of the scene, and the setting that the student imagines.
- ~ Report on viewing and reading plays.
- ~ Express understanding of a playwright's meaning by acting.
- ~ Explain what a character is thinking.
- ~ Understand blocking, lines, and stage business.
- ~ Cite research about the time period for a historical reference.
- ~ Document a playwright's intent and the theme of a play.
- ~ Summarize the character's emotional journey.

Application-Students can:

- ~ Select appropriate movement, vocal tone, expression.
- ~ Use props.
- ~ Manipulate scenes, songs, and dances.
- ~ Sequence the events that will lead to a successful production.
- ~ Organize peers into task situations for rehearsals.
- ~ Imitate people they observe.
- ~ Show emotions by use of body and voice.
- ~ Apply theories of acting and directing.
- ~ Dramatize characters in a play.
- ~ Illustrate emotions through movement.
- ~ Work collaboratively by communicating.
- ~ Imagine how acting skills apply to various careers.

Analysis-Students can:
~   Examine many selections of dramatic literature to create a
    monologue for performance.
~   Classify plays into genres.
~   Map the structure of the play in preparation to creating a character
    or directing.
~   Relate Theatre material from historical periods to contemporary
    audiences.
~   Characterize people in a play.
~   Question the actions and language of characters.
~   Research specific time periods, genres, cultures, and people.
~   Interpret a playwright's intentions.
~   Defend an artistic decision.
~   Discuss other points of view in artistic collaborations.
~   Infer meaning through language.
~   Scrutinize the overall effectiveness of a performance.
~   Question a piece of dramatic literature to determine themes.

Synthesis-Students can:

~   Propose ideas to peers and director regarding plays and the
    Theatre business.
~   Plan rehearsal schedules, promotional deadlines, designs, and
    direction.
~   Compose words of a play, choreography of a dance, sequence of
    presentations.
~   Formulate plans for character creation.
~   Design technical elements for a character, such as costume,
    makeup, props.
~   Emulate people whom the students know and/or
    celebrities in improvisation.
~   Imagine a special effect or a character's walk.
~   Create original monologues and scenes.
~   Invent a character for an original play.

Evaluation-Students can:

~   Judge the timing of a line, the value of each selection of dramatic
    literature, the work of others on stage.

Good teaching is one-fourth preparation and three-fourths pure Theatre.

Gail Godwin, author

- Decide the pros and cons of the artistic merit of various acting approaches.
- Prioritize personal time and Theatre projects.
- Cast a play and prioritize things that need to be done in rehearsals.
- Decide the artistic merit of various play scripts.
- Evaluate a character's state of mind in a scene or play.
- Assess a performance with the intent to improve.
- Validate a point of view about character choices.
- Justify artistic choices.
- Convince an audience out of their reality and into the world of the play.
- Persuade business people to help with productions.
- Assess him/herself and others working with a scoring rubric.
- Value self-discipline, cooperation, and the joy of working toward a common goal.

I hope that your Theatre students become engaged, involved, committed, passionate, and enthusiastic about becoming emerging actors. Your guidance will encourage your students to become active and responsible participants in this course of study. The students are asked to add ideas from their memories and imagination. They will learn to value their reflections and creations. The insightful learners engage in ongoing inquiry, make adjustments, assume responsibility for their learning, and take action to enhance knowledge with new understandings.

My license plate holder says, "Every Day You Deserve A Round Of Applause." I applaud you for what you do each day to teach evolving actors.

PREFACE TO STUDENT ACTORS: USING THIS BOOK

Theatre has no categories; it is about life. This is the only starting point, and there is nothing else truly fundamental. Theatre is life.

Peter Brook, director

Dear Student of Acting

Welcome to the world of Acting. I am a longtime Theatre educator who loves to introduce the acting process to students of all ages. Creating, studying, learning, innovating, making bold choices, committing, experiencing thoughts and feelings, engaging in reflective and creative inquiries, these are the exhilarating adventures that lie ahead of you in this book. I value your answers to questions that I pose in this book. Creative inquiries request that you use your imagination to answer questions. There are multiple correct answers to the creative inquiries. The reflective inquiries ask that you remember something that was stated in the text or from your experience.

Below I present my introduction as an example of a Reflective Inquiry. You as the student are creating your journey by studying this book.

REFLECTIVE INQUIRY **RI**   DATE: TODAY

Recall how you became a Theatre Sage? Make some notes on this in the space below.

I knew in the fifth grade that I wanted to teach and incorporate acting in my life, so I set out to find a career that allowed me to use acting skills every day.

CREATIVE INQUIRY **CI**   DATE: TODAY

Imagine your actor's journey as a story. Make some notes on this in the space below.

I share my journey in regard to Theatre from a child in Oklahoma to the present day. This story is entitled The Journey of a Theatre Sage.

The Journey of a Theatre Sage

I began my performance journey in the small town of Chickasha, Oklahoma. My first performance was in the kindergarten band. There were fifteen of us, dressed in red capes and little red hats. I played the sticks. My best friend played the triangle. There was only one triangle player. I knew then that my destiny was to become the one rather than one of fifteen.

My mother, a woman ahead of her time, arranged for me to take elocution lessons. Elocution is the study of formal speaking, pronunciation, grammar, and style. I stood on Mrs. A.B. Morgan's Persian rug and recited monologues and poems that she had assigned and that I had practiced and memorized. Mrs. Morgan coached me on how to analyze a script and create a character. Little did I know that later I would make a living teaching acting.

In the fifth grade, I was a gangly, tall girl from a working-class family. I typed scripts in exchange for the acting lessons. Being involved in Theatre helped me develop a sense of self-confidence and a feeling of pride for a talent that I possessed.

In high school, we had a drama teacher who announced that she knew very little about Theatre. I remember thinking at that time I think I could teach Theatre to youth. I was cast as Mrs. Jones in the junior class play. Then as a senior I was cast as the Prompter. I knew even at that age the role of Prompter had very little to do during a performance. I sat behind a piece of scenery following the script during the performance. I knew it was not correct for me to prompt any actors during their time on stage. I vowed then and there to become a Theatre teacher and never cast anyone as the Prompter. And I never did.

To those students who will think about attending college, below is my college acting experience.

I attended a small liberal arts college for women. I chose to seek a specialized degree by earning a BA in Speech and Drama. The advantage of a small college with all women was that we did everything in the Theatre ourselves: built sets, painted, hung and focused lights, and played the male roles in Shakespeare and in some contemporary plays. I was the old man character in *As You Like It* and a Lost Boy *in Peter Pan*. When we did plays with male characters that needed to be played by men, we recruited officers from a nearby Army base.

Shortly before graduation, I wrote to Cunard Ocean Lines, asking how to become a Cruise Director. I was influenced by the television show *The Gale Storm Show*, in which the female title character played a cruise director. Remember, I lived in Oklahoma, which has no ocean. Cunard Lines gave great career advice. Move closer to the ocean. I did. I moved to California to teach Speech, Drama, and English to middle school students.

In California, I auditioned for a community Theatre production of *Blithe Spirit*. At the theater, I noticed a distinguished gentleman who was cast in the main role. I was cast in a small role, Mrs. Bradman. When rehearsals began, I noticed the distinguished gentleman had switched to the role of Dr. Bradman. We married. In addition to teaching, we both worked as actors and studied Theatre.

I was the first woman to receive an MA in Theatre at CSU Fullerton. I auditioned for NBC television network, during the time they had contract players. These actors were signed with the network to play roles on their soap operas. I turned down the contract because I realized that what I really wanted to do was to teach youth about Theatre and acting.

Remember that I tell you these adventures to let you know that you as a lover of acting can have a life that allows you to embrace Theatre.

For thirty-four years I was fortunate to teach Theatre at El Dorado High School, in Placentia, CA. The program grew from one class of Drama to five classes; from one production a year to five productions each year. My students were members of the International Thespian Society (ITS); participated in five Theatre festivals each year; formed Drama clubs, Mime clubs, and a Thespian honor society. We won awards locally and nationally for having an outstanding Theatre program.

My former students are film, Theatre, television actors, voice-over artists, cabaret singers, opera stars, composers, Theatre educators, lawyers, judges, vice presidents of television companies, executives, owners of Theatre companies, Disney technical designers and performers. One is a special effects film creator; another is a children's book author; and there is an events planner, an Olympic Gold Medal winner and news broadcaster, and a Ringling Brothers Clown, among other occupations. I hear from them frequently about how they continue to use in their daily work the acting skills they learned in high school.

Here are some of the ideas that my former students shared about things they learned by being in high school Theatre. All of these concepts are addressed in this book.

- See as many plays as you can. By volunteering to usher, you will see the plays free.
- You are enrolled in a subject that has national standards.
- Even if you don't go into Theatre, you will become appreciative, discriminating Theatre goers.
- It is an honor to be part of the International Thespian Society.
- Apply for every Theatre scholarship for further study.
- Learn how to say thank you when someone compliments your performance. Do not tell them the mistakes that were made.
- Take a break from acting every once in a while, if you have performed in numerous shows in a row.
- Someone you know will become famous someday.
- Be nice to everyone. There may be some unique people in Theatre. As long as you feel safe with the person, learn something about Theatre.
- There are no unimportant roles. Each person has equal billing as supporting role to the ensemble.
- In comedy, tickle the audience with your words.
- Listen, act, and then react. That is also good advice for "off the stage" life.
- In comedy, be crisp, loud, big, and bright when you deliver your lines.
- Yawn to relax.
- Think of a secret before you face the audience. That will put a twinkle in your eye.
- Conquering stage fright means the ability to make the butterflies fly in an organized formation.
- Trust the playwright's words.
- The word rehearsal has "rehear" in it.
- Rehearse, rehearse, rehearse. Rehearse one hour for each running minute after the script is memorized.
- Never compare yourself with others. You are talented.
- If you don't audition, you will not get cast.
- The size of the role does not determine the talent of the actor.
- If you are going to be absent, notify someone in charge.
- Never use Theatre as an excuse for incompetence.
- Play the moment, not the scene.

PREFACE TO STUDENT ACTORS

~ Don't be afraid of silences in your performance. Let the emotional silences affect the audience.
~ Aim for the moon. If you miss, you will be with the stars.

I served as board member and officer of various educational Theatre associations, and received numerous awards. Upon my retirement from full-time work, the black box theater at El Dorado High School, Placentia, CA, was named The Gai Jones Theatre.

Since then, I have written three books on the topic of Theatre education. I began a commercial acting career and have appeared in some national commercials; I currently direct at three local Theatres, and I teach at a university and at a community college. I conduct local and nation-wide workshops, teach at a Theatre camp in the woods each summer, direct summer Theater workshops for young emerging actors, and perform with SAG/AFTRA. I created California Youth in Theatre, a state-wide advocacy action effort at the California state capital that also honors award-winning Theatre students. I continue to serve in various local, state and international Theatre associations and sponsor several scholarship programs to help high school youth to go on to study Theatre at the college level. I created Sage to Stage, an acting workshop for senior citizens.

The story above is an illustration of what you can do and be true to your love of acting.

By studying this book and taking part in the creative and reflective inquiries, you will build your own successful acting journey. Your actor's training, like mine, is a life-long process. Enjoy the process. Enjoy creating, viewing, and participating. The more engaged you are in the process, the more complete your imaginative journey. If you enjoy the study of acting, then you will celebrate your performances.

It is a pleasure to be active and involved in acting activities.

We learn...10% of what we READ; 20% of what we HEAR; 30% of what we SEE; 50% of what we SEE and HEAR; 70% of what we SAY; 90% of what we SAY and DO.

Eldon Ekwall, Diagnosis and Remediation of the Disabled Reader

May you embark on a lifetime journey full of adventures by taking part in the experiences of *The Student Actor Prepares: Acting for Life.*

P.S. This letter is continued throughout the book until the Epilogue at the end of this book.

XXV

PROLOGUE

The prologue is an opening to a story or play that establishes the setting and gives background details. This prologue sets the stage for this book of acting experiences by giving you a brief history of acting, vocabulary terms, traditions, and guidelines on how to read a play. You will use the process of creative and reflective inquiry experiences. Your creative inquiry invites you to give answers to questions that create new knowledge using your creativity. Your reflective inquiry asks you to recall what you have learned. In this practical book you are presented with objectives that can be accomplished by committing to the process of reading and answering questions based on the material presented.

You need three things in the Theatre—the play, the actors, and the audience, and each must give something.

Kenneth Haigh, actor

In this book, you are asked to give something: *your insightful, creative and reflective responses.*

In order to become comfortable with the creative and reflective inquiry process you must practice thinking about yourself. Making time for your thoughts is an obligation for the acting process. Exploring your own thoughts and feelings and knowing yourself are very important to your acting study. If you know yourself and can communicate your thoughts and feelings, you can begin to understand characters in a play. Using this book as a reflective booklet is one vehicle for setting aside time for reflection. Ongoing reflective inquiry involves your devising answers, making notes, and revisiting the text with new insights. Reflective thinking includes being constructive with what you create, making adjustments, rehearsing again and again, and then making more adjustments. Assessing your work will help you develop tools for you to use throughout your life-long journey. The experiences in this book are opportunities for exploration.

Engaging your thoughts and feelings in the inquiry process develops good habits for your acting study. As an emerging actor, you want to be curious. You need to question and become confident in changing your ideas to arrive at a new knowledge or way of thinking. You develop tools to uncover creative thoughts. This process asks you to reframe your thoughts from a different angle and discover new things. This book instructs you to re-read your entries to search for any emerging ideas, and make notes for further study.

There are numerous definitions of acting; some definitions suggest that acting is exclusive to Theatre and films. Other definitions include work in television. In this book, the actor is one who portrays a character who speaks lines from the written text of a play in a Theatre. Theatre or theater is an art that uses live actors to present a play in front of a live audience, usually on a stage.

Whether you are a youth or a sage, whether you are new to the stage or a seasoned veteran, there are basics of acting that you need to study. In your future, you may become a professional actor, a recreational actor, a worker who employs acting techniques, or even an appreciative audience of the acting profession. Knowing acting fundamentals will enhance your work and enrich your enjoyment of the acting process whether participating in or viewing a performance.

There is an ongoing discussion as to which spelling indicates the art form or dramatic production and which identifies the building, the place where an actor performs. The difference between Theater and Theatre is usually considered one of a spelling preference. Theatre with a "re" reflects the British spelling of the art form. American English speakers usually use Theater with an "er." Nowadays the terms are used interchangeably. Sometimes people use the "re" spelling to indicate the art form, and "er" to name the building in which the play is performed.

For your study with this book, "Theatre" indicates a performing art that employs live actors to perform before a live audience. The word Theatre also refers to the study that includes elements of acting, directing, and technical designs. Theater indicates the building.

The word Theatre comes from the Greeks. It means the seeing place. It is the place people come to see the truth about life and the social situation.

Stella Adler, acting teacher

Another question arises for the emerging actor. Do actors study Drama or Theatre? In this book, drama is considered one of the genres of Theatre. Drama is a type of literature that is performed by actors on a stage.

You are an actor, or you are on your way to becoming an actor. In this book, the term actor refers to both males and females. Do you think of yourself as an artist? Or do you consider acting a craft? A good way to distinguish between what is the art of acting and what is the craft of acting is to think that a craft is something that almost everyone can do. You learn the techniques of the acting craft. The art typically refers to the quality that some people possess. You can think of the art of acting as what you bring to the craft by adding something that is uniquely yours. All conscientious actors learn the techniques of the craft. In this book you will learn the craft needed to master the skill. With a sound foundation, you can develop your artistry.

Acting is behaving truthfully under imaginary circumstances.

Sanford Meisner, acting teacher

Your acting requires a positive attitude, creativity, relaxation, emotions, movement, mime, vocal expression, improvisation, script analysis, monologue skills, audition skills, and thinking about your future. You will train in schools and specialized programs to perfect these skills. You will also study to develop singing and dancing skills, audition techniques, and scene work for the Theatre. The tools needed for the art of acting include: a positive attitude, which is a way of thinking or feeling, typically reflected in your behavior; creativity, which can be defined as the ability to transcend traditional ideas with originality and imagination; critical thinking, the process of activity and conceptualizing, applying, analyzing, and evaluating information to reach an answer; and communication, the interchange of thoughts or information.

Creative (CI) and Reflective Inquiry (RI) Journey

This experiential book leads you through approaches to creating truthful, genuine, and bold characters. This book requires explorations of emotional memory and creative choices. The process is for you as a serious actor who wants to devote time and energies to the creative passion of acting. You must have discipline to study individually, reflect, and then to study and reflect some more. Acting asks you to enter imaginatively into the exploration of motivations, aspirations, and frustrations; you are requested to respond to questions about the process. This book advocates that you as a student actor become a vibrant example of the creative process. You are to study, reflect, assess, and continue your progression.The Creative Inquiry (CI) and Reflective Inquiry (RI) model wants you to recall information to answer questions. The Reflective Inquiry (RI) requires you to gather memories from your

past. The Creative Inquiry (CI) asks you to give imaginative answers to a question or prompt. The inquiry is identified by (CI) or (RI). A date is asked for, so that when you revisit the inquiries, you can write a different date with new information. It is recommended that when you are doing a (CI) or (RI) you read all of the directions before answering any questions. Assignments are also included. You are encouraged to revisit the Assignments often to try them another time and to celebrate your progress in your study of acting.

REFLECTIVE INQUIRY **RI**   DATE:

Recall three specific facts that you have learned from the preface and prologue

1.

2.

3.

Here is one of many quotations about life, acting, and/or Theatre, which are incorporated in this book. Think about each quote presented in the book and ask yourself, "What does this quote mean?" and "How can I apply the quote's lesson to my life and my study of acting?"

> *One of the most important things I've learned about acting is that you can't separate how you live your life and how you practice your art.*
>   Larry Moss, acting coach

Quotes are periodically included for your reflective and creative thinking. Sometimes a quote has a (CI) or (RI) following it. If this is the case then answer the question that follows the quote. Sometimes a quote will not have a (CI) or (RI) following it. In this case I invite you to read each quote and think about what it means to you and how you can apply it to your study.

~~~~~~
REFLECTIVE INQUIRY   **RI**   DATE:
~~~~~~

Revisit the quote by Larry Moss. What does this quote mean?

~~~~~~
CREATIVE INQUIRY   **CI**   DATE:
~~~~~~

Imagine how you might apply the quote's meaning to your life?

How do you think the quote relates to the study of acting?

My hope is that you as a student of acting, no matter what age will find
the gratification of thinking reflectively and creatively.

Brief History of Theatre Acting

You are studying a historical art form: Acting. As a student of acting, it is beneficial to study a brief history of Theatre Acting. By looking at the brief history of acting in Theatre, you will understand the evolution of acting from the first known documentation to today. There are years of acting history, so knowing the rich past of the art will enhance your knowledge. You will also get to know the great things that happened in ancient times, and the acting styles from which you can draw techniques. In the future chapters of this book, you will study a more in-depth history of acting styles as they relate to script work.

The brief history of your chosen art form begins with the first actor, primitive man, who reenacted the story of the day's hunt for his tribal members at his tribal campfire. The art is also documented in the storytelling traditions of the West African oral historian, known as a griot.

Thespis
Thespis, an ancient Greek poet was the originator of the individual role of the actor. He stepped out of the chorus to speak lines.

Roman times
In the Roman period, actors were usually slaves, and during the Christian times in Rome, acting almost disappeared. In the Middle Ages, the actor performed for church goers.

Commedia dell 'Arte
In Italy in the sixteenth century the actors used masks and improvised performances based on scenarios, known as Commedia dell 'Arte (comedy of craft), whose actors improvised entertainments with masks and well-known characters.

Shakespeare
Shakespeare wrote for actors who performed for royalty and groundlings, the audience members who stood to see the play because they could not afford to pay for seats.

Eighteenth century actors
Throughout the eighteenth and nineteenth centuries, acting was melodramatic with stock gestures and dramatic poses.

Twentieth century

During the twentieth century the more natural types of acting began to appear, and in today's Theatre the realistic portrayal of emotion is honored. In contemporary Theatre, the acting process is eclectic and pulls from various varieties of acting.

Theatre Vocabulary for the Acting Student: Top One Hundred and Sixty Essential Words

As an actor, you will hear words that you might or might not know. The next few pages contain acting terminology. Working with the words will help you to be prepared to talk the actors' talk. The Theatre Vocabulary for the Acting Student is an important communication tool.

Like any other professional, you need to develop a vocabulary to be used in your field. Terms used in the world of acting include much of the vocabulary for the study of Theatre, such as the word actor, which can indicate either a male or a female who acts. For this book, I have selected approximately one hundred and sixty essential words that will empower you in your study and when you talk the "lingo" with other performers.

Throughout your study of acting, it is important to know how to spell, define, and use each vocabulary word and phrase.

ASSIGNMENT Theatre Vocabulary for the Acting Student   DATE:

Read the following Theatre vocabulary words and phrases for the acting student. Mark each word that you recognize, have heard, or whose definition you know. If the term is marked with the symbol *, it indicates that there will be exercises using that term in other chapters of this book. You need to learn the definition of the indicated words, so you can work with their meanings in other chapters.

Following some of the essential vocabulary words, there are also Creative Inquiry sections, Reflective Inquiry sections and another assignment to complete. These have all been designed to help you remember the meanings of these words.

Academic Theatre or educational Theatre—Theatre that is affiliated with a school. It has educational goals.

*****Act**—A major division of a play.

*****Acting process**—The manner in which the actor studies a character and develops thoughts, emotions, and traits for the performing of the character. Also referred to as AEA.

*****Actor**—One who portrays a role. The term actor refers to a male or female.

Actors' equity—The professional stage actors' association and union in the United States.

*****Adjustments**—The suggestions that a director and actor make in rehearsals.

*****Ad lib**—The improvised dialogue, stage business that is not written in the script, usually to cover a mistake.

*****Agent; manager**—The professional person who books an actor's auditions and jobs. A manager is a professional person who manages an actor's professional career.

American Theatre Wing—The organization that gives out the Tony Awards, known as the Antoinette Perry Awards. It awards the best of New York Theatre each year. Perry was a well-known actor and director in the 1930s and 1940s.

Annie Oakley—A complementary ticket to a performance. Named after the sharpshooter who shot a hole through tickets performances, and who inspired the practice of punching holes in tickets.

*****Antagonist**—The character who opposes the main character, who is called the protagonist. The opposition is the conflict.

*****Arc**—The journey that the character takes from the beginning of the play to the end. In a well-written play the character's arc changes from the beginning to the end.

Aristotle's six elements of drama—Character, Diction, Music, Plot, Spectacle, and Thought were defined by Aristotle in Greek times. The terms describe parts of all types of plays.

Artistic truth—The believed reality on the stage.

*****As if**—An acting process that includes playing the part "as if" you were in the situation. It is known as the magic as if or what if.

Audience—The spectators who watch a performance.

Auditorium—The part of the Theatre that holds the audience; it is called the house.

*****Audition**—The process that includes trying out for a role in a play.

*****Backstage**—The area behind the set which is not seen by the audience.

Black box—A small Theatre without a proscenium arch, usually painted black.

Blackout—A lighting cue that darkens the stage for a moment, usually at the end of a scene or act.

***Blocking**—The stage movement by actors during the play. Some of the staging is indicated by the script; some added by the director. Some directors use the term staging instead of blocking.

Boards—The stage, also named acting area. To "tread the boards" is to be on the stage.

Body positions on stage—The eight positions that an actor may use: full front—facing the audience; 1/4 right or left—turning 1/4 away from audience; profile right or profile left—turning sideways to the audience; 3/4 right; 3/4 left; and full back—back is facing the audience.

***Break a leg**—A traditional greeting to wish an actor good luck. It comes out of the superstition that if someone says "good luck," the perverse forces will send the opposite of good luck.

***Broadway**—A street in Manhattan, which is called the Theatre district. It can also indicate that an actor has achieved success.

***Business**—The term that indicates stage action. Some actions are indicated by the playwright; some are given by the director.

***Call back**—The second part in the audition sequence in which the actor returns for further readings and interviews.

***Cast**—The list of characters and actors who are portraying characters in a play.

Casting—The process of auditions in which the director selects the actors. The person responsible for selecting the cast is the Casting Director.

Center stage—The space at the center of the acting area.

***Character/role**—A person in a play.

Choreography—The dance steps designed for a musical.

Chorus—In Greek drama, the group who sang, danced, and narrated between episodes of a play. The term now is used to designate the performers who sing and dance together.

Classical drama—The drama of past eras written before the twentieth century.

***Climax**—The climax marks a change for the better or worse for the main character's life. If the story is a comedy the plot will move toward a happy ending. If the story is a drama the plot will move toward a serious ending.

***Comedy**—A play with a lighthearted story and amusing dialogue. The play ends happily.

Comp—An abbreviation for the complementary (free) ticket to a show.

Community Theatre—Amateur productions by people in a local area.

Company—A group of actors and technical workers who present plays.

Conflict—The opposition between the antagonist and the protagonist in a play.

Copyright—The playwright's legal ownership of a play. After seventy-five years, most works are in public domain and can be performed without permission of the author.

Costume—Clothes worn by the actors in the performances.

*****Crisis**—A decisive point in the play's plot on which the outcome of the story depends.

*****Criticism**—An evaluation of a play.

*****Critique**—A critical analysis or evaluation of a theatrical work.

*****Cue**—A signal from the stage manager to an actor or member of the stage crew. It can also be a line or action that is a signal for something to happen.

Curtain—The drape that closes the stage from the audience's view.

Curtain line—The last line of the play or scene that is a signal for the curtain to close.

Curtain call—The final acknowledgement of the actors to the audience. The actors' bow.

*****Dialogue or dialog**—Lines between two or more characters.

Dinner Theatre—A performance consisting of a served meal and a performance.

Director—The person who is in charge of the artistic direction of the actors. This director supervises the actors as they rehearse and works with coordination of technical aspects.

Director's notes—The comments and adjustments the director gives to the cast and technical staff to work on for the next rehearsal and performance.

Double casting—The practice of casting two or more actors who alternate in performances of a role.

Double take—An action that directs the actor to look and look again with surprise for comic effect.

Doubling—The playing of more than one character in a play by the same actor.

*****Downstage**—The part of the stage closest to the audience.

Drama—The serious literature written in dialogue form to be performed for an audience.

Dramatic structure—The literary style in which the plays are written.

*__Dramatis personae__—Latin, meaning the characters in a play.

__Dress rehearsals__—The final rehearsals prior to opening night in which the show is run with full technical elements.

__Emotional recall__—An acting technique using some past personal experience to tap emotion in a monologue or scene.

__Empathy__—The act of the audience identifying with the characters.

__Ensemble__—The type of acting in which a cast and company works as a team to produce a dramatic production

__Entr'acte__—Musical interlude between the acts of a play.

*__Entrance__—The act of entering onstage during a performance.

__Equity waiver house__—A theater with less than one hundred seats in which an equity member with permission of the union can work without receiving minimum wage.

*__Exit__—The action of leaving the acting area.

__Focus__—The ability to direct attention of actors and audience.

__Forestage__—The apron or the space in front of the curtain line.

__Fourth wall__—The invisible wall of the set through which the audience views the play. The phrase "breaking the fourth wall" means the actor acknowledges the audience.

__Freeze__—The act of remaining motionless.

*__French scene__—A division of a play based on when a new character enters and exits.

__Front of house__—The parts of the theater that are open to the public.

*__Genre__—The main types of literary forms, principally tragedy, drama, and comedy. Under each principal form there are subdivisions, such as Greek tragedy, melodrama, and comedy of manners, among others.

*__Gesture__—Any movement of the actor with hand, arm, leg, foot or head.

*Given circumstances**—The situations the playwright has provided in the text about a character, characters, other characters, time, place, relationships, and story.

Greasepaint—A type of stage cosmetics with intensity of color and texture.

Green room—A backstage area where actors wait for their entrance cues.

Groundling—An Elizabethan term for spectators who stood to see the play.

Gypsy—A member of the chorus, so named because of the continuous existence, moving from show to show. There is a Broadway tradition of bestowing the chorus member who is known for his/her dedication, professionalism, and long career with the Gypsy Robe. The gypsy wears the robe and circles the stage three times. Cast members and the behind-the-scenes crew touch the robe for good luck.

Ham—A term to denote an actor who overacts to bring focus to himself.

Heavy, the—The villain in the play.

Hero, heroine—The protagonist in the play. These words sound like [hee row] and [hair o win].

Hot spot—An area downstage or within the main light of the theater light.

House—The seating area of a theater.

House right/left—The directions from the perspective of the audience.

House seats—The seats set aside at each performance to cover any problem in seating or for important guests.

Hubris—The Greek term for pride, which causes the downfall of the hero.

In the moment—The phrase meaning that the actor is completely involved in the character's emotions and thought processes. It is also referred to as being "in the here and now," and "play the moment."

Ingénue—The young, innocent female lead in the play.

*Leading roles**—The main characters in a play.

Legitimate Theatre—The term to indicate the straight drama.

*Lines**—The dialogue for the play.

*Lyrics**—The words in a musical Theatre song.

Makeup—the cosmetics that actors use onstage. Types of intense stage makeup include grease paint, pancake, and cream.

Matinee—A theatrical performance given in the afternoon.

*Method acting**—An approach to acting based on the system developed by Konstantin Stanislavski.

*Mime**—A type of show or actor that acts without words. Pantomime is an activity without words. Some famous mime characters are Harlequin and Bip.

Mise-en-scene—The total environment of a play.

*****Monologue**—The lines for one character.

Mugging—The use of exaggerated facial expressions for comedy.

Musical Theatre—A type of Theatre that includes lyrics, tunes, dances, and dialogue.

*****Narrator**—A character who explains or comments on the events in the play.

*****Off/on stage**—Any place where the audience cannot see the actors/anywhere the audience can see the actors.

Off Broadway—Commercial theater productions performed away from the theater district.

*****One-act play**—A short play.

Opening night—The first public performance of a play.

Pacing—The tempo of a theatrical performance.

Periaktos—A three-sided prism made of flats and mounted on casters that revolves to show a different background. It originated in Greek Theatre.

*****Playwright**—The person who writes the play.

*****Plot**—The events of the play that make up the story.

Point of attack—The point of the play at which the main action of the story begins.

*****Portfolio**—A file containing a resumé, photographs and designs for prospective employers.

*****Protagonist**—The main character of the play.

Previews—The first performance for selected audience members before the opening night.

Proscenium—The view of the stage for the audience. The proscenium arch is a frame defining the boundaries of the stage.

*****Prompt book**—The stage manager's copy of the script with notes of staging and technical cues.

*****Public domain**—Plays that were written over seventy years prior to the present date. These plays can be performed without paying royalty rights to the playwright or publisher.

*****Rake**—The incline angle of the stage.

Rehearsal/s—The various sessions during which the directors, actors and technical personnel work on the play. Rehearsals include blocking or staging, interpretation, run-through, and technical. Adjustment notes are usually given after rehearsals.

Regional Theatre—A professional, nonprofit Theatre located away from Broadway.

Repertoire—All of the parts an actor has played or the plays in production by a company.

Repertory company—A Theater group that performs the plays in the season's repertoire.

Resolution—The final part of a play, in which the conflict comes to some kind of conclusion.

*****Resumé**—The organized credits of the actor. The resumé contains your productions, workshops, training and skills.

Revival—A play after its original production. Sometimes the play is done years after its opening.

Revue—A production featuring a collection of songs, dances, or sketches.

*****Role**—A part in the play.

*****Royalty**—The money paid to the playwright for permission to perform his/her play.

Run of the play—The length of time a play is presented.

Run-through—A rehearsal during which a scene, act or entire play is rehearsed without stopping.

Scene—The division of a play, usually part of an act; indicates the setting of the play.

*****Score a role**—The actor's marking on the script as to emotions, beats, actions, and staging.

*****Script**—The written copy of the actors' lines and technical directions.

Showcase—A presentation that shows off the talents of actors.

*****Sketch**—A short piece of writing or a skit.

Stage—The physical area where the action of the play takes place.

*__Stage directions__—The nine directions of the acting area, indicating planes on the stage: Down right (D.R.), Down center (D.C), Down left (D.L.), Right Center (R.C), Center stage (C.), Left center (L.C.), Up right (U.R.), Up center (U.C.), Up left (U.L.).

__Stage manager__—The technical person who is responsible for overseeing all of the backstage elements of a production.

__Straight man, woman__—A character who sets up the comic character with lines that make the comic's lines funny.

__Strike__—The action that takes place after the final performance, during which all technical effects are removed.

*__Tag line__—The final line of the scene, act, or play.

__Technical theatre__—All of the designs and constructions that are used for the visual depiction of the playwright's work, referred to as the spectacle of the play. Technical terms include: costumes, make-up, lights, sound, house management, scenery, set, fly space, floor plan, properties, strike of the set, grid, grip, house management.

__Tech rehearsal__—The rehearsal/s devoted to setting the technical aspects of a production.

__Text__—The printed words including dialogue and stage directions for a script. Subtext is information that is implied by the character but not stated in dialogue.

*__Theatre games__—A type of improvisation led by the director for a specific objective.

__Theatre-in-the-round__—A type of Theatre in which the audience surrounds the acting area.

*__Theme__—The message of the play; it is often the lesson that the main character learns. Some plays have multiple themes.

__Thespis__—The Greek poet who is considered to be the first actor to step out from the chorus to speak individual lines.

__Thrust stage__—A type of stage surrounded on three sides by the audience.

*__Tragedy__—The type of play that is serious in nature and ends unhappily.

__Understudy__—The actor who is prepared to take over a main role.

__Upstaging__—The action that takes attention away from another actor.

__Villain__—The evil character who opposes the hero.

__Voice-over__—The voice acting done by an unseen actor.

__Walk-on__—A character with no lines.

__Warm-Up__—The actor's preparation.

__Workshopping__—The action of polishing a production; a place to prepare a play for performance before a professional opening.

As you progress through the study of acting by means of the Reflective Inquiry method, you will work with the definitions of each of the marked Theatre Vocabulary for the Acting Student listed on the previous pages. Below are some questions about some of the Theatre Vocabulary. Look back at the alphabetized list to remind yourself what the term means.

REFLECTIVE INQUIRY **RI**   DATE:

Try to remember the title of the first Broadway play that you saw on Broadway? If you have never been to Broadway, recall a touring production of a Broadway play. What do you recall about the first play you ever saw, no matter where you saw it?

REFLECTIVE INQUIRY **RI**   DATE:

Try to remember the first character you ever played in a play? In the space below write down 1.) What part you played, 2.) How old you were, 3.) What the play was about, 4.) What your costume was, and 5.) Other details you remember.

1.

2.

3.

4.

5.

CREATIVE INQUIRY *CI*   DATE:

Imagine what might be the advantages of double casting a role in a play? Write down three of these below.

1.

2.

3.

CREATIVE INQUIRY *CI*   DATE:

Imagine ideas to help you when you perform so that you face the audience without "breaking the fourth wall." Write down three of these below.

1.

2.

3.

REFLECTIVE INQUIRY   *RI*   DATE:

Try to remember the first time you heard the term "Green Room"? Recall the circumstances when Green Room was mentioned.

REFLECTIVE INQUIRY   *RI*   DATE:

Try to remember your favorite musical. Now list the reasons that you chose that one.

1.

2.

REFLECTIVE INQUIRY   *RI*   DATE:

Try to remember any play/s that have the name of a character in the title. If the play has the name of a person in the title, that character is often the protagonist.

ASSIGNMENT Resumé   DATE:

List some of your childhood and youth accomplishments and skills for your resumé, include any awards you received in childhood and any sports or artistic skills from your early school days. This resumé should contain every skill, award and non-Theatre related credit. In the process of experiencing this book, you will build a conflated resumé.

REFLECTIVE INQUIRY RI   DATE:

Remember a memorable voice-over acting role from a movie or commercial. Make some notes on this below.

Theatrical Humor

From various sources of Theatre materials

In is down, down is front
Out is up, up is back
Off is out, on is in
And of course –
Left is right and right is left
A drop shouldn't and a
Block and fall does neither
A prop doesn't and
A cove has no water
Tripping is OK
A running crew rarely gets anywhere
A purchase line buys you nothing
A trap will not catch anything
A gridiron has nothing to do with football
Strike is work (In fact a lot of work)
And a green room, thank god, usually isn't
Now that you're fully versed in Theatrical terms,
Break a leg.
But not really.

Participating in the world of acting, you need knowledge about the craft, and some Theatre people believe you need a bit of good luck. You can carry a four leaf clover or cross your fingers, wish on a ladybug, hope for a unicorn, a rainbow and a pot of gold. You can honor the patron saint of actors, Saint Genesius of Rome, who was an actor. He is also the patron saint to lawyers, printers, and secretaries. Some say Saint Vitus is a patron saint to actors, comedians, and dancers.

In a live Theatre performance numerous things can go wrong, so it is good to be prepared with possible scenarios of what to do if things go awry, as well as calling on the entertaining traditions known to actors.

"Good Luck" or "Break a Leg" Traditions
Some actors tend to share a history of traditions that bring good luck or ward off any harmful luck. It is interesting for you to research the list below and other Theatre superstitions to locate the origins. Some common Theatre warnings or wishes include:

- **Good luck**—It is considered tempting bad luck if anyone wishes "good luck" in a theater. One knowledgeable about the Theatre will say, "Break a Leg." There are historical references in many languages and past cultures explaining where this term originates.
- **Script under your pillow**—It is believed that if an actor sleeps with his/her script under the pillow, it will help with the fast learning of lines.
- **Ghost Light**—Placing a light, usually on a stand, up stage center after the performance and after all of the lights are extinguished is said to ward off ghosts.
- **Bad dress rehearsal**—Supposedly, it foretells a good opening night. That is not always true.
- **Whistling in the Theatre**— It is considered bad luck for an actor to whistle on or offstage.
- *Macbeth*—If the title of Shakespeare's Scottish play *Macbeth* is said, it brings bad luck to the production.

If you whistle in the Theatre or utter the title of the Scottish play, the person uttering the title must go outside the theater, spin around three times, spit, and then knock to be allowed into the theater. There are different versions of this so-called removal. Some say you must spit over your left shoulder.

You can avoid whistling backstage, avoid saying the title of the Scottish play, and avoid saying, "Good Luck."

"Break a leg."

Reading Plays

The literature of an actor is the play script. Reading, reading, and more reading of plays gives you material to analyze and appreciate. There are numerous benefits to reading plays. Reading a play will stimulate your imagination, can bring the world of the past into the present, and allow you to visualize what the playwright says. Each well-written play has a theme or sometimes multiple themes. The theme is the issue that the play talks about. It could be something as simple as a lesson that the playwright wants the reader to remember. Some plays have more than one theme that you can look at. The universal themes presented from the past can be related to today so that we learn about life. Another reason to read a play is to study the human condition through the playwright's eyes. An ongoing benefit of reading a play as an actor is to locate interesting roles for you to portray.

There are many plays that you as an educated actor should know in order to be considered well-informed, and well-versed. Some important plays that every actor should have a working knowledge of are included in Important Plays to Read List below. This is by no means a complete list of great plays. Reading a play a month is a good habit to develop for Acting for Life.

ASSIGNMENT Plays   DATE:

On the play list below make a checkmark next to any title that you know, or you have heard of, seen a production, know the story, have read the script or performed in it, or seen the play. Mark any play that you can talk about.

Playwrights   Titles

Greek Theatre
Aristophanes   *Lysistrata*
Euripides   *The Trojan Women*
Sophocles   *Oedipus Rex*

Medieval Theatre
Author unknown   *Everyman*
Shakespeare   *Romeo and Juliet, A Midsummer
                                                     Night's Dream, Macbeth*

Late nineteenth/early twentieth-century Theatre
Henrik Ibsen   *A Doll's House*
George Bernard Shaw   *Pygmalion*
Oscar Wilde   *The Importance of Being Earnest*

Twentieth-century English Theatre
Noel Coward   *Private Lives*
Peter Shaffer   *Equus* or *Amadeus*

Twentieth-century American Theatre
Edward Albee   (any of his plays)
Lorraine Hansberry   *A Raisin in the Sun*
Moss Hart and George S. Kaufman   *You Can't Take It With You*
Lillian Hellman   *The Children's Hour*
Beth Henley   *Crimes of the Heart*
William Inge   *Picnic*
Arthur Miller   *The Crucible*
August Wilson   *Fences, The Piano Lesson*
Thornton Wilder   *The Glass Menagerie*

American musicals

Richard Rodgers and Oscar Hammerstein	*Oklahoma*
Stephen Sondheim	*Sunday in the Park with George,*
	Into the Woods
Stephen Schwartz	*Pippin, Wicked*

REFLECTIVE INQUIRY **RI**   DATE:

Recall three plays from the above list that you think might be interesting based on the title.

1.

2.

3.

Things to Think About When You Read a Play

Reading scripts to discover the story requires asking questions, thinking about the story and characters of the play, answering questions, making ever-evolving discoveries.

When you read a play, it is good to look for the following aspects of the play:

~ The time period, the era in which the play's action takes place.
~ The playwright's biography, the life of the play's writer.
~ Setting, where the playwright has the play take place.
~ The genre of the play.
~ Plot, the story of the play.
~ Theme or themes, the moral that the playwright wants the audience to remember.
~ Characters, the persons portrayed in the play; the protagonist, the antagonist.

- ~ The climax, the point of the highest intensity in the plot of the play.
- ~ The resolution where the conflict comes to some kind of conclusion. It takes place near the end of a play.

Overtones

Below is part of a play entitled *Overtones*. Please read the play and then move to the assignment section, where there are some questions for you to answer and think about.

CHARACTERS

Dramatis Personae

HARRIET, a cultured woman

HETTY, her primitive self

MARGARET, a cultured woman

MAGGIE, her primitive self

HARRIET'S fashionable living room. The door at the back leads to the hall. In the centre a tea table with a chair either side.

At the back a cabinet. HARRIET'S gown is a light, "jealous" green. Her counterpart, HETTY, wears a gown of the same design but in a darker shade. MARGARET wears a gown of lavender chiffon while her counterpart, MAGGIE, wears a gown of the same design in purple, a purple scarf veiling her face. Chiffon is used to give a sheer effect, suggesting a possibility of primitive and cultured selves merging into one woman.

The primitive and cultured selves never come into actual physical contact but try to sustain the impression of mental conflict. HARRIET never sees HETTY, never talks to her but rather thinks aloud looking into space. HETTY, however, looks at HARRIET, talks intently and shadows her continually. The same is true of MARGARET and MAGGIE. The voices of the cultured women are affected and lingering, the voices of the primitive impulsive and more or less staccato.

[When the curtain rises HARRIET is seated right of tea table, busying herself with the tea things.]

HETTY: Harriet. *[There is no answer.]* Harriet, my other self. *[There is no answer.]* My trained self.

HARRIET: *[listens intently]* Yes?

[From behind HARRIET'S chair HETTY rises slowly.]

HETTY: I want to talk to you.

HARRIET: Well?

HETTY: *[looking at HARRIET admiringly]* Oh, Harriet, you are beautiful today.

HARRIET: Am I presentable, Hetty?

HETTY: Suits me.

HARRIET: I've tried to make the best of the good points.

HETTY: My passions are deeper than yours. I can't keep on the mask as you do. I'm crude and real, you are my appearance in the world.

HARRIET: I am what you wish the world to believe you are.

HETTY: You are the part of me that has been trained.

HARRIET: I am your educated self.

HETTY: I am the rushing river; you are the ice over the current.

HARRIET: I am your subtle overtones.

To be continued… (You will be reading the entire play in a later chapter for Script Analysis on page 239.)

ASSIGNMENT *Overtones* 1   DATE:

Reading plays is a rewarding practice. To begin your play reading, look at the play's title and brainstorm on what you think the title means. Make some notes about images, feelings, and associations.

What is one thing you notice about the cast list?

Notice the spelling of the word "center" in the stage directions. What does the spelling tell you?

What do you notice about the colors indicated for each character in the stage directions?

Why do you think the playwright asks the actors to follow the directions for Harriett, Hetty, Margaret and Maggie?

When Hetty says, "I want to talk to you," why does Harriet answer? She could have ignored Hetty.

Make a note about Harriet's use of the word "presentable."

What does Hetty's statement about her passions tell the actor in regard to what kind of voice to use?

What does Harriet mean when she says, "I am your subtle overtones"?

You have ventured into the exciting world of play reading, the basis of all actors' work in the scripted world. Your reading of plays should include study and inquiry, using your skill and imagination. Reading of plays opens new avenues of interest and appreciation of the written word. Reading plays is a life-long project that you can develop into a continual, rewarding habit.

Closure for *The Student Actor Prepares: Acting for Life: Prologue*

In a play, the script takes the characters on a journey that usually at the end concludes and resolves the story. Each chapter in this book presents reflection questions for you to assess what you have learned and asks for input on any thoughts you have about the subject matter. The charge to you as a student of the art of acting is to study and learn as much as you can about acting. Reflective inquiry leads you into thinking about and articulating your process. Your reflection is important. You may write anything that you wish to help you remember what you have learned. This journey invites your participation.

With my assistance, you begin your journey into the art, craft, and profession of a long-lasting acting study.

Congratulations. I applaud you.

When someone does something good, applaud! You will make two people happy.

Samuel Goldwyn, American producer

CHAPTER ONE: INTRODUCTION TO THEATRE ACTING

As an actor you prepare for performance by setting the stage, getting ready by discovering unlimited potentials, knowing yourself, identifying natural talents, approaching acting with a positive attitude by acknowledging your uniqueness, studying emotions, looking at new experiences, and dealing with inhibitors.

> *The thing about performance, even if it's only an illusion, is that it is a celebration of the fact that we do contain within ourselves infinite possibilities.*
>
> Daniel Day-Lewis, actor

Unlimited Potential

You are a person with unlimited potential. You have the natural gifts of your body, voice, intellect, imagination, emotions, five senses, and intuition. You have unique qualities that make you one of a kind. There is no one exactly like you. You can be an actor with distinctive traits, talents, and abilities. Identifying your distinctive traits, talents, and abilities will lead you toward reaching your potential in life and in acting.

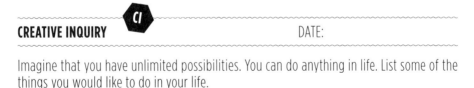

CREATIVE INQUIRY **CI** DATE:

Imagine that you have unlimited possibilities. You can do anything in life. List some of the things you would like to do in your life.

Believing in yourself will help you accomplish your goals. In this chapter, you will remember your past and present, list some of your natural talents, articulate what is unique about you, name emotions, deal with inhibitors, and affirm the positive. Getting to know yourself as a person will assist your progress in your acting journey.

The tools that you acquire in this unit will set the stage for positive thinking. Your objective is to develop positive attitudes, and to learn to recognize and deal with inhibitors, such as stage fright, reading challenges and negative attitudes. You will construct affirmations for dealing with any setbacks in the world of acting.

Skills Developed by the Acting Process

Skills that are used in daily life are fostered in the study of acting; likewise acting abilities help you to become an aware, passionate person with a dramatic presence in daily life. As you study acting, you will cultivate a keen awareness of observation, a heightened awareness of how people use their bodies, faces and voices, a method of working successfully on a project, and an enjoyment of your process and performance successes. Acting promotes disciplined work habits that encourage curiosity, imagination, creativity, and critical thinking.

Life skills that are developed and strengthened by the practice of acting include:

- ~ Creating imaginative, bold ideas.
- ~ Reasoning.
- ~ Thinking reflectively.
- ~ Developing positive working habits.
- ~ Being open minded and flexible.
- ~ Conveying emotions with your voice and body.
- ~ Listening appreciatively.
- ~ Cooperating.
- ~ Thinking on your feet.
- ~ Reading and analyzing written material.

As an actor you are an unrestricted thinker, one who is inventive, organized, patient, and self-confident. You are willing to take risks with innovative ideas, and to look forward to make adjustments. You embrace new ideas. As an actor, you thrive on assessment and working toward the best possible performance.

Actor's Personal Autobiography

There is a multitude of reasons for you to know yourself. You benefit by getting in touch with who you are. Knowledge builds self-confidence. Your self-discovery leads to empowerment to pursue your career. You need a secure sense of identity and self-awareness to engage all facets of your personality to create characters in plays.

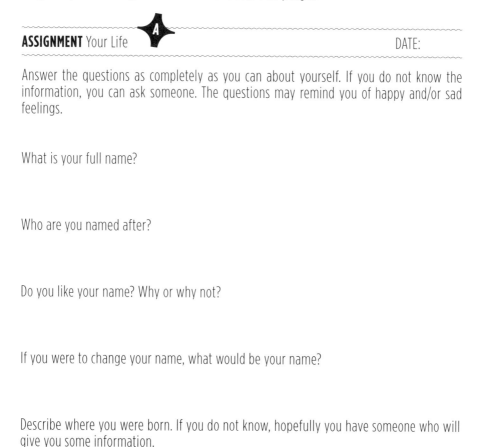

ASSIGNMENT Your Life   DATE:

Answer the questions as completely as you can about yourself. If you do not know the information, you can ask someone. The questions may remind you of happy and/or sad feelings.

What is your full name?

Who are you named after?

Do you like your name? Why or why not?

If you were to change your name, what would be your name?

Describe where you were born. If you do not know, hopefully you have someone who will give you some information.

What do you remember about your childhood?

Do you have any brothers or sisters?

Recall your favorite birthday.

Recall your saddest birthday.

Describe your childhood bedroom.

Recall your favorite childhood memory.

Recall your least favorite childhood memory.

Remember any childhood collections you had.

What was your favorite childhood song?

Recollect any serious childhood accidents or illness you have had.

Who was your first crush or idol?

Describe an important first.

What was a favorite childhood toy, furniture, or other possession?

What is your favorite color?

What is your lucky number?

What is one of your favorite hobbies?

What is one of your favorite places in your hometown or city?

What country would you like to visit?

What would be an ideal vacation for you?

What is one source of pride and joy in your life?

What is one skill you could teach others?

What is something that you value?

What is something that makes you laugh?

What kinds of jobs have you had?

What was a turning point in your life?

What is your best trait?

What is something you would like to change about yourself?

What makes you feel angry?

What makes you feel happy?

What is your favorite food item?

What is something positive in which you like to indulge?

What is your biggest achievement?

Describe a frightening moment in your life.

What do you hope to accomplish by the age of 50? If you are 50, what do you hope to accomplish in the next 20 years?

What is your major goal in your personal life? What do you want?

Write a phrase, quote, song lyric, or saying that you really like.

What would you like people to remember about you?

REFLECTIVE INQUIRY **RI**   DATE:

Revisit three revelations about your past or present by reading over all of your answers. Now list three revelations or surprises about your past or present.

1.

2.

3.

Think about one new awareness that you gained about yourself?

There was never yet an uninteresting life. Such a thing is impossibility.
Inside of the dullest exterior there is a drama, a comedy, and a tragedy.

Mark Twain, author, humorist.

Think about what this quote means to you? How can you apply the quote's lesson to your life and your study of acting?

Natural Talents and Aptitudes

You have all of the natural capabilities needed to be an actor: your body, mind, imagination, voice, emotions, and five senses. You are filled with capacities that will help you as an actor. It is one of the objectives of this book to aid you in the journey of identifying your natural abilities. A talent is defined as a special ability or aptitude. This talent or aptitude is innate or natural from birth.

ASSIGNMENT Abilities   DATE:

Making a list of your abilities in writing helps you create an inventory of your natural talents and aptitudes. Think of some of your natural talents and aptitudes.

REFLECTIVE INQUIRY   DATE:

Recall ten positive, natural talents or aptitudes you possess. Do you have an imagination? Are you a good listener? Do you sing? Are you an organizer? Do it as a quick write, a reflection to list your abilities. (A quick write means that you list items without paying attention to spelling or sentence structure.) This open-ended question should take you less than five minutes to complete.

1.

2.

3.

4.

5.

6.

7.

8.

9.

10.

REFLECTIVE INQUIRY   DATE:

Revisit the Natural Talents and Aptitudes Inventory. Go back to it now and update and add additional positive things about you.

When you're an actor in grade school, high school, college, whatever, you start to realize what you're really good at, what you're kinda good at, what you're okay at, and you start to compartmentalize. But if you know yourself and what you're capable of, it's just a matter of opportunity.

Bryan Cranston, actor

Think about the quote by Bryan Cranston. What are you capable of? If you have the right opportunity, what can you accomplish? List three positive things you are capable of.

1.

2.

3.

Acknowledging your Uniqueness

An agent asked new clients, including me, the following question, "What is unique about you? Not just interesting, but truly unmatchable with others? I thought and stated, "I am the only actor in this room who went to Chickasha High School, where our football team was "the Fightin" Chicks." I was the first woman to be granted an MA in Theatre at CA State University, and I have a theater named after me."

In this business there will be many others who are your age, size, height, with comparable talents, so you must walk into an audition believing that you are distinctive; you are the solution to the casting director's problem. A casting director has a role that he/she needs to fill. Show the casting director why he/she would benefit by hiring you. You are the unique solution to fill the role.

Think about four specific unique physical qualities or talents that you have. Some people can wiggle their ears, are double jointed, can lift one eyebrow, or they have an unusual scar. What about you? This is a quick write for you to list several unique qualities and aptitudes.

1.

2.

3.

4.
_____

As an actor, you will create a resumé. The document will have your contact information, a listing of your performances, training, and special abilities and skills that a director might be able to use in a play. Can you sing, dance, play an instrument, play a sport, or speak a foreign language? List five of your unique skills.
_____

1.

2.

3.

4.

5.

_____

Magnetic Personality

You have some traits that are unique, appealing, and engaging. In order to know yourself as an actor get in touch with those traits.

Think about the idea that you have something about you and your personality that draws other people to you. Think about the unique, likeable, interesting, engaging qualities you have that might draw people toward you like a magnet. You might have a lively mind, a winning smile, a sense of humor, a calming style, a soothing voice, or a positive spirit. This is an experience to claim your best traits. List three magnetic things about you.

1.

2.

3   .

Emotions in Life and the Study of Acting

How do you feel? You are an emotional being with an abundance of feelings. The moods you choose to express are uniquely yours. As an actor, being able to identify your feelings and tap into your emotions immediately are prized abilities. To discover the intricacies of any character created by a playwright, you must know your own feelings. You can understand a role and empathize with the character's emotions you are portraying. You use your feelings to connect to a character created by a playwright. You connect with the portrayal so that the audience members sense your emotional relationship to the lines that you are saying.

You as an actor must have a safe environment to be able to express your feelings. To be aware of feelings and to be able to choose to act on the emotions at the appropriate time and place are acquired practices. To be able to state how you feel about topics and situations is a respected skill for actors. It takes rehearsal to name feelings and communicate how you feel to fellow actors.

You may or may not be experienced in communicating your feelings. As an actor it is to your advantage to be able to inventory your moods and express emotions. If you cannot name your own feelings, how can you hope to trace Hamlet's or Juliet's myriad feelings?

Primary and Secondary Emotions

Primary Emotions
Primary emotions are those that you feel first, as a response to a situation. You might feel fear if threatened or sadness when you hear of a death. Primary emotions include fear, anger, sadness, and happiness.

ASSIGNMENT Name your Primary Emotions   DATE:

Think over the last twenty-four hours of your life. Recount three events and the primary emotions you felt as a result of the events.

1.

2.

3.

REFLECTIVE INQUIRY   DATE:

Recall three significant life events and the feelings attached to each of these events. Choose from the list of possible primary emotions: fear, anger, sadness, happiness.

Event   Name Your Feeling

1.

2.

3

Secondary Emotions

An experience is layered with multiple emotions. Primary emotions disappear rapidly and are replaced by secondary emotions. These feelings may be a combination of moods that appear after primary reactions. Hearing of a win of your team over your friend's team may have stimulated feelings of joy, but then feelings of sadness about your friend's loss may emerge. Stubbing your toe might stimulate anger, because you hurt your toe; then despair evolves because your hurt toe might keep you from dancing.

You look at the primary and secondary emotions to get a complete picture of a person's complexity. The first emotion is a reaction; the secondary appears right after the primary emotion and may be a result of the first response plus your rational thoughts.

REFLECTIVE INQUIRY **RI**   DATE:

Revisit your primary emotions list. Now, in the table below, name three secondary emotions you felt strongly that were in reaction to your listed events and primary emotions. Here is a list of possible secondary emotions from which you can choose: Acceptance, Anticipation, Anxiety, Confusion, Contempt, Courage, Dejection, Desire, Despair, Disgust, Elation, Envy, Expectancy, Grief, Guilt, Hate, Hope, Interest, Jealousy, Joy, Love, Nervousness, Optimism, Pride, Rage, Shame, Sorrow, Surprise, Tenderness, and Wonder.

Event	Primary Emotion	Secondary Emotions
1.		
2.		
3		

Remembering events and emotions helps you as an actor to tap into emotions so that you can create characters.

The Theatre—acting, creating, interpreting—means the total involvement, the totality of heart, mind and spirit ... the total development of a human being into the most he can be and in as many directions as he can possibly take.

Stella Adler, acting teacher

Positive New Experiences

Each time you enter into an acting project, you will experience new and yet familiar emotions. You know the aspects of the art and craft, and yet each project will provide new experiences. Being receptive to unusual experiences conveys a positive attitude to your chosen course of study. Being optimistic to new events is a valued way of looking at life. Your presence in new experiences and reflecting on them bring affirmative perspectives to your life.

REFLECTIVE INQUIRY **RI**   DATE:

Recall a time when you risked taking part in a positive, new experience. What was the risk you took?

1. How did you feel about taking the risk before participating in the new experience?

2. What were the details of the risk taking?

3. What emotions were involved in the risk taking?

4. How did the experience add to your life's view?

Now you have explored a positive outlook about yourself, outlined natural talents and aptitudes, listed your uniqueness, magnetic personalities, and identified emotions, and looked at taking part in new experiences. You are ready to explore ways to face inhibitors and negative attitudes.

Dealing with Inhibitors

An inhibitor is anything that keeps you from doing your best, any distraction, any insecurity, any negativity, or any unanswered question. One of the worst things you might do is begin to judge yourself, decide that you are not good enough, or tall enough, or short enough while you are acting. It takes you out of the moment and inhibits your commitment to your performance.

Here is a reverse equation that works in acting, in test taking, in sports, and any event that requires performance. P=P-I. The equation letters stand for Performance Equals Potential minus Inhibitors. You have the potential to do the best performance of which you are capable, on stage, on a test, and in sports, if you address and prepare for all of the inhibitors that keep you from succeeding.

CREATIVE INQUIRY *CI*   DATE:

Think about why and when people experience anxiety in certain situations; for example, public speaking, parental or friends' disapproval, not being prepared, and falling down in front of people who might laugh. Such situations are called inhibitors. List three inhibitors that you fear.

1.

2.

3.

Facing the Fear of Public Performances

One of the major Inhibitors to any public performance is stage fright. Many people are more scared of public speaking than facing insects. Some people would rather deal with a snake than give a speech in public. Most people find performing in public to be worrisome and frightening.

As an actor, performing for an audience will be part of your occupation. Your job as an actor is to educate, engage, and entertain. If you are very frightened, you cannot give completely to the play, the role, or the emotions, because stage fright interferes with your total involvement. The stress of stage fright can lead to nervousness as well as other distracting behaviors, which take away from your immersion in the performances.

Being on stage challenges your security. "What ifs" take over? What if you fall down? What if someone laughs at the wrong times? What if someone does not like you? What if you make a mistake? What if you look silly? Being onstage can be exciting, challenging and exhilarating, but it can be also frightening and cause tension.

REFLECTIVE INQUIRY **RI**   DATE:

Recall a time when you were embarrassed or scared by a "what if." Relate the time and place and how you felt, physically and emotionally.

Time	Place	How You Felt Physically	How You Felt Emotionally

Revisit the inhibitors list. Now list three possible inhibitors that might keep you from doing your best acting performance; e.g. fear of someone laughing at you; not knowing your lines; parents not approving of your love of Theatre; lack of studying or mastering the needed skills; feeling inadequate or unworthy of the opportunity to perform before an audience. Use your imagination to list some potential acting worries.

1.

2.

3   .

Stage fright occurs because you are afraid of judging yourself negatively; of being ridiculed, being underprepared or other reasons. You become overly aware of the audience. Stage fright affects you physically. Your stomach becomes upset, and your mouth becomes dry. Your heart begins to beat faster. Your lungs do not expand fully, thus shortness of breath happens. Your body becomes shaky, and muscles tense. Sweat pours. Hands become wet. Your voice shakes. How do you manage stage fright?

Managing Stage Fright
You can use your brain and intellect to manage the fear of public performance, by acknowledging it and giving it a name. You have the power to master stage fright. Below is a list of tools and reminders to help you conquer the fear you might feel when you are on stage.

~ You can be kind to yourself.
~ You can remind yourself that even the worst stage fright lasts a short time.
~ You can mentally visualize your success.
~ You can be rested and give yourself extra time for unforeseen things.
~ You can give yourself space to be alone, before any performance.
~ You can be prepared.

~ You can create and use your positive affirmations.
~ You can remember that you have the power to fix any mistakes.
~ You can remember that the audience has not read the script.
~ You can remind yourself that you have rehearsed and know more about the performance than the audience does.
~ You can be "in the here and now," staying focused.
~ You can remember that the audience wants you to succeed.
~ You can think of anyone who ever supported your creative projects and use that image as a support.
~ You can remind yourself that although you feel nervous, the audience does not see it.

You can use physical practices to handle stage fright. You can:

~ Yawn.
~ Stretch and breathe.
~ Keep your acting instruments of body, mind, voice, emotions free from harmful substances and behaviors.
~ Center yourself.
~ Practice vocal warm-ups.
~ Use the bathroom before performance.
~ Have a bottle of water nearby.
~ Use extra antiperspirant.
~ Eat lightly before the performance.
~ Direct your nervous energy by making the panicky "butterflies in your stomach fly in the same direction; soaring up toward success."

CREATIVE INQUIRY   CI   DATE:

Imagine five ways you might handle stage fright.

1.

2.

3.

4.

5.

Above all remember stage fright is manageable.

Reading and Spelling Challenges
Some actors experience reading difficulties and/or spelling. If you have a reading or learning difficulty, you might feel that you can't succeed in a reading-based profession. In acting, it can be stressful when you are asked to read aloud.

There is a long list of famous, successful people who experience difficulty in reading. Some actors and entertainers who know what it is like to have dyslexia or related learning disabilities include Walt Disney, Harry Belafonte, Tom Cruise, Anne Bancroft, Whoopi Goldberg, Jay Leno, Keanu Reeves, Kiera Knightley, Tom Smothers, Vince Vaughn, and Henry Winkler. Many people with dyslexia have become successful in part because they were highly motivated to overcome any disadvantage.

Some quotes regarding their reading challenges include:

- Tom Cruise—*I became very visual and learned how to create mental images in order to comprehend what I read.*
- Anne Bancroft—*You learn to go where your strengths are and you go for them hard.*
- Whoopie Goldberg—*We have a handicap and that handicap can be overcome.*

Reading Challenges
Here are some tips to help you with a stressful reading challenge, such as an audition.

- If you are required to read text without preparation time, ask for time to look it over.
- Be open and honest about any reading or learning challenge.
- Ask for assistance.

~ Practice saying, "I have a reading challenge, but once I have studied the script, I will master the material quickly." You can request the script in advance to study.
~ Memorize your own name, your character's name, the title, and the playwright, so you can establish eye contact, while speaking those four items.
~ If you have time, memorize the first and last line for a strong first and last impression.

Pay attention to the punctuation marks, commas, semicolons, colons, periods, question marks, exclamation points. Commas mean a half breath; semicolon is a bit longer beat; colon means more of a pause than commas. Period or question mark means to stop your voice; the end punctuation marks do not mean to drop your voice on the last word of the sentence. The last word is often an important word, and, if so, should be spoken with significance.

Read the sentences below. Notice the difference in what each sentence means when you say the final word with confidence.

~ Are you going *home?*
~ Are you going *late?*
~ Are you going *up?*
~ Are you going *in?*
~ Are you going *out?*
~ Are you going *hurriedly?*
~ Are you going *slowly?*
~ Are you going to *cry?*
~ Are you going to *laugh?*
~ Are you going *today?*
~ Are you going to the *party?*
~ Are you going to the *funeral?*

The punctuation mark at the end of the sentence is a good place to take a breath and think about what the character says next. Is there a change in mood, emotion, or topic? These punctuated transitions ask for a change of approach with your body and voice.

An example of paying attention to punctuation marks is the title of a book about punctuation, *Eats, Shoots and Leaves.*

With the punctuation it is implied that a person eats something, shoots something and leaves from one location and is going to another location.

If the punctuation marks are removed, it reads *Eats Shoots and Leaves.* It indicates that someone eats some kind of vegetation shoots and the leaves of a plant.

Other comma punctuation mark confusions are evident in the following two sentences: "Let's eat Grandma," or "Let's eat, Grandma." The first statement might direct someone to eat Grandma; the second invites Grandma to eat a meal with you. Another confusing example is "My interests include cooking dogs and shopping." or "My interests include cooking, dogs, and shopping." Are your interests cooking dogs and then going shopping? Or are your interests cooking, along with interest in dogs, and you love going shopping?

When you pick up a script, watch the road signs of punctuation.

When you are prepared to do your best, you will be respected for overcoming a challenge with a secure performance.

Part of your success with the audition is attitude, so hopefully you will remember to breathe and relax; you can look forward to showing your enthusiasm and natural spirit. Think about your objective: to present your talents and skills. You might make mistakes; make then with assurance; be bold. Speak securely.

Spelling Challenges

Some people are expert spellers; some are not. As an actor, it is beneficial to know how to spell common performing words for your resumé or your audition sheet. Your audition sheet is the form that you fill out when you enter the tryout or interview room. The audition sheet asks about your experiences performing, your skills, and your contact information.

Key acting vocabulary words should be spelled correctly. You can look back at the vocabulary words in the Prologue of this book and memorize the correct spelling of those words.

The following is a list of common misspelled words on a typical audition sheet: performance, audition, Shakespearean, monologue, resumé, audience, rehearsal, dialogue, scene, critic, critique, Theatre/theater, soliloquy, improvisation, congratulations, thespian, drama, and genre. Learn the difference between its/it's, your/you're, Theatre/Theater. Spelling words correctly will be beneficial to your career.

~~~~~~

ASSIGNMENT Spelling   DATE:

~~~~~~

Write any of the words from the above list or the Theatre Vocabulary for the Acting Student in the Prologue of this book that you need to learn to spell. Learn to spell the words before your next audition.

Dealing with Negativism and Rejection in the Acting Biz

"Art Isn't Easy" is included as some of the lyrics in the Stephen Sondheim musical, *Sunday in the Park with George.*

Some people might express concerns about your becoming an actor. The Acting business is difficult. Your parents and loved ones care about your sustained happiness and income. They may be worried about you taking part in a profession known for rejection and less than sustainable income. Only a small percent of Actors' Equity members earn top dollar. The rest of the professional actors earn very little money for acting.

You need to keep trying, constantly evaluating your choices, and decide if and how you want to pursue your acting goals. It is a life full of successes and setbacks, accomplishments and negativism, highlights and "wish I had made another choice" thoughts. There is a refrigerator magnet saying that addresses this. "Success consists of going from failure to failure without loss of enthusiasm." When taking on a project that you consider to be worthy, evaluate the situation and your positive attitude.

Sometimes the acting profession is depicted as a challenging profession because of the rejection factor. You may not be cast for every role for which you audition. Acting is known for only a few getting the prized roles. In Los Angeles, you are considered somewhat successful if you go to ten auditions, and get one call back. For one role, many, many actors audition.

Those who love you do not want you to experience the rejection of going to auditions and not being cast. There will be challenges. It is up to you how you react to the challenges.

You might have had friends or acquaintances who self-destructed with drugs, alcohol, and other addictive behaviors. You may have known or read about someone who has ruined his or her career because of addictions. It is up to you to experience the natural "high" of executing a delivered line or creating a character to feed your spirit. You will need to be positive and figure out a way to keep positive as you proceed in your emerging acting career.

There are places in acting for displays of undesirable characteristics; those are the roles in which you are portraying a character who is not positive. In those roles, you have permission to embrace the feelings listed here: agitation, anger, anguish, annoyance, anxiety, avoidance, boredom, despair, disappointment, disgust, disinterest, doubt, embarrassment, envy, exhaustion, exasperation, fear, frustration, guilt, helplessness, hurt, inattentiveness, indecision, indifference, irritation, jealousy, nervousness, powerlessness, rage, refusal, reluctance, repulsion, sadness, shame, and lack of interest. Eliminate the words above when presenting yourself offstage. Look forward to being onstage.

Keep away from people who try to belittle your ambitions. Small people always do that, but the really great make you feel that you, too, can become great.

Mark Twain, author, humorist

ASSIGNMENT Rejection in Casting   DATE:

Acknowledge that you may not be cast. Think how you might react if your name is not on the cast list or you do not get the role that you wanted. How will you feel? How will you keep going? How will you turn the rejection into an opportunity for exploration?

Many times the reasons for not being cast are not within your control: being too tall; too short; too old; too young; too serious; too funny; too experienced; too new. These might be some reasons why you might not be chosen for a role, but you must remember that they are not things that you can change.

All of your life you are told the things you cannot do. All your life they will say you're not good enough or strong enough or talented enough. They'll say you're the wrong height or the wrong weight or the wrong type to play this or be this or achieve this. THEY WILL TELL YOU NO, a thousand times no until all of the no's become meaningless. All of your life they will tell you No, quite firmly and very quickly. They will tell you No. And YOU WILL TELL THEM YES.

Discovered on the wall of an LA casting director's office

Winning Attitudes

You need to display encouraging attitudes when presenting yourself to others. Develop the following outlooks: Attentive, Alert, Cheerful, Confident, Considerate, Friendly, Grateful, Helpful, Hopeful, Inclusive, Interested, Loving, Optimistic, Open, Satisfied, Sincere, and Trusting. Your life and acting career will be encouraged and influenced by your winning attitudes.

REFLECTIVE INQUIRY **RI**   DATE:

Remember a time when you displayed any one of the positive attitudes above. What were you doing, and why did you feel a positive attitude?

If you don't like something, change it. If you can't change it, change your attitude.

Maya Angelou, poet, historian

Affirmations for Keeping the Spirit

An affirmation is a positive statement that you say, read or keep in mind to remind you of a positive state of being or a desired outcome. Affirmations reinforced by an encouraging spirit help you bring to mind, upon a moment's notice, a comforting thought.

The repetition of a helpful statement triggers the subconscious mind into a confident state. Positive statements are effective when repeated with sincerity, while in a relaxed frame of mind. An actor repeats the affirmation with conviction and desire. The affirmation must be short enough for one to remember.

You can create positive behavior and attitude by practicing your positive affirmation. It might take days, weeks or longer for you to see results. You have to refuse to hold on to any negative thoughts to attain your positive desire.

Phrase your affirmations in the present tense rather than future. One positive affirmation to use before any audition is "I am healthy, hearty and happy to be here." Include encouraging words. Do not include any negative words, including the word, "not." For example, "I will not be sick, fragile or sad," is not a positive affirmation.

Another personal affirmation which can be repeated to yourself is "I have a beautiful spirit. I am prepared to let everyone see how proud I am to be me. I am proud for me."

CREATIVE INQUIRY   DATE:

Think about some positive words you can use in your personal affirmation. It may take time to develop the exact words you want to repeat for comfort or growth. List some reassuring words below.

Take short affirmation breaks each day to get into the habit of encouraging yourself.

ASSIGNMENT Positive Words   DATE:

Periodically add to your list of positive words so that you create:

*An affirmation for before you begin the audition process

*An affirmation before you rehearse, an affirmation before you perform

* An affirmation for when you finish a performance

* An affirmation when someone is grouchy towards you

* And an affirmation for other negative situations

Repeat an affirmation, such as, "I'm glad I'm here. I'm glad you're here. I care about you. I know that I am prepared." The first part shows the joy of being there. The rest of the affirmation declares that you know how to perform. Here is a sample affirmation:

I feel confident. I know what I am doing. I will listen to directions and follow them. I am flexible and able to meet challenges. I own the room. I believe in the creative power of Acting. I carry on its ancient tradition. I am magic. I am an actor, a storyteller. When I act, I take my audience on the journey with me. I am an amazing artist. My job is to play. I smile. I love challenges. Every time I step on stage, magic happens. I am the magic.

ASSIGNMENT Affirmations for Keeping the Spirit   DATE:

Create a short positive mantra that speaks to you at this time in your life.

You involve your heart as an actor – the way you see the world – your attitude towards life, your very being as a person. Your positive attitude leads to your affirmations that confirm that you are proud of being you, a multifaceted, interesting person and emerging actor.

The lyrics of "Accentuate the Positive," by Johnny Mercer state,

You've got to accentuate the positive
Eliminate the negative
And latch on to the affirmative
Don't mess with Mister In-Between

You've got to spread joy up to the maximum
Bring gloom down to the minimum
Have faith or pandemonium's
Liable to walk upon the scene ...

Closure for Chapter One: Theatre Acting

Look back over your notes made in the study of this chapter. Revisit the topics in Chapter One to review. The topics mentioned in this chapter are listed below. Respond with one fact that you remember about each topic.

Introduction to Theatre Acting

Skills Developed by the Acting Process

Know yourself by Actor's Autobiography

Natural Talents and Aptitudes Inventory

Acknowledging your Uniqueness

Magnetic Personality

Emotions in Life and the Study of Acting

Name your Primary Emotions

Name your Secondary Emotions

Positive New Experiences

Dealing with Inhibitors

Facing the Fear of Public Performances

Managing Stage Fright

Acknowledging and Managing More Inhibitors: Reading and Spelling Challenges

Dealing with Rejection and Negativism in the Acting Business

Winning Attitudes

Affirmations for Keeping the Spirit

ASSIGNMENT Closure 2   DATE:

As part of your progression, it is important to assess your learning. You evaluate your knowledge by making notes about what you understand, what new knowledge you have gained, what questions you have, and what you want to study more.

Complete the following unfinished sentences with ideas about the information presented in this chapter:

I understand

I have gained new knowledge about

I have questions about

I would like to study more about

Bravo to you. I give you a standing ovation for beginning your exciting journey. You are on your way to becoming an informed actor.

The next chapters provide you with experiences in creativity, relaxing your body for movement and mime, developing your voice, experiencing improvisation, analyzing scripts, working with prepared and original monologues, getting ready for auditions, and preparing for further study to continue learning for a lifetime.

CHAPTER TWO: CREATIVITY

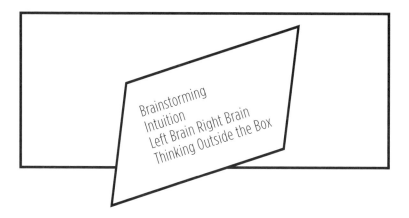

Introduction to Creativity

Creativity is something you are born with: it is a talent, an aptitude, and skill that you can learn to strengthen. Every day you use creativity and creative thinking. Each time you think of multiple answers to a question that is asked of you, when you play with an empty box, when you see a common object and imagine an innovative use for it, when you read a riddle and think of answers, you are being creative. You are creative in everyday life.

Definition of Creativity

Creativity is the process of bringing a new way of thinking into being. Creativity is a way of viewing the world. Originality requires flexibility, innovation, and uninhibited ways of looking at ideas.

You may have heard the various types of thinking that are used in connection with creativeness: brainstorming, intuition, left and right brain thinking, and thinking outside the box. Once you have learned the various types of creative thinking and challenging your brain for imagination, you will have creative skills to build a strong, imaginative life. In this chapter there are creative exercises you can use when you feel the need for out-of-the-box thinking. In this book's creative experiences there are multiple answers and ways to respond, so enjoy the freedom.

This chapter provides learning experiences, creative inquiries, and reflective opportunities, which address a prized ability for you in life and as an actor, that of creativity. The purpose of the activities in this unit is to provide creative experiences so that you think creatively and make imaginative choices. The aim of creativity work is to strengthen the imagination and give you a vast range of creative tools.

I know what I love about acting, and it's the creative process.

William Hurt, actor

Say Yes to Creativity

Give yourself time to be creative each day. Set aside time to be creative often. Develop an appetite for thinking imaginatively. You are a creative individual. Creativity is nurtured by your feeling positive and unique about who you are, so making use of the affirmations from Chapter One will help you tap into creative thinking.

ASSIGNMENT 1 DATE:

Get yourself into a positive frame of mind. Think of the word, yes. Think of how many different ways you can print the word, yes.

ASSIGNMENT 2 DATE:

In the space below, print the word Yes several times. Be creative with your Yeses; use different print, sizes, and colors.

The remarkable thing about the simple Yes experience above is that your Yeses are unique and unlike anyone else's Yeses. Your creativity is matchless. Your imagination is incomparable.

REFLECTIVE INQUIRY   *RI*   DATE:

Recall a time in your life when you used creative thinking. What was the event? What kind of creativity did you use?

Event   Your Creativity

Various Types of Creative Thinking:
Brainstorming, Intuition, and Left Brain-Right Brain

Brainstorming is a problem-solving technique that involves open contributions of ideas from many group members; it is used to find a solution to a problem or challenge. Brainstorming for you as an individual is a valuable way to work on a problem and also to think of many ideas focused on a topic. One idea leads to one or more new ideas, which lead to more ideas. Individual brainstorming is effective in generating creative ideas.

You utilize brainstorming when you think of a topic for research, and you allow your mind to flow with ideas. When you have some kind of problem, you think of all of the possible ways to solve it. You brainstorm on ways to ask for something that you think you might receive a negative response.

Brainstorming is an effective part of the creative thinking process.

Intuition is the ability to understand something without using a logical, step-by-step, conscious process. Intuition is also called insight and instincts on which you act. If you have ever walked into a room and felt some kind of unhappiness or tension, or if the telephone rang and you somehow knew who it was before answering, or you have a feeling as to what decisions you should make in your life, you are using your intuition. Everyone has intuition. Some people pay more attention than others to their intuition. Awareness of your intuition leads you to creative thinking.

You may have heard of or been referred to as a left brain or right brain thinker. The left side of the brain controls analytical thinking, decision-making capabilities, and critical thinking. Left brain people tend to analyze things and use logic to find solutions. Left brain activity might be used when you solve a math problem or take a multiple choice test. When using mostly your left brain thinking, you are mathematical, logical, and conventional.

Processes that are mostly in the right brain allow you to experience nonverbal concepts and three-dimensional activity. You use your imagination and emotions. You might be called "emotional," or "artistic." Right brain activity might include a time when you decorate your room so that looking at it makes you feel comfortable. You may be thought of as poetical, emotional, and spontaneous.

You may have also heard the phrases "Thinking out of the box" or "Thinking beyond the box." The expressions all suggest you are thinking differently, using new perspectives, thinking creatively. To think outside the box is to let your imagination soar and to not settle for obvious ideas. Thinking inside the box indicates that there might be safe thinking and no new ideas

You might use your ability to think outside the box when you wear a hat in a new way. Observe a cloud and imagine what the shape reminds you of; look at a chair and think of other ways to use it instead of for sitting.

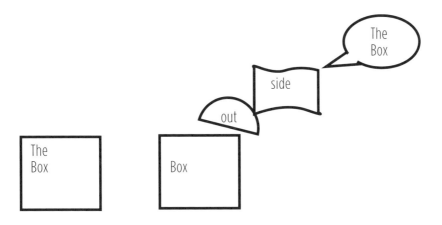

Tips on How to Increase your Creativity

CREATIVE INQUIRY *CI*   DATE:

Think about a time when you were in a "creative mood." List some creative thoughts you had.

Creativity is about finding new ways of looking at ideas and challenges. In order to increase your creativity, you need to decide that you really want to develop your creativity. Find joy in the process of creativity. Have confidence to take creative risks. Stay positive and away from negative thinkers. Increasing your creativity means taking care of yourself so that you can be in an open and receptive frame of mind to think creatively. Reward yourself for being creative.

To increase your creative thinking to be a believer, a listener, a learner, a laugher, a dreamer. Love yourself. Laugh with magic. Listen to all kinds of people. Learn from sages. Learn from children. Learn from your feelings.

- Take time to be silent.
- Take a nap.
- Quick write freely for five minutes. Write anything.
- Alter your routine of how you get up in the morning.
- Affirm yourself at least five times each day.
- Take a positive approach toward something you might not enjoy doing.
- Notice how you really feel at various times during the day.
- Be aware of your wildest imaginations.
- Use your non-dominant hand for a simple task, such as brushing your teeth or eating something.
- Eat with your eyes closed.
- Take an imaginative approach to something, such as sitting differently on a chair, take a different way to a familiar destination.
- Invent some new way of doing a routine that you do each day.
- Go to the park and play.
- Exercise.
- Laugh.
- Turn negative thinking into positive thinking.
- Look at abstract art.
- Dream.
- Pay attention to your night-time dreams.
- Journal. Keep notes regarding creative ideas, a Creativity Notebook.
- Read quotes about life and acting. Quotations provide inspiration and motivation. Journal your thoughts and feelings about the quotes. As you grow as an actor, revisit your reflective inquiries to see if your new understanding has changed your perception about the quotes you read earlier. Quotes from experts in your field help you think about your profession in an imaginative way.

Sensory Awareness

Be open to your environment and feelings for creative input, which is gained through all five of your senses. When you are receptive, then thoughts, feelings, imagination, the voice, and body become engaged so that you will be alert. Much of your brain is devoted to processing sensory input by engaging the senses and embracing feelings.

The experience below is designed to increase sensory awareness in a relaxed state.

ASSIGNMENT Awareness   DATE:

Close your eyes and breathe slowly, concentrating on the sense of hearing. Listen to each sound, and let it affect your body and feelings. Listen to your environment for approximately thirty seconds throughout this assignment.

Shift your focus to the sense of smell. Be aware of smells for about thirty seconds. Without judging whether you encounter good or bad aromas, take an inventory of smells.

Engage your sense of taste, noting all of the textures and tastes within your mouth for a short time.

Move to the sense of touch. Without moving your hands, be aware of how your skin feels. Activate the sense of contact in places where you have material touching your skin, from your feet to the hair on your head.

Open your eyes and look at the first inanimate object that is within your view. Look at the object as if you have never seen it before. Be aware of shadows, lights, colors, textures, and anything else you see.

Think about your sight, hearing, smell, taste and touch senses.

CREATIVE INQUIRY *CI*   DATE:

Think about all of the feelings you experienced. Name your feelings when you concentrated on the sense of hearing.

Name your feelings when you focused on the sense of smell.

Name your feelings when you concentrated on the sense of taste.

Name your feelings when you were aware of the sense of touch.

Name your feelings when you engaged your sight.

Periodically take part in Sensory Awareness experiences to get in touch with senses. Awareness of your five senses helps you to activate your senses for creative input and ideas.

Experiences to Increase your Creativity

Some of these assignments will be easy and joyful. Some of the experiences may take time and require you to think of multiple answers to creative inquiries. Experiencing is part of developing your creativity. Taking part in this chapter's experiences periodically will develop your creativity.

ASSIGNMENT Paperclips and Pencils   DATE:

Look at a paperclip or a pencil, two common everyday objects. In the next one minute, use individual brainstorming to imagine many uses for a paper clip or a pencil. For the paperclip, think outside the box, so instead of holding pages together, imagine the paperclip as one earring or a maze for a tiny mouse. Imagine the pencil as a toothpick for a giant or as a mustache.

CREATIVE INQUIRY   *CI*   DATE:

Think about what else a paperclip could be? Within a one-minute time period, list as many ideas as you can.

What else could a pencil be? List as many ideas as you can within a one-minute time limit.

~~~~~~

ASSIGNMENT Random Symbols   DATE:

Looking at random symbols stimulates your creativity. There are two boxes below. Each box has a shape or shapes. Imagine what the object could be part of and complete a picture with something recognizable. This experience is about letting your mind create without logical concern. Look at the symbol in Box A. Think creatively. Using a pencil or pen, finish the drawing in the Box A.

What is the title of your completed drawing?

Look at the symbols in Box B. Think creatively. Finish the drawing.

What is a title of your new creative Box B drawing?

Periodically repeat this creative experience to create new ideas. Use the boxes below.

```
¶



Title
_____
```

```
⊥L


≥


Title
_____
```

Risking silliness is part of the fun of being creative. Tapping into your illogical thinking side of you opens pathways to even more creativity. Being open to originality, playful thinking along with enthusiasm, spontaneity, and imagination are entertaining. Having a good sense of humor and laughing are tools that you can rely on throughout life to benefit you. See things from a humorous perspective other than the obvious; grasp unusual creative ideas or ways of thinking; enjoy being playful; and view the humor in life.

CREATIVE INQUIRY *CI*   DATE:

Think about each question below and answer with your first response. This is a silly quiz. Your objective is to create silly answers.

If you had to eat one crayon, what does the blue crayon taste like?

You suddenly become telepathic and can read thoughts. What is the best way to make lots of money?

If you were an inanimate object, what would you be and why?

If you could be any cartoon character, who would you be and why?

What is the capital of Mars?

If you could be turned into a cheerful, bright vegetable, what would you choose?

What does a dog bone think?

Where does your lap go when you stand up?

What is your favorite internal organ?

What is behind door number 1?

Where does lint come from?

If you could be extremely happy between the hours of 6 a.m. and 6 p.m. and really miserable between the hours of 6 p.m. and 6 a.m., how do you know when it is 2 p.m.?

_____

ASSIGNMENT Doodles   DATE:

A doodle is a drawing or drawings usually made while your attention is focused on something else. A good way to open channels of creativity is to doodle. The drawings can be abstract shapes, simple, and/or recognizable drawings, or not.

Below is a space for free doodling. Doodle for one minute.

Brainstorming

When you brainstorm you can rule out criticism because you need to suspend your judgment. There is no bad idea. The more creative the idea, the better. Work for many, many ideas; quantity is good. Building on your own creative ideas will add to your later creative thinking.

In your everyday life you use brainstorming to solve a challenge. If you have ever had a key stuck in a lock, you brainstormed about all of the possible ways to get the key out. You brainstormed about what would happen if you didn't get the key out. Your mind thought of several different ways and scenes of your getting the key out and what would happen if you couldn't get the key out. Brainstorming allows you to work on solving your challenge.

CREATIVE INQUIRY   DATE:

Imagine that your job is to create new words and titles. You have a challenge to think of new ideas for various categories. Think of as many creative words as possible for each category listed. Allow thirty seconds per category. List a minimum of four creative ideas for each category. Make up new names and titles.

Names for Yet-to-be-invented Colors

Names for Yet-to-be-discovered Animals

Names for New Shapes

ASSIGNMENT Breakfast Cereal   DATE:

Imagine that you have the job of creating a new breakfast cereal. Brainstorm with many ideas that help you create the name for your breakfast cereal; what ingredients are in the cereal; the colors; the packaging; the logo; the box graphic; the jingle; and how to market the new product.

Below are four shapes. Use one shape for each new brainstorming session. Include in each shape 1.) The name for your breakfast cereal, 2.) Ingredients, 3.) Colors, 4.) Packaging, 5.) Logo, 6.) Graphic, 7.) Jingle or motto, and 8.) Marketing ideas.

1.
2.
3.
4.
5.
6.
7.
8.

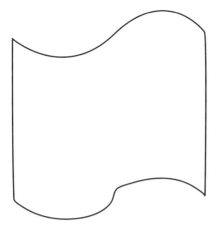 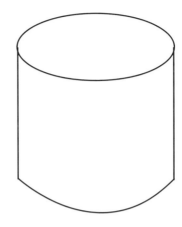

Intuition

Remember that intuition is the ability to understand something without using a logical, step-by-step, conscious process. You can benefit from creative or innovative thinking, because you can figure out what to do in a new situation. Using your intuition or your gut feelings, even though they don't make obvious sense helps you achieve a level of new creativity. When you see a challenge or a creative task, you begin to sense an answer, even before you can put it into words.

Here are some ways to improve your ability to access depth in creativity: practice being quiet; pay attention to your natural breathing. Inhaling and exhaling allows you to free your mind of any routine thoughts.

When you get in touch with your intuitive abilities, it is important to trust the first thing that comes into your mind, whether it is an image, thought, feeling or symbol. After receiving your intuitive message, notice how creatively alert you feel. Paying attention to little hunches or gut feelings will cause them to increase. Acknowledge and honor the intuitive ability that you have.

ASSIGNMENT Tap into your Intuition with Symbols   DATE:

Get a piece of paper and a pen or pencil.

Breathe easily.

Ask yourself silently, "What do I need right now in my life?"

Ask yourself the question above three times in row, pausing between each question.

Imagine you are going toward a more meaningful answer each time you ask.

When you've finished with the third question, pick up your pen and draw some symbols in the space below.

REFLECTIVE INQUIRY RI   DATE:

Revisit the created symbols that you drew. What do they suggest that you might add to or subtract from your life?

CREATIVE INQUIRY CI   DATE:

Imagine that you have inner music playing in your imagination. Remember a song with lyrics that have meaning for you.

Breathe easily.

Listen to your inner music.

ASSIGNMENT Lyrics   DATE:

Write some of the lyrics of your inner song.

CREATIVE INQUIRY   DATE:

Think about why you think that your intuition chose that song at this moment.

Left Brain/Right Brain Experience

Your left brain guides your thinking in a logical way and gives you the ability to communicate that logic. When in your left brain mode, you are logical and analyze things. You are practical and can work with a method to get things done.

ASSIGNMENT Left Brain/Right Brain Experience   DATE:

Your right brain processes information very quickly and stores your memories and experiences with all input from all five senses. Your right brain likes pictures and guides your intuition. Your right brain is visual and does not use conscious, logical thinking. Using your right brain, make a selection for the line you like better, the one from Rectangle A or Rectangle B. Which do you choose?

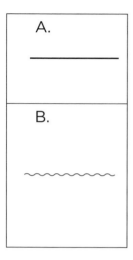

Thinking Outside the Box

By utilizing the creativity of thinking outside the box, you generate artistic freedom for yourself. You open yourself to fun opportunities; you can make bold choices.

CREATIVE INQUIRY *CI*   DATE:

Think about thinking outside the box, look at the categories below and create. Think outside the box for unusual names, animals, desserts and made-up words.

| A name | Think of another | and another |

| A dessert | Think of another | and another |

| A made-up word | Think of another | and another |

CREATIVE INQUIRY **CI**   DATE:

Think about the images below and give an outside-the-box title to it.

What is your title?

Look at the picture again. Write down another two titles.

Another?

And another?

Dream Work for Thinking Outside the Box

This section involves remembering and thinking about your nighttime dreams. Dreams have long been associated with creative inspiration in life. The purpose of dream work is to get in touch with an outside-the-box part of you and to unlock more creative dimensions. Dream work helps you get into the place of freeing emotions and imagination and looking at your creative dream life.

Only the dreamer him/herself is able to make meaning of his/her dreams. All dreams break new ground and invite you to new creativity. Your dreams have meanings unique to you. Others cannot assign meanings to your dreams; only you can. Dreams connect you with your world of symbols, images, and stories. Dreams contain the richest of imagination with no limits on budgets for costumes, settings and props. Dreams are like abstract paintings with symbols. Each aspect of the dream may be a symbol. Dreams pay no attention to the dramatic structures of form, time, sequence, location, or circumstances. Dreams are canvases of heightened imaginative expressions of your uncensored world.

In a dream, the dreamer is the writer, the producer, the director, the characters, the technical staff, and the audience. Nighttime dreams can be viewed as the ultimate individual, outside-the-box theatrical creation.

Tips for Remembering Dreams

The decision to remember dreams is an act of creative commitment. Make up your mind before you go to sleep that you will remember your dreams. It may take several nights of reminding yourself to remember your dreams before you do. Keep a dream journal by your bed. Before jumping out of bed or when you wake up in the middle of the night, write your dream. Write your dream in the present tense; remember all details of the who, what, when, where, all colors, all shapes, what you see, hear, smell, taste, and touch, all feelings and particularly the last scene and how you as the dreamer feel. Write down all that you remember, fragments, a part of your dream, thoughts, and images. Don't worry about time or sequences. Dreams pay no attention to time or staying in one location. Title your dream.

ASSIGNMENT   DATE:

Sit quietly.

Write down a dream that you remember. Choose a dream in which you take part. The dream can be a complete dream, a fragment, a part of dream, a thought, or an image.

Write the dream as if it is happening to you.

Pay attention to details.

Who or what do you see?

Who or what do you hear?

Who or what do you smell?

Do you taste anything?

What do you touch?

Trace your feelings in the dream.

Pay attention to any colors or lack of color in the dream.

Pay attention to the last scene in the dream. What is the last thing you remember?

In that last scene, what is your feeling?

After you have written the dream, read the dream and create a title.

Write your dream in the space below.

What are the last words or sounds or lack of sound that you hear or are aware of in your dream?

Looking back at your dream, list some of your feelings that you experience in the dream.

What is the title of your dream?

ASSIGNMENT A   DATE:

Recall your dream again and answer the following questions:

Why did you choose the title that you gave to the dream?

What part/s do you play in the dream?

What are the colors that you see in the dream?

What are the feelings that you felt in the dream?

What are the repeated images in the dream?

What are the sounds/music in the dream?

Are there any beings, animals, or objects that talk in the dream?

What are the surprises in the dream?

What are the themes, morals, or messages of the dream?

Things to Remember When You Work with your Dreams

When you work with your dreams, you need to remember some of the Dream work tenets. All dreams have several meanings to you. There is no such thing as a dream with only one meaning. Only you as the dreamer can say what meanings your dreams may have. The purpose of some dreams is to help you in waking life.

Sometimes you dream numerous times each night. The dreams of the same night may depict one theme or more than one theme. Sometimes your dreams are telling you something about your physical issues. Each dream might have elements of your past, present, and future.

You, the dreamer, are the only person who can really say what the dream means. Here's to remembering your dreams.

How an Actor Benefits by Thinking Creatively

As an actor there are numerous benefits to thinking with creativity. When you audition, making secure, bold choices will help you stand out as a creative actor. Being able to approach text with lots of different ideas to show versatility will be favorable. There will be many actors who come into an audition or approach a role with a "playing it safe" attitude for many reasons; one is that they don't want to make a mistake. You need to approach every audition with imaginative ideas and have enough security to present them. You might make bold creative so-called mistakes. Mistakes are creative gifts.

The purpose of the audition is to show the casting director that you are prepared, confident, and creative. By making brave, inventive choices you will distinguish yourself as a positive, confident actor.

Listen, follow directions and make any adjustment. It is better to adjust a daring choice rather than present an unimaginative choice. If your audition has too much energy, the director will ask for an adjustment.

As an actor, one way to aid your creative thinking is to think without judgment. Self-judgment will inhibit your creative thinking, brainstorming, intuition, right brain thinking, and thinking outside the box. You apply your imagination without criticism from yourself or others. Come up with unexpected answers.

Being a creative actor, you are to be fully present. Being completely in the moment and vitalized with all of your senses will set you apart as an engaged person. Your full awareness adds to your creativity. Engaging all five senses increases your mind's sharpness. Your creative energy will establish you as a creative actor.

Imaginative thinking helps develop empathy. This is what is known as being in someone else's shoes. As an actor, you will benefit if you can read a character's emotional story and relate to it. You use imagination to find the character's story. You have to be able to empathize with any character whether or not he/she is an admirable character in the play. You must be able to play the character truthfully, so you must be capable of empathizing with the character.

Creative expression helps your acting because it is your own originality. Imagination is important in establishing your character's point of view. You are who you are; this makes you different in your approach to creativity. Using your uniqueness in your creativity sets you aside as an actor who feels secure in your individuality. This is valued by casting agents, directors, fellow actors, and audiences.

A fun aspect of being an actor is playful freedom. As a child, you may have pretended and played for hours. When you become an actor, the ability to pretend is part of your acting tool bag. Curiosity and imagination are wonderful ways to fuel your creativity. Using the youthful imagination in your acting will bring freshness to your work.

Your ability to tap into your intuition is a distinctive quality of your good acting. Acting is about making insightful, creative choices. Your intuitive abilities bring your work to life. Aliveness is what engages an audience.

In your acting studies, you learn about people, life, and acting. You learn about yourself. By taking on characters, cooperating with others, and performing, you learn about who you are and who you might want to be as a person with a creative future. Thinking imaginatively engages you as a person and an actor.

Creativity is a natural extension of our enthusiasm.

Earl Nightingale, American motivational speaker, author

CREATIVE INQUIRY *CI*   DATE:

Think about the quote above. What do think this quote means? Make some notes in the space below.

_____

_____

_____

Thinking creatively will benefit you in your acting career. As an actor when you read a script and imagine how the character stands and talks, you are a creative thinker. When a director asks you to give a new idea to some kind of action, you will brainstorm, will use your intuitive feelings, will use your left and right brain thinking, and will think "outside the box."

As an actor you have both sides of your brain operating simultaneously. One side of the brain may dominate, but both are in constant interchange. You use the left side of your brain to analyze the script, looking at the plot or story, the theme or playwright's message, conflicts and a character's objectives, what the character wants to achieve in the play.

In rehearsal the director may ask you to experiment with ways to say lines or how to do an action. This asks for you to use your right brain thinking. The director may want you to be spontaneous and organic. Organic acting can be defined as you putting yourself in the mind/ body of a character. This is called organic because you are allowing your character to direct your movements, speech, and thought processes. The phrase "be in character" is an expression used to remind an actor to think, feel, and behave totally as the character would.

If you are using right brain dominance, you tend to look at the character first and identify feelings and use intuitions about the movements and how to say and how to act. Spontaneous right brain actors change things as the feelings hit them.

The creative process is beneficial for you as an actor. You can employ your mind's eye to create visual images of how the character would act. Using your freed imagination leads you to a playful creation.

As an actor, your job is to employ playfulness. Remember as a child, you had more time to play and create. As an actor, you can get paid to play and use your creativity. You have many character creations in your imagination now. Some acting teachers ask that you imagine your past experiences to bring a truthful aspect to your present work. So invite all of your creative thinking skills from your childhood and create alive characters.

Begin to use the letters CWOW to help establish the elements of any story line. You can use CWOW in your creativity, mime, improvisation, monologue, and audition work. C equals Character. What character do you portray? W is the Who you are talking or relating to. O indicates your character's objective. What does your character want to achieve? The final W is Where. Where does your story take place? Character, Who, Objective, and Where: CWOW. This acronym is pronounced See Wow.

An example of your CWOW might include:

- ~ Character—I play a five-year-old girl.
- ~ Who—I am talking to a department store Santa.
- ~ Objective—I want Santa to bring me a new doll tomorrow, Christmas Day, cause I have been a good girl and brushed my teeth each day.
- ~ Where—We are at a department store.

CREATIVE INQUIRY *CI*   DATE:

Think again about the idea that actors create characters and stories. In the creative planning, character is defined as any personality other than yourself. Below is a short list of characters. List an unusual location where this character might be. Think of a reason why the character would be in the creative location.

Character	Who are you talking to?	Creative Location Reason	Why the Character is in the Creative Location
Lawyer			
Clown			
Queen			
Fan			
President			
Dog walker			
Teacher			

Movie star

Salesperson

Miss USA

Disney character

CREATIVE INQUIRY CI

Think about one of the characters from the above list and tell a short story in three sentences of what happens to the character. A story has a beginning, middle, and an end. You are beginning to create a story using CWOW. Which character did you choose?

Character

Location

Sentence 1. The beginning sentence establishes the elements of a story: CWOW. Who is the character that you will portray? Who is the other person in the story? What is your character's objective? What does the character want? Where does the story take place?

Sentence 2. The middle sentence builds the story. The objective is developed.

Sentence 3. The end sentence includes what happens at the conclusion or resolution of the story. The character may or may not achieve his/her objective.

~~~~~~
CREATIVE INQUIRY **CI**   DATE:
~~~~~~

Think about one character who would say each of the lines below. Remember the character can be any age, any type, and have any occupation.

Line of Dialogue	Character Who You Chose to Say the Line	Talking to Whom

"She's as cute as a bug's ear"

"You are who you are."

"The proof is in the pudding."

"You can lead a horse to water but you can't make him drink."

"You know what to do."

"It's dark out there."

"I've lost my glasses."

Using Both Left and Right Brain Thinking in Acting

In this chapter you learned about creativity and various kinds of creative thinking. Acting utilizes both the creative, and the analytical kinds of thinking. You are asked to create, invent, discover and imagine. You also have to be able to analyze, evaluate, and assess. You are using both the right and left brain thinking.

Both the left and right brain thinking skills should be for you to access when required. First, you analyze a role to find the facts about the character; you discover the story or plot. Your right brain provides the feelings and emotion. You balance your performances with skills from both the left and right brain thinking.

Actors who use both the left and right brain can achieve a logical, consistent performance as well as be able to access spontaneity. The actor knows the staging; the character is surprised by a look or emotion. Knowing the details and analysis of the character and story helps you have organization; allowing continual surprises when making your performance new each time keeps your work alive. Actors who use predominately the right brain, as well as actors who use predominately the left brain, can both use both left and right brain thinking.

You, as an excellent actor, are seeking both analysis and emotion, that is using both the left and right brain to achieve discipline and vitality in your overall acting process. You know the details; you have creative ideas; you keep it alive and in the moment. You want to be known as an actor who works with both left and right brain acting.

CREATIVE INQUIRY *CI*   DATE:

Think about how you might compliment yourself. Your ideas are creative. As you look back over your choices from the assignments in this chapter, list some creative thoughts for which you applaud yourself.

Think left and think right and think low and think high. Oh, the thinks you can think up if only you try.

Dr. Seuss, Theodore Geisel, American writer, poet, cartoonist

Closure for Chapter Two: Creativity

ASSIGNMENT Closure   *A*   DATE:

Complete the following unfinished sentences with ideas about the information presented in this chapter:

I understand

I have gained new knowledge about

I have questions about

I would like to study more about

One surprising thing about working with creativity is

_____

Wishing you the best in all of your creative journeys!

In the next chapter, you apply your creative thinking to relaxing your body for movement and mime.

CHAPTER THREE: MOVEMENT

Introduction to Movement

You are continuing on your journey of the creative inquiry into the world of acting. This chapter pays attention to one of the instruments of communication: the body. Character creation is grounded in a bodily stance, so you first concentrate on the body without concern for the vocal work. Your physical work is a basis of any character's physical creation.

Your actor's goal in movement training is to free your body, so that you can create the character's physical stance and movement. To establish a character, you create a physical foundation that leads to character movement. The aim of movement training is to make the body flexible, to enliven the physical design with imagination, and to enable your creation of a character's physical life. Exercises in movement contribute towards making your physical apparatus more mobile, flexible, and expressive. Warming up your instrument with limbering exercises for body muscles helps you relieve tension and prepares you for flexible movement. If you have physical limitations, you can make adjustments to your warm-ups and exercises.

Having and maintaining a healthy body by eating properly and staying away from junk foods is one of your acting goals; staying hydrated, and sleeping adequate hours will aid in acquiring your ideal actor's body for physical work.

To deliver a believable character, you as the actor must involve your entire body with movement. You need to experiment with the way your body moves, and this requires that you get out of your seat, do exercises, evaluate the results by self-assessment, and make adjustments. Then you try the physical experience again with changes, evaluate the adjusted effects and make more adjustments. The end result is that you have control of your body, and you can use it exactly the way you want in order to create the character.

In order to train physically you must remove all distractions for full engagement and dress appropriately with clothes and shoes that allow for movement. Reduced muscle tone, poor posture, sagging chests show

insufficient training and undeveloped use of your physical instrument. Unless it is your intention to show a character with physical incapacities, you should move in an easy manner that adds to rather than detracts from your physical creation. To do this, you must have a healthy body in good working order.

Definition of Movement

Movement is an action with the body by which an actor communicates what the character is thinking, feeling, or doing.

History of Movement Training

Stage movement has a rich history from ancient to modern Theatre. Historically the Theatre has many teachers who created styles of movement and methods of physical training. There is a legacy from the work of the early twentieth- century movement pioneers, such as Rudolf Laban, Jacques Copeau, Jerzy Growtowski, Frederick Matthias Alexander, and Moshé Feldenkrais.

Rudolf Laban was a choreographer, dancer, teacher, and writer from Hungary. He developed a language for describing and notating human movement. His language is used by dancers, actors, and other professions to identify movement.

There are modern leaders in the Physical Movement field: Vsevolod Emilevich Meyerhold, Tadashi Suzuki, Anne Bogart, Tina Landau, and Julie Taymor. Physical Theatre is performance that utilizes movement as a basis for their performances. Modern physical Theatre is built on mime and Commedia dell 'Arte.

Introduction to Relaxation for Movement

Relaxation is an essential element of your work. It is necessary that you, on your own initiative, practice relaxation of your body to prepare for movement training. It is one of the primary principles of the acting craft that require ongoing attention. To create, you find techniques from various sources to help you become open and stress free. You might like group-led warm-ups, or you might prefer solitary moments. You can take classes in yoga, meditation, or other centering physical and mental practices to experience relaxation. You need to develop a routine which best suits you to achieve relaxation.

The body is one of the instruments of your acting communication. You want to keep your body free of physical tension. Preparation for achieving your physical freedom is essential for your acting. It is your obligation to continue adding to your ways of achieving physical relaxation. Care is required for your actor's instrument: your body. You owe it to yourself, your director, your fellow actor, and the audience to be in the best condition you can.

This chapter presents some relaxation, movement and mime assignments to achieve freedom from tension. Once you have taken part in some of the relaxation and physical experiences, you can think creatively in order to develop your own practices.

Relaxation and Centering Breath

Diaphragmatic breathing, also known as belly breathing, is a necessary instrument for the actor. If you lie on your back and relax, your natural diaphragmatic breath is automatic. Your ribcage expands, allowing your diaphragm muscle to expand, which then lets your lungs fill to capacity. Your belly rises and lowers. Your shoulders stay in place; they do not rise and fall when you use diaphragmatic breathing.

You can achieve the relaxation needed by engaging the breath. The breath supported by the diaphragmatic muscle leads to a deep sense of relaxation.

When you stand erect, your body might revert to shallow, chest breathing, which causes the shoulders to rise and fall. This action results in the tightening of your throat. You can train your muscles to expand your stomach area rather than your chest. You need to practice correct breathing techniques daily to return to natural breathing habits. This inhalation and exhalation technique is used to lessen anxiousness, to relax, and for vocal support.

ASSIGNMENT Relaxation and Centering Breath   DATE:

This is a breathing experience that you can do sitting in a crowded location, without others knowing. Use the technique for focusing, relaxation, and centering. Focus on the breath is what integrates the mind and body.

Take one minute to breathe. Sit on a straight-backed chair with both feet on the floor. Hands are held loosely in your lap. Close your mouth. If you can lie down, that is even better. Roll your tongue toward the back of your throat and up, so that the tongue's tip touches the top soft palate. Inhale slowly through your nose with your mouth closed, filling your lungs with air. Open your mouth slightly and exhale. Repeat three times, releasing tensions and gathering tranquility in your mind and body.

REFLECTIVE INQUIRY (RI)   DATE:

Recall all the details of using your diaphragmatic breath. Now think of a prompt to remind you to do belly breathing instead of letting your shoulders rise and fall from shallow breathing. A prompt would be a thought or a saying that reminds you to belly breathe. Write some kind of reminder below.

Yawning

When you are preparing for auditions, performances, or any possible stressful situation, you can find release by yawning. Even if you don't feel like yawning, go ahead and try it, no matter how you think you might look. Give yourself approval to look unrefined. Remember the confidence you worked on in the Prologue of this book. Be assured that you will feel good yawning.

Give yourself permission to yawn. Yawning revives the brain; it can perk you up. Some think it is rude to yawn. In the Victorian era, the custom that exposed any orifice was uncivilized which is why people cover their mouths today when they yawn. You can explain to others that it is important to keep you more alert, more aware, and relaxed. Feel free to yawn. In other surroundings you might have to choose the suitable time and location to yawn.

ASSIGNMENT Yawning ✦ DATE:

Yawn the polite way with your mouth opened and covered with your hand. Then involve your entire face; open your mouth wide and uncover your mouth; "yawn" with your arms and hands; "yawn" with your entire body. Continue yawning until you feel you could qualify as an expert yawner. Imagine a casting director is looking for the most committed yawner. You might be cast.

REFLECTIVE INQUIRY RI DATE:

Revisit the yawning assignment. Was your face relaxed? Did your jaw pop? Did you use diaphragmatic breathing to inflate your lungs and exhale? Make some notes below.

ASSIGNMENT Adding Gentle Voice ✦ DATE:

If you are in a location where you are able to add gentle voice to your physical work, sigh ten times. If you have not sighed each day, you are under-sighed. Gently sigh with your voice. Let your sigh be relaxed and unforced. Sigh with your face along with your voice. Sigh with your shoulders. Sigh with your stomach and hips. Sigh with your legs and feet. Sigh with your entire body. Enjoy sighing while you engage all parts of your body.

Engaging the Relaxed Body
With any type of physical exercise, be sure to make adjustments for physical limitations. After reading the steps below, you decide whether you need a supporting apparatus for balance.

ASSIGNMENT Engaging the Relaxed the Body   DATE:

When you are able to stand in a space where you can stretch your arms without bothering anyone else, stand in neutral position. Neutral position means weight is equal on both feet with feet approximately hip width. Hands hang loosely at your sides; knees are slightly relaxed, so they are not locked.

Shake your hands easily. Let your hands hang loosely. Rotate each wrist then relax your wrists.

Shake one foot, and then the other. Stand easily on both feet with arms, wrists, feet relaxed.

Move your hips in big circles, one way at a time. Then stop. Check your lower back for any tension points.

Breathe, engaging your diaphragm.

Roll your shoulders forward then back. Stand easily and take a stress inventory.

Using only half circles, roll your head and neck slowly and carefully. Roll your head to the right and then tip your chin up slightly. Roll your head to the left and turn your chin slightly up.

Move your face into several different contortions.

Remember to roll your eyeballs and blink. Yes, it is okay to roll your eyes.

Keep breathing.

Stretch up onto your toes.

Reach toward the sky, bringing your arms above your head.

Reach out and write your first name in air with one arm, then write your last name in air with your other arm. Write your first name with one foot while standing on the other foot. Hold on to something for balance if needed. Write your last name with the other foot.

Stand in neutral stance again. Take inventory of any areas of tension in your body, as you breathe. If comfortable, close your eyes and sigh quietly ten times.

Open your eyes.

Stand relaxed for a moment.

Hopefully you feel relaxed and ready to delve with positivity and creativity into movement. Revisit the relaxation experiences whenever you feel a need to relax.

The Bow

Let's start at the end of your performance. A physical move that is symbolic and has emotional meaning for you as an actor is the bow at the end of the production, at the curtain call. Look back at the Prologue chapter to refresh your memory of what a curtain call is. Bowing is the act of lowering the torso and head as a symbol that the play is finished. For actors it is a sign that states a nonverbal "thank you" to the audience at the end of a performance. Imagine if each actor appeared onstage and verbally thanked each audience member for attending. The curtain call might be longer than the play itself. Thus actors take nonverbal bows.

The curtain call should be staged with tempo and sequence so that the spirit of the performance is continued while the audience applauds. The entire curtain call must be quick and energized. If the audience stops applauding, you have slowed the pace of the curtain call. Your goal is to bow quickly, sincerely, professionally, demonstrating dignity in order to thank the audience for coming to watch the performance. After all, without the presence of the audience, the actor's creative process is incomplete. They deserve to be thanked with an energized, sincere curtain call.

Some directors have the actors take the curtain call and do a bow in character. If you play a high-class character, and your curtain call is to be taken in character, your bow would be very straight and stern. Whereas if you are playing a happy-go-lucky upbeat young character, your bow would be fast, very energized, and delivered with a big smile.

Most directors prefer a non-character, neutral bow with hands at your sides, lowering your head toward the ground, then arising with a smile and direct eye contact with the audience to show appreciation.

What could be called the beginner's bow is distinguished by the actor bending his/her elbows and placing one arm in front of the waist and the other behind his or her back, thus appearing to bend the body in the middle by using the arms to fold the body. It is cute to see little ones take their first bow with arms helping their bodies bend, but it is not appropriate for professional actors.

ASSIGNMENT The Bow   DATE:

Practice the neutral bow ten times with genuine smiles. You can practice your thank you smile as you bow. Think creatively within the guidelines of being genuine.

Now is your time to rehearse, watch the rehearsal, assess your rehearsal, make adjustments to your rehearsals, and rehearse again. So before you video record your bow, there are some guidelines to your video recording.

Video Recording as Part of your Rehearsal Process

An important part of your actor's progress is assessing your rehearsals and performances. You can watch a rehearsal recording and make adjustments for the next practice. As you proceed in study of movement theories, you can check your progress by recording your rehearsal and your created movement pieces. This video diary is part of documenting your progress as an actor. Sometimes in the study of this book, you will be asked to video record without audio and video record with audio.

Guidelines for Preparing Your Rehearsal Video

~   Avoid Visual Distractions.
    If you can, video your work in front of a blank wall or closed curtains without any print on the backgrounds.
~   Check the background sounds.
    Leave your television turned off, so any viewer does not hear the play-by-play of the football game. Be sure your phone is turned off.
~   Identify each performance piece.
    Announce the title/s of any movement, mime, or monologue during the opening ten seconds.
~   Optimize the production values of the video.
    Mount your camera on a tripod or steady table. A hand-held camera will produce video that is, at the very least, unsteady and difficult to watch. Whatever you do, do not try to hold the camera yourself while performing.
~   Face forward toward the camera.
    Profile shots shows only one half of your face; turning your back for an extended time shows your least expressive side.
~   Place your camera a moderate distance from you.
    A football field distance is too far away. Likewise extreme close-ups are too near.

Make sure you can see each move and understand any spoken words on the video documentation of your artistic work.

ASSIGNMENT Neutral Bows   DATE:

Video record your neutral bows and watch the video recording. Make some notes addressing how professional and genuine your ten bows appeared. Did you smile and seem to enjoy the imagined applause?

ASSIGNMENT Bowing in Character   DATE:

For a character bow, shift from a neutral stance into a character stance for a unique bow. Brainstorm on the many ways your character might bow. Practice a character bow for each one of these character types:

A proud upper-class person;

A shy, timid person;

A happy, energetic person;

A servant with low status.

Next video record your character bows. Watch your video recording. Make some notes on 1.) How the bow of the proud, upper-class character differs from the shy, timid person, and

2.) How the bow of the happy, energetic character differs from the servant with low status?

ASSIGNMENT Assessing your Bows   DATE:

Revise any three of your bows. Evaluate what you did, not because the bows were bad, but because actors view, evaluate, make creative revisions or adjustments, then perform again. Utilize your positive, evaluation techniques in this assessment process.

Now make three adjustments in the types of bows. Video record the bows, incorporating the three changes.

What creative changes did you make?

Preparation for Actor's Character Stance and Movement

This is a reminder to return to do a basic physical warm-up each day. A routine physical preparation focuses your mind and gives flexibility to your body. The objective is to create a physical routine that works for you.

Neutral Stance to Character Stance

You are ready to assume your neutral stance, the position the actor begins with, to establish a physical character. The neutral stance is a body that is balanced with arms hanging to your sides and your body weight equally distributed on each foot.

From neutral stance, with slight adjustments of your physical posture, you can create an attitude and posture for any character. You will find this neutral position to be a good center of balance. In this position, you can align posture and release any areas of tension in your neck, shoulders, back, and/or hips. This grounded position allows you to move into a variety of character stances and carriages.

ASSIGNMENT Neutral Stance   DATE:

Stand up. Let your hands hang loosely at your sides. Be sure knees are not locked. Put the distance of two fists between your two feet. Your arms hang loosely at your sides with imagined weights on your fingertips. Check that there is no tension in your neck, shoulders, back and/or hips. If you locate points of tension, gently shake the tensed muscle and then relax that isolated area.

Now follow the directions below and complete the (CI) sections. Stand in a neutral position. Shift your weight to one hip.

CREATIVE INQUIRY   DATE:

Think about what character type might stand with his/her weight over one hip.

Name a feeling that is generated by standing with your weight over one hip.

Now return to neutral stance. Raise your head up so your nose is in the air. Inhale so your chest expands. Stand up as straight as you can and put your hands on your hips. What character type might stand with his/her head raised up, nose in the air with chest expanded and hands on hips?

Name a feeling that is generated by standing with your head raised, nose in the air, chest expanded, and hands on hips.

Return again to a neutral stance. Lower your head. Exhale your breath, letting your chest cave in and shoulders slump. Drop your hands in front of your body. Bend your knees slightly. Turn your toes in. What character type might stand with head lowered, with stooped shoulders, hands hanging loosely with bent knees and toes turned in?

Name a feeling that is generated by standing with lowered head, stooped shoulders, etc.

ASSIGNMENT Neutral Stance to Character Stance   DATE:

Set up the recording device and record your neutral stance to character stance. Announce the date of video recording and say the title "Neutral Stance to Character Stance". Use ten different character types and attitude positions for the (RI) below. Begin in your neutral position and announce the character type. Be sure to return to neutral stance after each shift. Concentrate the entire body for each adjustment. For each character type, shift from neutral stance to character stance.

REFLECTIVE INQUIRY *RI*   DATE:

Revisit your recording of Neutral Stance to Character Stance. Begin by noting the differences between a neutral stance and a character stance.

Now make a note about any character stance that conveyed a bold physical character choice.

Stage Stances and Movement

There are five categories of stage stances and movement for the actor. All five categories originate from neutral stances. These are 1.) Basic stage stance and movement, 2.) Emotional stance and movement, 3.) Non-verbalized words stances and movement, 4.) Status, age, and character stance and movement, and 5.) Creative stance and movement.

Basic Stage Stances and Movement

Stances and movement communicate thoughts and feelings to fellow actors and audiences. Much of your actor's communication is based on nonverbal body positions and attitudes. The audience watches your body language to tell them how your character feels in reaction to a situation. The audience can usually tell by watching a person's body communication, if your character is happy, excited, sad, or agitated.

On stage, the movements and stances must be heightened so that they will be understood by the audience. Because in some theaters the audience is sitting far away from the stage, the actor must broaden his/her movements. As an actor you must practice movement until it becomes natural in appearance to the audience.

Onstage, there are certain staging conventions which are learned by rehearsing physical movements.

- When walking onstage, starting with your upstage foot, the foot away from the audience, opens the body so that the audience can see your face when you cross the stage.
- When seating yourself onstage, you should feel the edge of a chair with the back of your legs, so that you do not have to look down at the chair to sit.
- If you must cross the stage while speaking, you are to walk in front of the other characters.
- If you need to cross the stage while others are speaking, you are to walk behind the speaking actors.
- The moving actor dominates the stage. If two actors cross the stage together, the one with more lines should take the upstage position, a short step ahead of the other actor.
- In the Prologue chapter, the eight body positions are defined. Below are abbreviations and an explanation of the body positions.
  - » **FF**—Full Front: Your entire body is facing toward audience; this Full Front position is considered the strongest position.
  - » **1/4 R**—One Quarter Right: Your body is slightly angled toward your right.
  - » **PR**—Profile Right: Your body turns profile toward your right or at a 90-degree angle; the left side of your face is showing to the audience.
  - » **3/4 R**—Three Quarters Right: Your body turns another quarter turn to your right; you are almost facing backwards.
  - » **FB**—Full Back: Your back is toward the audience; full Back is considered the weakest position.
  - » **1/4 L**—One Quarter Left: Your body is slightly angled toward your left.
  - » **Pl**—Profile Left: Your body turns so you are facing profile left or a 90-degree turn toward the left.
  - » **3/4 L**—Three Quarters Left: Your body is turned so far toward your left that you are almost facing backwards.
  - » **DS**—Downstage is the area closest to the audience.
  - » **US**—Upstage is the area farthest away from the audience. The Downstage and Upstage areas originated with the theaters of the past where the stage floor was sloped toward the audience.
  - » **Open up**—The stage direction when you are facing as much towards the audience as you can and still relate to other actors on stage.
  - » **Cheat out**—The direction given when you are to position yourself towards the audience. You may have to readjust your body so that the audience can see your face.

» **Upstaging**—The situation in which you either take the attention of the audience to yourself, or you move toward the back of the stage to make another actor face away from the audience.

» **Sharing the Stage**—The direction that indicates that all of the actors on stage have equal attention from the audience.

Emotional Stances and Movement

Rehearsing expressions of emotions without speaking, in front of your video camera helps you evaluate how an audience member might view your physical communication. Taking a neutral stance and then moving in the manner of the emotion without being concerned about saying lines allows you to concentrate on basic stage stances and movements.

ASSIGNMENT Emotional Stances and Movement   DATE:

Study the list of emotions below and imagine how you might communicate the emotion so that the audience understands the feeling. For this experience you are asked to take a stance demonstrating the engagement of your entire body. After each pose, return to neutral stance.

Announce each emotion. Make up a line that another character might have said to you just before you go into stance; this will give you a motivation to react with the emotion. The prompt line motivates you to move into your emotional stance. Feel the emotion; internalize the emotion before becoming the emotional stance. Create CWOW: who you are as the character (your age and occupation, for example); to whom are you speaking; what objective you want to express by your pose; and where you are. After holding the stance for a count of three seconds, return to neutral stance. Hear another implied prompt line and move to a new stance to display the emotion. Return to neutral after each emotional stance. Video record your demonstration of the following Emotional Stances and Movement.

Aggression
Boredom
Confidence
Confusion
Disgust
Exhaustion
Fright

Guilt
Love
Negativity
Pride
Shyness
Stubbornness
Thoughtfulness

REFLECTIVE INQUIRY   *RI*   DATE:

Recall whether you let yourself feel the emotion? Did you let the feeling emotionally affect your physical stance? Now view your video and make adjustments to three emotions. Which three emotions did you choose to adjust?

Describe your adjustments.

What body parts did you move to make each adjustment?

Non Verbalized Words Stances and Movement
Sometimes the director will want you to use your body to express a word, phrase, or emotion. The physicalization might take place before the verbally expressed line, after the expressed line, or instead of the line.

Rehearsing natural-looking reactions to words, phrases, or emotions is part of maintaining your flexible, expressive body.

ASSIGNMENT Non Verbalized Words Stances and Movement DATE:

For this experience, convey the following phrases by taking a stance. The challenge is to demonstrate the word or phrase without using any sound or mouthing any words. Video record your stances and moves. Announce the word or phrase, and then take the stance that symbolizes the word or phrase.

"What?"

"No."

"Yes."

"Come over here."

"Shhh"

"Come over here right now."

"Hurry."

Now rehearse three different ways to express each word and phrase above. For one of the three revisions, imagine you are in a large theater and must communicate the reaction to an audience member who is seated far away from the stage.

Status, Age, and Character Stances and Movement

To play a status, age, or character different from yourself requires a physical creation based on stances and movements. Status is defined as the position of an individual in relation to another, in regard to social, family, or occupational standing. Age in the character's creation is a defined period of the human's life, his or her years of birth. Character is a personality type, with distinctive traits, language, mannerisms, and physicalization. The status, age, or character is reflected in how the actor stands and moves.

The actor needs to observe different statuses, ages, and characters in real life. You will benefit by people watching in various locations. Watch people in action in public places. Notice how people of different economic statuses stand and move. Notice how different types of people and occupations stand and move.

Notice how various ages stand and move in various situations. Watch young children stand and move. Observe teens; notice the difference from age five to teen years. Discern how middle-aged people move and interact. Look at those nearing retirement age. Then watch the stages of age, the older generation. For the experiences of observation, observe a five-year-old, a sixteen-year-old, a thirty-year-old, a fifty-year-old, and an eighty-year-old. You can estimate a person's age.

REFLECTIVE INQUIRY RI   DATE:

Recall what you noticed about various statuses' stances and movements?

What did you notice about various ages' stances and movements?

What did you notice about various characters' stances and movements?

ASSIGNMENT Status, Age, and Character Stances and Movements DATE:

Using your creative thinking tools, create stances and movements for various statuses, characters, and ages. Use your intuition to feel how it would feel if you were the various statuses, characters and ages listed below.

Imagine a crown on your head. You are standing on a balcony looking down on your subjects. You want the audience to recognize your status. Now change your status to portray a servant being subservient to the king.

REFLECTIVE INQUIRY DATE:

Recall how your body felt with the imagined crown on your head?

How does the body change when you are portraying a servant?

How do your emotions change from the high status character to the low status character?

ASSIGNMENT Stages of Life—Status, Age, Character Stances and Movements DATE:

After observing various ages in real life, concentrate on five ages: youth, teens, middle age, retirement age, and oldsters.

Focus on an exact age for a young child, and then a teen, and an older person. Imagine your character at an age- appropriate location for each. Free your mind of any stereotypical poses, concentrating on the exact age of the character. Let your body physically become younger or older. Engage your toes and feet, then your legs and hips; move to your stomach. Let your arms reflect the age, and engage your shoulders and head. Show the age with your face. Think and feel like the character of a selected age.

Show a child of five years of age with a stance and movement without getting on your knees. Everyone and everything seems taller than the five-year-old.

Act like a teen, shifting your weight from one leg to another. Depict the stance and movement of the teen.

Demonstrate a middle-aged person. Movements are brisk and busy-like.

Interpret an older person about ready for retirement. Movements are slower and settled.

Show the eldest of your character stances. You have slower movements and require more conscious effort to move. Movement is often shaky and careful.

Video record your rehearsal of your Stage of Life. Announce the created age and then move into the age for stances and movements. Sustain your age character for one minute. Shift to neutral; announce the next age and then move into your next character age.

REFLECTIVE INQUIRY   **RI**   DATE:

Revisit your video work. Write down what you notice about your portrayal of 1.) Your young child, 2.) Your teen and, 3.)Your middle-aged adult, and 4.) Your older person.

Character Stances and Movements—Lead Walk

A character can be established by walking. By imagining an invisible string attached to various parts of your body, and moving as if the invisible string is pulling you forward, a character can be created.

When you video the Lead Walk assignment, stay within camera parameters.

ASSIGNMENT Lead Walk A   DATE:

Start with a neutral stance.

Imagine an invisible string pulling your forehead forward.

Your lead walk is with the forehead.

Walk for ten seconds.

Shift to neutral stance, and then imagine the string is attached to your nose. What character would lead with his or her nose?

Shift to neutral stance, and then lead with your chin.

Walk for ten seconds.

Continue to shift to neutral stance and then shift to the lead walk with the invisible string pulling each of the following body parts: elbows, chest, stomach, hips, knees, and toes.

Think about what kind of a character might lead with the following parts of the body. Make some notes below.

Chin

Elbow

Chest

Stomach

Hips

Knees

Toes

When you work with characters' movements, you create a walk with energy concentrated in a certain part of the body. Being propelled forward with an energized part of the body integrates stances and movement to establish a character.

Creative Stances and Movement
The imaginative stances and movement are accomplished when you as the actor convey a phrase, a weather condition, an animal, or an inanimate object with creative stances and body movements only. Concentrate on moving creatively. You do not have to make a story about the imaginative movement as you would when performing a story mime or pantomime. You will have opportunities to create pantomime stories later in this chapter.

ASSIGNMENT Creative Stances and Movement   DATE:

This experience directs you to adapt an imaginative attitude and move for five seconds to represent each of the following phrases or familiar sayings. You are your own age in this movement experience; you want to convey the phrase by using your face and body only:

turning the other cheek.

busy as a bee.

quick as a wink.

curious as a cat.

pretty as a picture.

stubborn as a mule.

sticky as glue.

clear as mud.

snug as a bug in a rug.

ASSIGNMENT A Walk in Weather   DATE:

The following list contains suggestions for stances and movements you can practice to show reactions to different kinds of weather. Use your imagination to feel the weather condition. Portray your own age and take a stance and then move as if it is . . .

Rainy.

Cold.

Very hot.

Windy.

Stormy.

Create each weather conditions as the following ages: five, sixteen, thirty, fifty, and eighty. Record your A Walk in Weather.

REFLECTIVE INQUIRY   **RI**   DATE:

Watch your video recording of each creative stance and movement for A Walk in Weather. Make some notes addressing how well you accomplished age and weather changes.

> *An actor is never so great as when he reminds you of an animal—falling like a cat, lying like a dog, moving like a fox.*
>
> Francois Truffaut, film maker, critic

Creative Stances and Movement—Animal-Like Movements

Moving like an animal requires that you forgo inhibitions and truly transform your body to show the creative movements of a person with animal-like moves. Try to be as imaginative and physically free as possible without becoming the animal that might be down on all four feet. Your goal is to capture the essence of animal-like movements using all parts of your human body for a specific animal.

Observing animals is an important exercise for you to get the feel of an animal moving. Watch animals in real life and on any media. Observe each animal's activities. Think about each part of the animal's body: hair, fur, face, neck, shoulders, back, chest, stomach, hips, legs, feet, toes.

ASSIGNMENT Animal-Like Movements   DATE:

Make a list of five animals you have observed, noting the movements in various states of rest and motion.

How does each animal move? What is the animal's lead walk?

Animal   Observation

1.

2.

3.

4.

5.

Select a single animal that you have witnessed. Start with a neutral stance, and then let each part of your body transform. Think like the animal, in a relaxed state; then, move into action. Make bold physical choices for non-human moves. Move around the acting space for thirty seconds like the animal you observed, and then shift back to neutral stance.

Think again about your animal movements and choose one that you wish to video. Staying within camera parameters, move like your animal. Videotape your animal-like movements. Watch the video and assess your creation.

Did you think like the animal? What were you thinking about as you moved like the animal? Did your eyes move like the animal? Did you transform your head and neck moves? Did you transform each part of your body into animal-like features?

The animal creations can be used as warm-ups. If you truly commit to moving in the manner of the animal, inhibitions are put aside, and your body is transformed. In addition, exploring animal movements can directly affect how you create the uninhibited, physical life of a human character. Add moving like an animal to your actor's rehearsal warm-up.

Creative Stance and Movement — Inanimate Objects
Your movement giving life to inanimate objects can be a liberating experience. Thinking outside the box allows you to move freely as an object. You imagine how the object would move in various situations.

ASSIGNMENT Inanimate Objects   DATE:

Imagine a stance, facial expression, and body movement that might convey the following inanimate objects.

1. Dry breakfast cereal waiting for milk to be poured on it. Then imagine what happens when milk is poured onto you.

2. A piece of bread inside a toaster, waiting to be popped up. You are waiting to be taken out of the toaster, then you pop up.

3. A washing machine waiting for clothes to be put in, then with water, detergent and clothes added, agitating through cycles.

4. A piece of frying bacon enduring the heat of fire. The fire becomes hot, and then is turned off.

CREATIVE INQUIRY   DATE:

Think of a title for each of the above inanimate object's physicalizations. Video record yourself announcing the title standing with a neutral stance, and then transform your body including animated facial expressions, show the inanimate object's characteristics, including size, shape, and attitude.

Return to neutral; announce the next title and transform accordingly.

Create each of the inanimate objects listed in the above list: cereal, bread, washing machine, and bacon.

CREATIVE INQUIRY   DATE:

Revisit your creative moves. List three observations about physicalizing inanimate objects.

You have practiced simple stances and movement, status, age, and character stances and movement, and imaginative stances and movement. Flexible stances and movement are important for any character's physical design.

Introduction to Mime Study for the Actor

Mime is regarded as the silent movement. Pantomime is the art of conveying a story with only body movements. Both include a sense of reality by creating imaginary objects in imaginative situations. The mime uses space and its transformation to create the imaginary objects. Sometimes the word mime is used to designate a short play without speech. A mime or mime artist can also be used to name the performer in a pantomime.

History of Mime

- **John Weaver** was the father of English pantomime (1673–1760) who created the first pantomime ballet. He fused dance and mime to tell stories.
- **Joseph Grimaldi** was an English clown and pantomimist (1778–1837). He is best known for his invention of the modern day, whiteface clown.
- **Jean-Gaspard Deburau** was a French pantomimist who lived from 1796–1846. He created Pierrot, a character who is recognized today as a clumsy Commedia dell 'Arte creation.
- **Étienne Decroux** is considered the father of modern mime. Living from 1898–1991, Decroux created mime in which movement was generated from the character's emotions rather than outside gestures or poses.
- **Jacques Lecoq** (1921–1991) was a French actor and mime. His work is noted for physical methods, beginning with the neutral mask.
- **Jean Louis Barrault** (1910–1994) was a pupil of Decroux who brought mime to the film world.
- **Marcel Marceau** (1923–2007) a French mime, created the most famous character of Bip the Clown. He established his own school of mimodrama to foster one-person mime stories and established the Marceau Foundation to promote mime in the United States. He toured the United States and appeared on television with his own one-man show, Meet Marcel Marceau.

In modern times, there are several noted mime performers.

- **Jewel Walker** is a nationally renowned movement, mime, and acting teacher.

~ **Desmond Jones** established the longest running School of Mime and Physical Theatre in Britain.

~ **Tony Montanaro** is considered by some to be one of the great mimes of the twentieth century. He founded the Celebration Barn, a world-famous school of mime, improvisation, and other performing skills.

~ **Adam Darius** is an American dancer, mime artist, writer, and choreographer. He originated expressive mime, a combination of dance and mime.

~ **Robert Shields and Lorene Yarnell** made mime more popular with the television show, *Shields and Yarnell*. Shields began working as a street mime who was seen by Marcel Marceau while performing at the Hollywood Wax Museum. He was offered a full scholarship to Marceau's school of mime in Paris. Yarnell was a tap dancer and actress. They originated the robotic moves and mastered the ability to refrain from blinking their eyes for long periods of time.

~ **Samuel Avital** was an international mime and teacher of kinesthetic awareness. He created a unique method of bodywork called Body Speak, for kinesthetic awareness.

~ **Mummenschanz** is a mask and mime troupe from Sweden who perform with masks, forms, light, shadow and choreography. The name is German for "mummery," which includes mummers, a term for mime artists.

~ **Richmond Shepard** is an American writer, director, producer, and mime.

~ **Gregg Goldston** is a teacher of mime who was a student of Richmond Shepard and Marcel Marceau. He created a solo show, "One Mime Show."

~ **Claude Kipnis** was a stage mime who wrote "The Mime Book."

~ **Geoff Hoyle** was a student of Etienne Decroux. Hoyle trained in England and joined San Francisco's Pickle Family Circus, where he plays Mr. Sniff, a clown. He also toured in one-man shows, in which he used English-style clowning, pantomime, Commedia dell 'Arte, puppetry and tap dance.

A magician makes the visible invisible. A mime makes the invisible visible.

Marcel Marceau, mime, teacher

Why an Actor Studies Mime

You can become a mime performer—a street mime, a mime who works children's parties, or a mime who develops and performs shows. All of the mime work requires the study of classical mime techniques. Mimes study the traditional mime moves. Basic, classical, identifiable mime moves include the Marceau walk, walking against the wind, working with a rope in tug-of-war, walking a tightrope, creating the wall or box, skating, riding a bicycle, running in fantasy, riding an elevator or escalator, moving in slow motion, moving in space, and moving in water, among other illusions.

As an actor you can study mime to develop the precise movements that stimulate feelings and communicate the attitudes of a character who is telling a story. By concentrating on your body and physical movements, the expression of emotions without vocal enhancements, you refine your ability to use your body as a precise acting tool. Recreating some of your everyday activities without props or tangible items strengthens your imagination and exercises your body.

Mime Warm-Up

As emphasized in the Prologue of this book, an actor's body must be relaxed and ready for any physical acting. Mime warm-ups are recommended for each of the actor's tools: body, voice, and imagination.

ASSIGNMENT Mime Warm-Up   DATE:

Standing in neutral position, lean over by rolling down, vertebra by vertebra, until you are bending at the waist.

Make any physical adjustment so you do not hurt yourself.

Roll back up, vertebra by vertebra, until you are standing in neutral position.

Tense your body, one part at a time, from toes to head, taking fifteen seconds for each isolated body part.

Breathe, taking slow deep breaths.

Put your hands on your ribs; inhale through the nose, out through the mouth.

Stand with your feet separated by a few inches. Keep feet parallel with your heels on the ground.

Bend forward easing into a stretch.

Stand up.

Raise your arms in front like a hoop.

Keeping your feet in place, rotate arms and trunk side to side slowly.

Let your head turn easily with your shoulders.

Arch one arm over your head; the other arm is extended in front of your body.

Slowly alternate your arms overhead stretching along your torso vertically.

Breathe slowly.

Clasp your hands behind your back and raise your arms slowly to feel the stretch across the top of the chest.

Slowly stretch your neck at a slight angle left, then front, then right.

Rotate your wrists, flopping your hands in circular motion at the wrists clockwise then counterclockwise.

Bend your arms and rotate your elbows.

Rotate your shoulders, forward then backward.

Rotate your neck gently and slowly, letting your head roll easily. Move your neck and head in half circles only.

Yawn.

Open your eyes wide; look left, right, up and down.

Stretch your mouth; make a horse face; blow air through your lips.

ASSIGNMENT Isolation of Body Parts   DATE:

Moving your eyes only, watch an invisible fly in action.

Use your mouth to blow out birthday candles that refuse to be extinguished.

Engage your face in a quick snapshot to show the following emotions: happiness, sadness, surprise, anger, fear, and extreme joy.

Using your hands only, put on a puppet show without props.

Imagine that you have a screen in front of your body blocking your body, exposing only your feet. Concentrating on your feet, demonstrate the following feelings: Anxiety, Joy, Bashfulness, Hysterics, Peace, Shock, Worry, and Fear.

Re-creation of Daily Activities Using Mime Actions

Your character's physical objective is to communicate the action to an audience for the purpose of making a statement or getting an emotional response. Communication with action must be meticulous so that intentions and details are read and understood.

Rehearsing everyday actions without props forces you to pay attention to life's daily activities. For example, the next time you eat a bowl of cereal, notice the number of steps it takes to prepare the bowl of cereal and all of the needed utensils, then the steps it takes to eat and clean up.

ASSIGNMENT Re-creation of Daily Activities Using Mime Actions 1   DATE:

Perform a carefully detailed mime action for each one of the following daily activities listed below. Take time to develop each element of the movement. Prepare the required invisible props for the action; perform the action and clean up. Each mime might take approximately two minutes. Concentrate on detailed actions only; explore the object. Play your own age. You are not concerned with creating a story. Many of the activities require the use of a mimed table. Keep the table at the same height while maintaining a consistent size.

Using mime, read different types of imaginary books, concentrating on detailed action:

a telephone book

a mystery book

a textbook

a how-to manual

Using mime, write several different types of communication:

a text

a love letter

an instruction sheet

a diary entry

Using mime, play with different types of balls:

a golf ball

a super ball

a football

a medicine ball

a ping pong ball

Using mime, wash different objects:

a window

a dog

your hair

a car

a plate

Using mime, try on a variety of articles:

a cowboy hat

a swim suit

a pair of glasses

a ring

a pair of tight shoes

Using mime, prepare various food items:

pancakes

eggs

soup

hot dogs

cake frosting

ASSIGNMENT Re-creation of Daily Activities Using Mime Actions 2   DATE:

Choose three of the above detailed mime actions and video record your meticulous pantomime. Verbally announce the action that you are performing. Spend a minimum of three minutes on each mime performance. Watch your performance.

CREATIVE INQUIRY   DATE:

Think about whether you included all of the details needed to perform the action? Did you keep invisible objects the same shape, size and weight? Did you put any objects down on an invisible table? Did you keep your pantomime table in the same location and at the same height? Make some notes below on these questions.

_____

Food and Five Senses Re-creation Mime

As an actor in a play, you have to remember what it is like to prepare and eat food. Often, you do not have the real food on stage, so you have to recreate the action and details of what you did in daily life when you did have the tangible food to use.

CREATIVE INQUIRY *CI*   DATE:

Think of one food item that might involve your five senses: hearing, seeing, smelling, touching, and tasting, in the preparation and consuming of it. What is the food item you chose?

_____

Imagine seeing the food.

Imagine hearing any sound the food makes.

Imagine smelling the aroma of the food.

Imagine feeling the texture of the food.

Imagine tasting the flavor of the food.

In your mime, you will use your imagination to recreate the sensations received through your five senses.

Plan where you will locate the food. Be aware of size and shape of the food item. Choose utensils that you need for the preparation and eating of the food.

ASSIGNMENT Food and Five Senses Re-creation Mime   DATE:

Perform and video record your three-minute mime addressing the five senses with your chosen food item.

How detailed was each sensory reaction? As you showed detail, did you imagine having tangible objects?

Rehearsing a detailed mime often keeps your mime skills equipped to perform at any time. Make it part of your actor's daily warm-up.

Character Mime from a Familiar Story
For this assignment, think of a familiar story for which you are acquainted with all of the dialogue and plot. You might choose a fairy tale or childhood story, such as *The Three Little Pigs* or *Goldilocks and the Three Bears,* or another well-known story. Physicalize each character's moves, using mime and action. Communicate your physicalized story, showing how each of the characters moves and uses their body. Decide what happens in the story and the location of any mime props. Be completely involved in the telling of the story, using only your body. Concentrate on each character's moves and facial expressions. Use your face, gestures, and movements without words. Do not mouth any dialogue. Record your mime.

REFLECTIVE INQUIRY **RI**   DATE:

Revisit your video-recorded character mime and make a note as to which characters are the most detailed in mime movement.

___

What changes and adjustments in character moves will you make when you rework this familiar story as a mime performance?

___

Mime and Solo Pantomime

Creative thinking for a solo performance requires tapping into your uninhibited imagination. Creativity in mime work stimulates your artistic nature to think innovatively, inventing characters you can portray and locations for your characters. Pantomime will use mime movements and tell a story.

ASSIGNMENT Solo Mime **A**   DATE:

Create a solo character and place your character in a location for each of the titles below. You can play humans, animals, or inanimate objects. Think as creatively as you want.

Title	Solo Character	Location for this Story
Toys		
Winter		
Wild Wild West		

The Snowman

The Zoo

If. . .

Before and After

Birth, Life, Death

Inspiration

Planning a Solo Pantomime Story Line

To create a story for a solo mime performance, you need to think creatively to develop CWOW (character, who, objective, and where) for your story. CWOW prompts you to develop a character for your portrayal and to create an implied other character with whom you interact in your solo mime. You need to give your main character an objective, something you want from the invisible partner in your scene, and place both of you in a location that is appropriate to your character and partner.

ASSIGNMENT Planning a Solo Pantomime Story Line DATE:

First choose a character that you will play in a solo mime. Now pick an invisible, imagined character with whom you will be interacting. The invisible, imagined character is the implied other in your pantomime, if you want to include an implied partner in your solo mime. Now decide an objective. Make some notes below on what you want to achieve.

Select a location where you want to place your scene.

Create a title that you will announce verbally before your silent mime begins.

Choose a time of day or night for your solo pantomime.

Develop some ideas for complications and obstacles that the other implied character might present to your main character.

What will be the climax or the exciting part of your story?

What will be the result of the journey to achieve your character's objective?

Create what your final tag look will say to the audience. Your tag look is the final expression of emotion at the end of the mime that is expressed by your face and body. Are you happy or sad?

Write out the story of your mime below. Include a beginning, middle, a climax, a conclusion, resolution, and a tag look.

Rehearse your pantomime. Remember to face the camera (the audience) and verbally announce your title.

After your slate of your title (a slate is a greeting, your name, title, and character name), establish a stance for your character that shows the age and type of personality you are portraying.

Place your invisible implied partner, if any, near the camera, so your face is visible.

Approach your unseen acting partner and, by using mime actions and mouthing words, establish who you are, who your partner is, what you want, and where you are.

Listen to the invisible partner present an obstacle.

Try a tactic to overcome that obstacle.

Develop your story showing the audience how you are feeling by a tag look at the end of your mime.

Rehearse your pantomime several times.

Video record your pantomime.

Watch your pantomime.

REFLECTIVE INQUIRY **RI**   DATE:

Revisit your performance. List three aspects of the performance that you feel you performed well.

1.

2.

3.

Now list three aspects of the performance you would like to work on and develop further.

1.

2.

3.

CREATIVE INQUIRY *CI*   DATE:

Think about the actor's assessment below as you watch the video of your solo pantomime performance. Mark the column that corresponds to your evaluation.

Actor's Assessment of Solo Pantomime Story

Aspects of Performance	Creatively Executed	Adequately Executed	Needs Work on Execution	Performance Aspects to Work On
Title announced				
Character established				
Mime techniques detailed				
An implied partner established				
Where your pantomime takes place				
Objective clearly acted				
Story has beginning, middle, climax, resolution, and end				
Tag look conveyed a feeling				

The areas that you feel need work can be developed through experimenting with adjustments for a revised performance

Periodically revisit the pantomime experiences and create other ideas for your physical creations.

Pantomime to Music
Choose a short piece of instrumental music, one without any lyrics. Listen to the music. Let the music stimulate a character in a location. Imagine

what the character is doing. Let the music guide the story's creation. The story needs a beginning, middle, climax, resolution, and an ending.

Let this be an experience in letting the music create the character in a situation. Something happens to the character. The music will contain surprises for the character. Create CWOW (character, who, objective and where). Let the music dictate if the mood is serious or humorous.

CREATIVE INQUIRY   DATE:

Think about the music again. Write a story that the music inspires. Title your story.

Video record your Pantomime to Music. Watch your video.

REFLECTIVE INQUIRY   DATE:

Revisit your video recording. Make three notes indicating adjustments for further rehearsal of your Pantomime to Music.

The Pantomime to Music exercise can be recreated often with different types of instrumental music. It is a creative physical experience.

Working on body expressions is a way to develop your actor's physical communication. This includes methods of movement work and mime work. You learn to create characters with your flexible body coupled with imaginative, creative stories.

What is important in mime is attitude.

Marcel Marceau, mime, teacher

Closure for Chapter Three: Movement

ASSIGNMENT Closure   DATE:

Imagine that you are an Acting teacher and you are making notes about Movement for the actor.

List one interesting fact that you would like to make sure that your acting student is told about each of the topics below.

Look back at each topic to refresh your memory about one interesting fact.

Introduction to Movement

Definition of Movement

History of Movement Training

Introduction to Relaxation for Movement

Relaxation and Centering Breath

Yawning

Adding Gentle Voice

Engaging the Relaxed Body

Video Recording as Part of your Rehearsal Process

Guidelines for Preparing Your Rehearsal Video

The Bow

Preparation for Actor's Character Stance and Movement

Neutral Stance to Character Stance

Stage Stances and Movement

Basic Stage Stances and Movement

Emotional Stances and Movement

Non Verbalized Words Stances and Movement

Status, Age, and Character Stances and Movement

Stages of Life—Status, Age, Character and Movements

Stages of Life— Age Stances and Movements

Status, Age, Characters Stances and Movements—Lead Walk

Creative Stances and Movement

Creative Stances and Movement—A Walk in Weather

Creative Stances and Movement—Animal-Like Movements

Creative Stances and Movement—Inanimate Objects

Mime Study for the Actor

History of Mime

Why an Actor Studies Mime

Mime Warm-Up

Mime Warm-Up Isolation of Body Parts

Re-creation of Daily Activities Using Mime Actions

Food and Five Senses Re-creation Mime

Character Mime from a Familiar Story

Solo Pantomime

Planning a Solo Pantomime Story Line

Assessing Solo Pantomime Story Performance

Pantomime to Music

You are relaxed and have experienced movement, and mime. You are ready to work on another of your actor's tools: your voice.

CHAPTER FOUR: VOCAL WORK

Develop one of the most beautiful voices in the American theater, and you will demand the role. Actors with clear voices are needed by directors. You will be able to stand out if you can be heard and understood.

David Mamet, playwright, Theatre educator

Introduction to Vocal Work

Just as a relaxed and flexible body is needed by an actor, a relaxed and expressive voice is a requirement. You have worked on your physical instrument with movement and mime, so it is time to concentrate on vocal work. Vocal exercises are required to develop your vocal instrument. The voice is an instrument you use to communicate thoughts and feelings. Your relaxed and expressive voice is able to give meaning to the script and displays emotion.

When you are at home with your friends, you are at ease vocally. You use variety in energy and volume, according to how excited or calm you are about events. Your job now is to transfer that same ease to the stage using vocal projection so that an audience of any number can hear and understand each word.

The ability to create a flexible vocal range and proper voice production requires daily practice. It is necessary for you as an actor to develop vocal abilities so that every audience member can hear every word you say, understand each word, and believe your character because of your vocal creation. Projecting with ease and speaking without vocal strain can be learned with daily exercise. Think of this as an opportunity to add a vocal workout to part of your regular actor's training. Your objective is to be able to create and recreate distinct and flexible vocal qualities for each character you portray. Just as you work out to get ready as a physical actor, your vocal instrument needs care, attention, and exercise.

Strengthening your vocal muscles is important for you to make sure you are communicating clearly. Think of an Olympic athlete who works daily to stay in condition; your vocal tools need daily training and care. Actors often perform eight shows a week, so taking care of your voice, body, and emotions is needed for good vocal health and stamina. Care of the vocal instrument is important to you as an artist.

Breath support leads to increased actor's stamina for vocal needs of any script and large performance venues. The voice supported by your diaphragmatic breathing allows you to communicate with clarity, variety, and vocal control to any audience in any auditorium. It is your job as an actor to make sure an audience can receive all of the words to appreciate your work.

Voice exercises for the actor can sometimes be perceived as repetitive and boring. The word "rehear" appears at the beginning of the word rehearsal. Rehear—is part of the word rehearsal. Think of any vocal experience as an opportunity to create with enthusiasm, evaluate with caring criticism, and rehear your vocal exercises until you are happy with your vocal production.

The assignments in this section present experiences that help you obtain clear diction, articulation, and projection. The experiences in this section help expand vocal flexibility, projection, and all of the vocal techniques you need. You will implement tongue twisters, oral interpretation of literature, song lyrics, and a Shakespearean sonnet to exercise your voice.

Taking Care of your Voice

Imagine an instrumentalist caring for his or her musical instrument, keeping it in a safe place under lock and key, maintaining it, and rehearsing with it daily. You need to take care of your voice, just as carefully as an instrumentalist takes care of his/her prize-winning, expensive, delicate musical instrument.

Learning how to take care of your physical being requires a personal system that includes making healthy choices. Doing physical exercise prepares your voice for the needs of any role. Eating properly and staying away from junk foods and radical diets are wise choices for an actor. Getting a natural high from executing a perfectly said line rather than from addictive substances is a goal for you. Drinking water and staying hydrated are two important ways to take care of your vocal instrument.

Before any performance, get sleep and proper rest. Before any performance, avoid milk, nuts, and sugar. These products create phlegm. Warming up your vocal instrument is essential; this relieves stress on your instrument. Losing your voice when you are an actor is one of the worst things you can do. If you have lines to say, you cannot perform without a voice. Being kind to your voice is essential.

Warm-Up for Vocal Experiences

How relaxed is your body, particularly your face, neck, and shoulders? If your body is relaxed and warmed up, then your vocal tools of your face, neck and shoulders will be ready to be expressive. Acknowledge the condition of your body. Once you have "checked in," you can determine how much warm-up time you need in order to relax any parts of your body that will affect vocal production.

The purpose of a warm-up is to relax and relieve any physical tension, to prepare the voice for speaking, to prepare the body for moving, to access creativity, and to focus your mind.

ASSIGNMENT Warm-Up for Vocal Experiences   DATE:

The following vocal warm-up experiences for your teeth, tongue, lips, jaw, and vocal chords can be accomplished seated in a chair, standing upright, or lying on your back.

Stretch. Slowly and gently stretch your legs, arms, shoulders, neck, jaw, and face, isolating each part of your body.

Yawn and swallow. Now stand comfortably in neutral position and roll your head slowly in half circles to release tension. Swallow, inhale and yawn.

Add a long H-0-0-0-0 with your mouth open. Let your voice slide from highest note to lowest in your range. Repeat this exercise.

Breathe slowly and deeply.

Hum. Keep the vocalization gentle and unforced, supported by diaphragmatic breath.

Chew invisible gum. Relax.

Make horse-lips sound. Pucker your lips and blow. Relax.

Check your jaw to see if it is unclenched and relaxed. Separate your teeth at intervals during your day's activities.

Use any short phrase that you have memorized and say it going from highest to lowest pitch in your range and back again. You can choose a nursery rhyme or a short poem. Use your higher and lower registers, making your voice use high notes then low notes, then high notes, then low notes. Relax.

Vocal Vocabulary and Assignments

Among the words in this chapter are key vocal vocabulary terms, which will benefit your acting. Each word is defined and has an assignment to help you understand and implement. A Creative Inquiry or Reflective Inquiry follows some of the Assignments, so that you can give feedback and contribute creative or reflective ideas. The topics are presented in alphabetical order.

Vocal vocabulary terms that you will study include accent, articulation, building, clarity, diaphragm, diction, emphasis, enunciation, fluency, gibberish, inflection, intention, intonation, pace, pause, pitch, pointing, projection, pronunciation, register, rhythm, tempo, throw away, tone, topping, variety, vocal challenges, vocal control, vocal objective, vocal quality, and volume. Assignments and Vocal experiences include oral interpretation of literature, song lyrics for vocal work and Shakespeare for vocal interpretation.

Following some of the essential vocabulary words, there are also Creative Inquiry sections, Reflective Inquiry sections and another assignment to complete. These have all been designed to help you remember the meanings of these words.

Record your vocal work and then listen so that you can rehear and make vocal adjustments. You can audio record or video record and be "off camera," so you can concentrate on your voice. "Off camera" is a direction to stand outside of what the camera sees, or you can stand in camera vision. When assessing only your audio work, you can stand off camera.

Vocabulary

Accent—A speech pattern that is associated with a geographical region. Another term for accent is dialect.

Articulation—The distinct precise pronunciation of words.

Building—A vocal technique that increases in volume, excitement, and pace; it is used in the climatic section of a monologue, scene, mime, or play.

Clarity—The clearness of the voice.

Diaphragm—The muscle under the rib cage that aids support for lung capacity.

Diction—The pronunciation of words. Informal, conversational speech is relaxed. On stage the audience does not have the script in front of them, so over-enunciation is needed for understanding of the playwright's words and for communicating across the expanse of the Theatre space.

Emphasis—The vocal highlighting of some words or sounds to focus on the meanings and to imitate sounds that the word suggests.

Enunciation—The clear, distinct production of each word, including the end consonants.

Fluency—Speaking without hesitation, pause or uncertainty.

Gibberish—The created language made of nonsense sounds substituted for recognizable words to speak thoughts and express emotions. The success of communicating by gibberish includes distinct nonsense sounds that you substitute for each word. The gibberish sentence sounds as if you are speaking a new language. Gibberish accompanied by a gesture and action helps with the communication of the thoughts.

Inflection—The variety of voice quality or pitch, using highs and lows.

Intention—The use of the voice to convey meanings, attitudes and emotions.

Intonation—The rise and fall of the voice in pitch at the end of a sentence.

Oral interpretation of literature—The use of the voice to read printed material, making the words come "alive" for the listener.

Pace—The speed at which a person talks.

Pause—The temporary vocal stop in dialogue. The pause creates tension or anticipation.

Pitch—The lowness and highness of a voice.

Pointing—The emphasis of a word.

Projection—The increase or decrease of the voice's volume, clarity, and distinctness for the purpose of communicating to an audience.

Pronunciation—The way in which a sound or word is delivered.

Register—A series of tones and patterns produced by the vocal chords. The register is identified by upper, middle, or lower vocal ranges.

Rhythm—The vocal pattern created by the cadence of the words, sounds and silences. The sounds and silences form a pattern that is repeated to create a stressed and unstressed rhythm.

Vocal control—The ability to use all of the vocal techniques when and as they are needed.

Vocal objective—The actor's purpose in using his/her voice a certain way in order to accomplish an objective.

Telephone calls—When making a telephone call onstage, use your upstage hand and put the mouthpiece of the phone near your chin, so it does not cover your mouth. Make sure each pause, when you are listening to the implied phone caller, is not too long or too short. Establish CWOW.

Tempo—The pace of speaking, rapidly or slowly.

Throw away—A vocal technique that de-emphasizes words, though still heard by fellow actors and audience members.

Tone—The emotional quality in the voice that expresses the speaker's feelings or thoughts.

Topping—A vocal technique that picks up tempo, and/or volume.

Variety—Flexibility in voice incorporating tempo, pace, and tone to show various feelings and emotions.

Vocal challenges—Stage directions that an actor carries out. Each stage direction requires a change in vocal presentation to communicate it correctly to the audience.

Vocal quality—The characteristics of a voice. Sometimes a voice is described as shrill, soothing, nasal, well-modulated, booming, or withdrawn.

Volume—The degree of loudness or intensity of the voice.

ASSIGNMENT Accent   DATE:

Record your accent creations. Say "Twinkle, twinkle, little star, how I wonder who or what you are," with a British accent. Exaggerate each word so that you speak very clearly and precisely. Imagine yourself having a cup of tea with the Queen of England.

Repeat the same lines with your best Texan accent by making each word very loud and emphasizing each consonant. Imagine riding a horse that bounces you on each word.

Repeat the same lines with a Southern accent. Slow your speech and elongate each vowel, a, e, i, o, u and sometimes y in your words. Think of sitting on a Southern porch in a slow rocking chair sipping a tall drink and fanning yourself.

REFLECTIVE INQUIRY   DATE:

Revisit your recordings. Close your eyes and see if you can picture a British character, a Texan character, and a Southern character. What were some differences in the British, Texan, and Southern accents?

ASSIGNMENT Articulation   DATE:

Create an articulation dance.

While standing in neutral position, say the phrase: "The tip of the tongue, the teeth, the lips, the jaw." Repeat three times.

As you say the words, exaggerate each word. Imagine saying the words to people who need to hear distinct words.

Continue saying the words and move one arm. Shake your arm and hand while saying the phrase three times.

Add another arm. Continue the phrase and the moving of two arms.

Add shaking one leg.

Then alternate with your other leg, while continuing the repetition of the phrase.

With two arms and alternating both legs, continue the Articulation dance.

Gradually stop moving one leg, then stop your other leg, then one arm and your final arm and whisper the phrase, while standing still. Maintain clear articulation.

The articulation experience can be used to warm-up your vocal tools.

ASSIGNMENT Building **A**   DATE:

Say the word "Wow" ten times increasing volume and pace to make the voice louder and faster.

ASSIGNMENT Clarity **A**   DATE:

Read aloud Hamlet's advice to the players. A section of the soliloquy is printed below. A soliloquy is a long speech that is said as the actor stands alone on stage. The Shakespearean play written in 1603 presents vocal guidance for clarity and other vocal performances guidelines. If you are not sure of the words, give it your best guess as to the pronunciation. As you speak the monologue, look for Hamlet's advice to the actors.

HAMLET: Speak the speech, I pray you, as I pronounced it to you, trippingly on the tongue. But if you mouth it, as many of our players do, I had as lief the town crier spoke my lines. Nor do not saw the air too much with your hand, thus, by use all gently, for in the very torrent, tempest, and (as I may say) whirlwind of your passion, you must acquire and beget a temperance that may give it smoothness. O, it offends me to the soul to hear a robustious periwig-pated fellow tear a passion to tatters, to very rags, to split the ears of the groundlings, who for the most part are capable of nothing but inexplicable dumb shows and noise. I would have such a fellow whipped for o'erdoing Termagant. It out-herods Herod. Pray you avoid it. Be not too tame neither, but let your own discretion be your tutor. Suit the action to the word, the word to the action, . . . Go make you ready.

CREATIVE INQUIRY **CI**   DATE:

Think about five standards of vocal and acting advice that Hamlet gives to the actors. Make some notes below.

1.

2.

3.

4.

5.

ASSIGNMENT Diaphragm   DATE:

You remember that you worked on diaphragmatic breathing as part of relaxing your body. Relaxing your body with breathing from the diaphragm will support vocal production.

Engage your breath support using your full lung capacity. Expand your diaphragm muscle to achieve full lung capacity. Leave your shoulders down. Use belly breathing.

Hold a finger a few inches away from your mouth, and attempt to blow out an imaginary candle. Keep a steady stream of breath for as long as possible.

Say the word "Ha" loudly. Do not shout. Repeat each "Ha" ten times. Use diaphragmatic breathing.

Speak clearly, if you speak at all; carve every word before you let it fall.
Oliver Wendell Holmes, Justice of the Supreme Court

ASSIGNMENT Diction   DATE:

Record your reading of *The Jabberwocky,* which is a nonsense poem by Lewis Carroll.

Be bold when saying the nonsense words. Use your confident voice. Over-articulate the unusual words.

`Twas brillig, and the slithy toves
Did gyre and gimble in the wabe:
All mimsy were the borogoves,
And the mome raths outgrabe.
"Beware the Jabberwock, my son!
The jaws that bite, the claws that catch!
Beware the Jubjub bird, and shun
The frumious Bandersnatch!"
He took his vorpal sword in hand:
Long time the manxome foe he sought—
So rested he by the Tumtum tree,
And stood awhile in thought.
And, as in uffish thought he stood,
The Jabberwock, with eyes of flame,
Came whiffling through the tulgey wood,
And burbled as it came!
One, two! One, two! And through and through
The vorpal blade went snicker-snack!
He left it dead, and with its head
He went galumphing back.
"And, has thou slain the Jabberwock?
Come to my arms, my beamish boy!
O frabjous day! Callooh! Callay!"
He chortled in his joy.
`Twas brillig, and the slithy toves
Did gyre and gimble in the wabe;
All mimsy were the borogoves,
And the mome raths outgrabe.

CREATIVE INQUIRY  DATE:

Think about the poem again. Now make a list of twelve words from *Jabberwocky* that need clear diction in order for an audience to hear them correctly.

1.

2.

3.

4.

5.

6.

7.

8.

9.

10.

11.

12.

ASSIGNMENT Emphasis 1  DATE:

Read the last stanza of *The Jabberwocky* emphasizing the following words: brillig, slithy, gyre, gimble, mimsy, outgrabe. You will see a difference in the vocal interpretation.

ASSIGNMENT Emphasis 2 DATE:

Say the explosive consonants "b, p, d, g, j, k, t," using your lips and breath support to spit each letter. Repeat the following words ten times: butter, putter, dutter, gutter, jitter, kitten, titter.

The end consonants of all words need to be emphasized for clarity. On stage the audience must hear the end sounds of words. In everyday conversation, we are relaxed about finishing words. Onstage each word takes on a special importance. In the musical *Oliver*, there is a song, entitled "Food, Glorious Food." After weeks of performances the cast of young workhouse boys began to drop the final "d's." Thus the audience heard "Foo, Glorious, Foo." In the musical *The Wizard of Oz*, there are song lyrics saying, "You will be a bust in the Hall of Fame." Actors had to make sure the audience did not hear, "You will be a bus in the Hall of Fame." Paying attention to end consonants is an important part of enunciation.

As you repeat the words below, notice the change if you do not articulate the final consonant. Car, card; coal, cold; fee, feed; goal, gold; ha, hot.

Tongue twisters are fun, challenging and a great way to work the teeth, tongues, lips and jaws. Many familiar tongue twisters, such as the ones below, can be used to work on enunciation.

"Around the rugged rocks the ragged rascal ran" or "Unique New York."

Below are some unusual tongue twisters for your enunciation workout. With each tongue twister, begin slowly and pronounce the words carefully. Make the start and end of each word crisp. Repeat the phrase, increasing speed while keeping words clear. Then repeat each with a slow, distinct pace, then medium pace, then rapid pace, while maintaining clarity.

ASSIGNMENT Enunciation 1 DATE:

Say each tongue twister below three times. Focus on speaking clearly, over-enunciating each word.

"Abigail Adams acquired an apple after alleviating."

"Blue glass fruit bowl. Blue glass fruit bowl. Blue glass fruit bowl. "

"Critical critics criticize cars careening carelessly. "

"Double bubble gum, bubble double, bubble double, bubble double. "

"Eight gray geese in a green field grazing. "

"Fanny Flower fried five floundering fish for Francis Finch's father. "

"Grab the groundhog from the glazed grass. "

"Three gray geese in the green grass gazing and grazing. Gray and gay and gazing were the geese and green was the grazing as they gazed. "

"High roller, Higher roller, Highest roller, High roller, Higher roller, Highest roller. "

"Inexplicable irate Irish instantly interrupted irritated iguanas. "

"Jingle jungle jangle joker. "

"Knit kilts of knights' kites. "

"Lucy likes light literature. "

"May you imagine an imaginary menagerie manager managing an imaginary menagerie? "

"Netty's next nest will not necessarily be next to nothing. "

"Octopi occupy an octopi's mind. "

"Perhaps you can see Peter Piper's puppy peeping playfully? "

"Queen Quinn quietly quakes the queen's quick cracker. "

"Roberta ran rings around the Roman ruins. "

"Synonym, Cinnamon, Synonym, Cinnamon. "

"A snifter of snuff is enough snuff for a sniff for a snuff sniffer. "

"Three thick thistle tricks. "

"United unique unicorns ultimately used youthful unicorns. "

"Venti, vanilla, very vanilla, and very venti vanilla. "

"What whim will Whitey Whitney whisper, whimper, whittle and whistle to win wealth and wed well?"

"Extreme existentialists exit excitedly. "

"Zoologists zip zippy around to zip the zippers on the zebras. "

RELECTIVE INQUIRY RI   DATE:

Revisit the tongue twisters. List five from the above list that you will work on for clear enunciation.

1.

2.

3.

4.

5.

ASSIGNMENT Enunciation 2   DATE:

Create your own tongue twister. Each word in the tongue twister should begin with the consonant indicated.

MMMM

PPPPP

FFFFF

SSSSS

ASSIGNMENT Fluency   DATE:

Say the alphabet in order with fluency. Say the alphabet backwards, Z–A. Practice for fluency.

ASSIGNMENT Gibberish   DATE:

Video record an explanation of how to make a sandwich in gibberish. Vary the words so you do not use the same sounds. Use a variety of consonants. The first time you explain how to make a sandwich, stand still and do not use hand movements. The second time you explain the procedure of sandwich making, use action to further communicate what you are demonstrating.

Record your gibberish while standing off camera. Listen to your recording.

RELECTIVE INQUIRY   DATE:

Revisit your recording. Make a note on how well you understood "How to Make a Sandwich."

Now video record your gibberish "How to Make a Sandwich" again. This time stand within camera view and act out each step of the process of making a sandwich. Watch this video recording and make a note about the differences between each.

ASSIGNMENT Inflection   DATE:

Say each of the groups of words below using an extreme range of pitch and quality.

"A dimly lit room with candles flickering."

"Cinnamon coffeecake. "

"A baby's first tooth. "

"Snow-white carpeting. "

"Being kind to the child within me. "

"Milkshakes. "

"Pumpkin pies, cakes, pancakes, muffins, ice cream. "

"Watching a favorite movie. "

"Reading an engrossing book. "

ASSIGNMENT Intention   DATE:

Say the following sentence: "Look at him!"

Each time you say the sentence, convey the described intention, attitude or emotion.

(whispered, embarrassment) "Look at him!"

(indicating what a silly thing for him to do) "Look at him!"

(meaning not me, him) "Look at him!"

(thinking isn't he gorgeous?) "Look at him!"

(disgusted) "Look at him!"

(telling someone to hurry, or you won't see him.) "Look at him!"

ASSIGNMENT Intonation 1   DATE:

Read the following sentence letting your voice rise at the end word of the sentence. Make your voice go up on the word, home.

"I am going home."
 Read the following sentence moving your voice to drop at the end of the sentence. Make your voice go down on the word, home.

"I am going home."

ASSIGNMENT Intonation 2   DATE:

Make some notes on the difference between the above two examples of intonation.

ASSIGNMENT *The Frog Prince 1*   DATE:

Children's literature is a rich source of material for an actor to work on to achieve vocal expressiveness and flexibility. Stories for children usually contain active, animated words and various characters. When working with children's literature, develop expressive body and voice to entertain and engage little children with your story reading. Using an expressive voice coupled with your animated face and body is a wonderful warm-up for your vocal instrument.

Now analyze the story below, *The Frog Prince*, and do the following things to make your voice expressive.

Highlight the narrator's voice using a color highlighter. Use your natural voice to narrate. Use vocal variety to create mood for the narrator's lines, those without quotation marks. Rehearse the narrator's lines without saying any of the characters' lines.

Count the number of characters in the story. Highlight each character's quoted lines in a different color for each character. Determine a variety of pitch, rhythms, and tempo for each character. One character may usually speak low and slow: another high and excited. Rehearse each character's lines separately.

Locate key action words, which are verbs and adverbs, and mark them to indicate a vocal change to imitate the word itself.

Rehearse only the action words.

Mark the climax, the most exciting part of the story. Increase tempo to provide excitement with volume during the climatic part.

Imagine reading to a loud group of three-year olds who will only pay attention when you are using a variety of voices.

Look at the final line of *The Frog Prince* and determine an attitude for saying this line.

Determine what your tag look will be. What will you final facial look express?

The Frog Prince

By The Brothers Grimm

One fine evening a young princess put on her bonnet and clogs, and went out to take a walk by herself in a wood; and when she came to a cool spring of water with a rose in the middle of it, she sat herself down to rest a while. Now she had a golden ball in her hand, which was her favorite plaything, and she was always tossing it up into the air, and catching it again as it fell.

After a time she threw it up so high that she missed catching it as it fell, and the ball bounded away, and rolled along on the ground, until at last it fell down into the spring. The princess looked into the spring after her ball, but it was very deep, so deep that she could not see the bottom of it. She began to cry, and said, "Alas! if I could only get my ball again, I would give all my fine clothes and jewels, and everything that I have in the world."

Whilst she was speaking, a frog put its head out of the water, and said, "Princess, why do you weep so bitterly?"

"Alas!" said she, "what can you do for me, you nasty frog? My golden ball has fallen into the spring.'"

The frog said, "I do not want your pearls, and jewels, and fine clothes; but if you will love me, and let me live with you and eat from off your golden plate, and sleep on your bed, I will bring you your ball again."

"What nonsense," thought the princess, "silly frog is talking! He can never even get out of the spring to visit me, though he may be able to get my ball for me, and therefore I will tell him he shall have what he asks."

So she said to the frog, "Well, if you will bring me my ball, I will do all you ask."

Then the frog put his head down, and dived deep under the water; and after a little while he came up again, with the ball in his mouth, and threw it on the edge of the spring.

As soon as the young princess saw her ball, she ran to pick it up; and she was so overjoyed to have it in her hand again, that she never thought of the frog, but ran home with it as fast as she could.

The frog called after her, "Stay, princess, and take me with you as you said."

But she did not stop to hear a word.

The next day, just as the princess had sat down to dinner, she heard a strange noise - tap, tap - plash, plash - as if something was coming up the marble staircase, and soon afterwards there was a gentle knock at the door, and a little voice cried out and said: "Open the door, my princess dear, Open the door to thy true love here! And mind the words that thou and I said By the fountain cool, in the greenwood shade."

Then the princess ran to the door and opened it, and there she saw the frog, whom she had quite forgotten. At this sight she was sadly frightened, and shutting the door as fast as she could came back to her seat.

The king, her father, seeing that something had frightened her, asked her what the matter was.

"There is a nasty frog," said she, "at the door, that lifted my ball for me out of the spring this morning. I told him that he should live with me here, thinking that he could never get out of the spring; but there he is at the door, and he wants to come in."

While she was speaking the frog knocked again at the door, and said: "Open the door, my princess dear. Open the door to thy true love here! And mind the words that thou and I said by the fountain cool, in the greenwood shade."

Then the king said to the young princess, "As you have given your word you must keep it, so go and let him in."

She did so, and the frog hopped into the room, and then straight on - tap, tap - plash, plash - from the bottom of the room to the top, till he came up close to the table where the princess sat.

"Pray lift me upon the chair," said he to the princess, "and let me sit next to you."

As soon as she had done this, the frog said, "Put your plate nearer to me, that I may eat out of it."

This she did, and when he had eaten as much as he could, he said, "Now I am tired. Carry me upstairs, and put me into your bed." And the princess, though very unwilling, took him up in her hand, and put him upon the pillow of her own bed, where he slept all night long.

As soon as it was light the frog jumped up, hopped downstairs, and went out of the house.

"Now, then," thought the princess, "at last he is gone, and I shall be troubled with him no more."

But she was mistaken, for when night came again she heard the same tapping at the door, and the frog came once more, and said: "Open the door, my princess dear, open the door to thy true love here! And mind the words that thou and I said, by the fountain cool, in the greenwood shade."

And when the princess opened the door the frog came in, and slept upon her pillow as before, till the morning broke. And the third night he did the same. But when the princess awoke on the following morning she was astonished to see, instead of the frog, a handsome prince, gazing on her with the most beautiful eyes she had ever seen and standing at the head of her bed.

He told her that he had been enchanted by a spiteful fairy, who had changed him into a frog; and that he had been fated so to abide till some princess should take him out of the spring, and let him eat from her plate, and sleep upon her bed for three nights.

"You," said the prince, "have broken his cruel charm, and now I have nothing to wish for but that you should go with me into my father's kingdom, where I will marry you, and love you as long as you live."

The young princess, you may be sure, was not long in saying "Yes" to all this; and as they spoke a brightly colored coach drove up, with eight beautiful horses, decked with plumes of feathers and a golden harness; and behind the coach rode the prince's servant, faithful Heinrich, who had bewailed the misfortunes of his dear master during his enchantment so long and so bitterly, that his heart had well-nigh burst.

They then took leave of the king, and got into the coach with eight horses, and all set out, full of joy and merriment, for the prince's kingdom, which they reached safely, and there they lived happily a great many years.

RI

RELECTIVE INQUIRY   DATE:

Revisit the characters in *The Frog Prince?* (Include the narrator as a character.) Now make some notes on the kind of voice you will use for each character. (You can use your own voice for the narrator.)

Now list some action verbs and adverbs that you will use your voice to "color" for the audience.

What are the lines that are the climax of the story?

What is your final emotion that you want to express after the final line of the story? Create a tag look that ends the story telling.

ASSIGNMENT *The Frog Prince* 2   DATE:

Record your audio oral interpretation of the story. Listen to the recording. Answer the questions below as you listen.

Is your articulation clear throughout the story

Are your pitch and inflection varied and lively?

Is a mood set by the narrator?

Is the volume varied and always audible?

Is the pace varied and used effectively?

Are pauses used to emphasize ideas?

Does the vocal quality fit the respective character?

Are words pronounced correctly throughout?

Do builds in volume and pace convey emotion?

Is each character voice consistent?

Is the vocal work consistent and does it convey objectives?

Does the climax build with excitement?

What changes would you make for the next time you record this story?

Speech is a mirror of the soul. As a man speaks, so is he.

Pubilius Syrus, 1 BC, Latin writer

ASSIGNMENT Pace   **A**   DATE:

Say the following television commercial text with a slow pace to indicate mystery.

"Your first job away from home in the city. You have worked late and it's raining. You're tired. You're returning home to your brownstone apartment. You open the door, enter the lobby, expecting a letter from home, you go to the mailbox, open it and find it empty. You are disappointed. You go to your apartment door; open it, go in, turn on the light. Look around. You are very aware of how empty it is. You really miss your mother. The phone rings. It's she. "Hi, Mom."

Say the following commercial with a rapid fast pace indicating excitement.

"You have been waiting for this day for months. Your sailboat was delivered last night, and it's on the trailer in the driveway. All of your friends are coming today to help you launch it. You go to the window, open the drapes, and discover it's storming outside. No laughing. No party. You are extremely disappointed. You look around the room. What are you going to do now? You turn on the TV. It's Saturday—only cartoons. You don't want that! You turn it off. You pick up a magazine. That's not what you want either! You're restless—bored—still unhappy and disappointed. The phone rings. It's your buddies! They're coming anyhow—you'll have the party in the garage."

ASSIGNMENT Pause   DATE:

Record your assignment. Stand off camera, so you have a recording.

Say each sentence below and follow the instructions in the parenthesis.

"I am very (pause) angry."

"I am very (pause) happy. "

"I am very (pause) tired. "

"I am very (pause) excited. "

RELECTIVE INQUIRY   DATE:

Revisit the audio recording. Write below what you notice about the tension created by the pause before the final word.

The most precious things in speech are the pauses.

Sir Ralph Richardson, British actor

ASSIGNMENT Pitch   DATE:

Use a high pitch of your voice to say the following one-line commercials: 1.) "When your own initials are enough," and 2.) "You never had it so good for so little."

Use a medium-pitched voice to say the following lines: 1.) "Doesn't it feel good to pay less?" and 2.) "It's sharper than you think."

Use a low-pitched voice to say: 1.) "A little bit more," 2.) "You're going to like the way you look, I guarantee it," and 3.) "Sometimes you feel like a nut, sometimes you don't."

Say the following sentences, using your voice to emphasize the italicized words: 1.) "I'm sure she thought you were *fascinating*," 2.) "Do you come here *often?*" 3.) "You can't always get what *you* want" and 4.) "I'm very *pleased* with it."

ASSIGNMENT Projection   DATE:

Imagine that you have a mouth full of your favorite color of paint. Your objective is to speak with vocal projection, while imagining that with each word you are painting the back wall of the theater. "Paint" the entire wall. Be sure to use belly, diaphragmatic breathing. Say each sentence below, maintaining projection for a small performance space, and then repeat the sentences for a medium performance space, and then repeat the sentences for a very large auditorium. Imagine the most important, friendly person in your life in the back row of the audience.

"I know there will be a surprise for me in the future."

"I will carry a cup of coffee out to the porch to enjoy the morning sunshine. "

"Good health is a goal. "

"Help, I need help.

ASSIGNMENT Pronunciation   DATE:

Pronounce the following rhyming words. Each word is rhymed with a similar word to help you with correct pronunciation.

Example: The word "for" rhymes with "ore." The correct pronunciation is heard when for and ore are pronounced so they rhyme.

Again-pen

Because-pause

New-mew

Poor-sewer

Roof- proof

Wolf-woolf

Rinse-mince

Picture-stricture

Worst-first

Get-bet

ASSIGNMENT Character Pronunciation   DATE:

Pronounce each word in the above list with a character dialect full of incorrect pronunciation. Imagine the kind of character who might use such improper pronunciation.

RELECTIVE INQUIRY *RI*   DATE:

Think about what type of character would use the incorrect pronunciation of each word in the list above.

List what type of character would use the very correct and precise pronunciation of each word in the list above.

ASSIGNMENT Register   DATE:

Say the following sentence using your upper vocal register: "Let's do something fun today."

Say the following sentence using your middle vocal register: "I have to talk to you."

Say the following sentence using your lower vocal register: "You have some nerve."

An example of stressed and unstressed is as follows:

X   /   X   /   X   /   X   /   X   /

But SOFT! What LIGHT through YONder WINdow BREAKS?

ASSIGNMENT Rhythm   DATE:

Say the following line using stressed, unstressed, and silences to form a pattern of sounds:

"Like the beat beat beat of the tom-tom

When the jungle shadows fall.

Like the tick tick tock of the stately clock

As it stands against the wall.

Like the drip drip drip of the raindrops

When the summer shower is through."

ASSIGNMENT Tempo DATE:

Say the following sentences using the indicated tempos and intentions. Look back at the definition of intention.

"What are you doing?" slowly as if to a cute puppy.

"What are you doing?" measured as if to a frustrated student.

"What are you doing?" rapidly as if to a frightened child.

Record the three different tempos of the sentence above.

RELECTIVE INQUIRY DATE:

Revisit your recordings. Make some notes on how you made distinct differences in the tempos and intentions.

ASSIGNMENT Throw Away   DATE:

Say the following sentences, and de-emphasize the final word in each sentence. Sometimes in acting, a character will "throw away" words to indicate boredom or disinterest: 1.) "I feel happy," and 2.) "I feel fantastic."

ASSIGNMENT Tone   DATE:

Say each word below showing the different emotional tones indicated in parenthesis.

"Oh." (Happiness)

"Well." (Worried)

"Really." (Skeptical)

"Okay." (Excited)

ASSIGNMENT Topping   DATE:

Say the familiar nursery rhyme using topping. With each phrase build tempo, talking faster and faster until the end word.

"Twinkle, twinkle, little star,

How I wonder what you are.

Up above the world so high,

Like a diamond in the sky."

ASSIGNMENT Variety   DATE:

Perform the following one-line commercials with three different tempos, pace and, tone. You decide on the tempo, pace, and tone for each sentence. 1.) "I never have to worry about it again. Ever." 2.) "I liked it so much, I got two!" 3.) "I work with trees, shrubs and my dog Fritz. I'm allergic to them all." 4.) "They pretty much keep to themselves."

Now talk very softly to a small child who is frightened. Increase your volume to shout at the person who frightened the child.

Speak quietly to a classmate, not overheard by teacher. Say something so teacher hears.

Now say the sentence, "I love it", starting quickly, then move to more enthusiastic volume and variety.

Say the sentence, "I love it", showing the emotion of joy.

Count the numbers, "1, 2, 3, 4, 5, 6, 7, 8, 9, 10," building intensity for vocal variety.

Show grief as you count.

Show surprise.

Show anger.

Show puzzlement.

Show indifference.

Show confusion.

DATE:

1. Calling offstage—As you are onstage, use the correct amount of volume, so that the audience hears each word, yet you appear to be calling someone far away.

Imagine a small child offstage at an imagined playground. Call, "John, come back here right now."

Incorporate the following emotions into the preceding line: anger, worry, and joy. Use one emotion at a time.

2. Stage Whisper—Use a strong breath, a low pitch and while you are appearing to whisper, project the words so the audience can hear them.

Say the following words: "Come on; hurry; we have to get out of here."

3. Laughing—Expel your breath in explosive spurts. Keep the words clear, laughing between the words or phrases.

Say a nursery rhyme, such as, *Mary Had a Little Lamb.* Laugh between the phrases or words, as you think of the funniest joke you ever heard.

"Mary had a little lamb,
His fleece is white as snow.
And everywhere that Mary went,
The lamb was sure to go."

4. Crying—Inhale in little gasping sobs. Sob between the words or phrases. The tears are in the voice. The audience must understand the words while believing you are crying.

Repeat a memorized nursery rhyme, such as Humpty Dumpty, indicating crying in your voice. Say it as if you are crying, while still making each word clear to the audience.

"Humpty Dumpty sat on a wall.
Humpty Dumpty had a great fall.
All the king's horses; all the king's men
Couldn't put Humpty together again*."*

ASSIGNMENT Telephone Calls   DATE:

Use the phone. Listen to the implied actor who asks a question. Rephrase the question so an audience knows what you heard. Answer the question and ask three questions, listening to the answers to each, repeating the answers so the audience knows what the other actor says. End your conversation.

RELECTIVE INQUIRY   DATE:

Revisit your telephone conversation. Answer the following questions and make a note of the answers.

Could you hear all of the words of the telephone call?

Were the pauses the right length?

Who was the C in your CWOW? What character did you portray in the telephone call?

Where was your location during the telephone call?

What was the objective of the phone call?

To whom were you speaking on the phone call?

Could an audience tell what the other person on the phone wanted from you?

ASSIGNMENT Vocal Objective   DATE:

Say the following lines to achieve the objective of soothing an upset person: 1.) "Pajamas at breakfast," 2.) "Fresh ginger muffin," 3.) "Rubber duckies," and 4.) "Finding a lucky penny."

Say the following lines to excite a relaxed person: 1.) "A squeeze Ketchup bottle, " 2.) "Bags of magic tricks, " 3.) "Action heroes, " and 4.) "Comic action books. "

Say the following lines to express love to the recipient of your words: 1.) "Seeing the moon rise, " 2.) "Red velvet, " 3.) "A valentine, " and 4.) "Rainbows. "

Say the following lines to get sympathy from your partner: 1.) "Babies who cry, " 2.) "The first week of school, " 3.) "A broken toy, " and 4.) "A band aid on my skinned knee. "

Say the following words to quiet an excited person: 1.) "Do not disturb signs, " 2.) "Eating the center of an Oreo cookie, " 3.) "Watching TV with a bowl of snacks, " and 4.) "Collecting prizes for winning. "

ASSIGNMENT Vocal Quality   DATE:

Say the following line, using a shrill voice: "Get in here right now."

Change to a soothing voice: "Get in here right now."

Use a nasal voice: "Get in here right now."

Indicate a feeling using a well-modulated voice: "Get in here right now."

Use a booming voice: "Get in here right now."

Be withdrawn: "Get in here right now."

CREATIVE INQUIRY   DATE:

Think about what kind of character would use a shrill voice to say, "Get in here right now?"

What character type would use a withdrawn voice to say, "Get in here right now?"

ASSIGNMENT Volume   DATE:

Imagine you are a radio announcer. Say the following words with loud volume, medium volume, and quiet volume: "Now a word from our sponsor."

REFLECTIVE INQUIRY   DATE:

Recall how it felt to say those words at different volumes. What attitudes are conveyed by saying the line loudly, and then with medium volume, and then with quiet volume?

ASSIGNMENT Oral Interpretation of Literature—I'm Nobody DATE:

Analyze the following poem for the meaning. When you think you know what the poem is saying, practice the three vocal objectives that you discover in the poem. Using articulation, diction, inflection, pace, pause, projection, variety, communicate the objective. Look back at the Vocal Vocabulary to review how you will use your voice.

I'm Nobody
by Emily Dickinson

I'm nobody! Who are you?
Are you nobody, too?
Then there's a pair of us—don't tell!
They'd banish us, you know.

How dreary to be somebody!
How public like a frog
To tell your name the livelong day
To an admiring bog!

When vocally rehearsing literature, use a variety of voices for practice.

Imagine you are talking to a real person from your life and try to motivate the person to give you a hug.

Change the person to whom you speak and irritate the person while you say the poem.

Change your person to whom you are speaking a third time and scare the person with your voice while you say the poem.

REFLECTIVE INQUIRY   DATE:

Recall how you varied your voice for three different objectives. Which one of the three ways described above do you think is an appropriate interpretation to communicate the meaning of the poem? Or is there another intention you will try? Write the chosen vocal intention you will use for a fourth way to interpret the poem's meaning.

One difference between poetry and lyrics is that lyrics sort of fade into the background. They fade on the page and live on the stage when set to music.

Stephen Sondheim, American composer, lyricist

Song Lyrics for Vocal Work

By working on lyrics by interpreting the words as if they are a poem without singing, you can create a character who speaks lyrically and tells a story.

ASSIGNMENT Song Lyrics for Vocal Work   DATE:

Imagine your character believes in the power of magic, and you are talking to someone who is in the need of empowerment. Your objective is to convince the implied other that putting all of his/her powers to work will result in magic.

Rehearse the words to the song "Bibbity-Bobbity-Boo," which the Godmother sings in the movie *Cinderella*. Remember this is a song about the power of magic.

Salagadoola mechicka boola bibbidi-bobbidi-boo
Put 'em together and what have you got
bibbity-bobbity-boo

Salagadoola mechicka boola bibbidi-bobbidi-boo
It'll do magic believe it or not
bibbity-bobbity-boo

Salagadoola means mechicka booleroo
But the thingmabob that does the job is
bibbity-bobbity-boo

Salagadoola menchicka boola bibbidi-bobbidi-boo
Put 'em together and what have you got
bibbity-bobbity bibbity-bobbity bibbity-bobbity-boo.

ASSIGNMENT A Novelty Song for Vocal Work ⬧**A**⬧   DATE:

Rehearse the words to the song, "Mairzy Doats", a novelty song written in 1943 by Milton Drake, A. Hoffman, and Jerry Livingston.

Mairzy doats and dozy doats and liddle lamzy divey
A kiddley divey too, wouldn't you?
If the words sound queer and funny to your ear, a little bit jumbled and jivey,
Sing "Mares eat oats and does eat oats and little lambs eat ivy."

REFLECTIVE INQUIRY ⬤**RI**   DATE:

Revisit the "Mairzy Doats" song. What do you think the last line is saying?

ASSIGNMENT "Mairzy Doats" ⬧**A**⬧   DATE:

Look at the rest of the "Mairzy Doats" song, printed below.

Mairzy dotes and dozy dotes and liddle lamzy divey,
A kiddley divey, too - wouldn't you?
Mairzy dotes and dozy dotes and little lamzy divey,
A kiddley divey, too - wouldn't you?

(Bridge:)
Now if the words sound queer, and funny to your ear,

A little bit jumbled and jivey,
Just say, "Mares eat oats, and does eat oats,
And little lambs eat ivy."

Mairzy dotes and dozy dotes and little lamzy divey,
A kiddley divey, too – wouldn't you?
A kiddely divey, too – a kiddley divey, too,
A kiddley divey, too – wouldn't you?

Create a character who might say these lyrics. To whom is your character speaking? What is your objective by saying these words? Where are you? Create CWOW (character, who, objective, where).

Shakespeare for Vocal Interpretation

Shakespearean sonnets are poems that present love themes. Each sonnet has fourteen lines and a fixed verse and rhyme scheme. The sonnet is written in iambic pentameter, a fixed measure with stress and unstressed rhythm, and a rhyme scheme.

The speaker is expressing internal thoughts and emotions; he/she is working on a problem, which is solved in the final two lines.

ASSIGNMENT Shakespeare for Vocal Interpretation DATE:

Read and interpret Shakespeare's sonnet below. Pay attention to the end of the sentence's punctuation marks. Concentrate on the vocal challenges within the sonnet. Look for repeated words and images.

Now look at the problem the speaker is working on. Discover the turning point at the end of the sonnet. Find the mood and contrast of moods.

Define each word for complete understanding. *A Shakespeare Glossary* by C.T. Onions is a book that you might find useful to complete this task.

Sonnet 116
Let me not to the marriage of true minds
Admit impediments; love is not love
Which alters when it alteration finds,
Or bends with the remover to remove.
O no, it is an ever-fix'ed mark
That looks on tempests and is never shaken;
It is the star to every wand'ring bark,
Whose worth's unknown, although his height be taken.
Love's not Time's fool, though rosy lips and cheeks
Within his bending sickle's compass come,
Love alters not with his brief hours and weeks,
But bears it out even to the edge of doom.
If this be error and upon me proved,
I never writ, nor no man ever loved.

ASSIGNMENT Shakespeare's Sonnet Rewrite in Modern Language   DATE:

In order to do oral interpretation of literature you must understand what you are saying, then infuse the words with emotion. Rewrite the lines of Sonnet 116 in modern language. Put what Shakespeare has written in Sonnet 116 in your own words.

Now that you have the meaning, work on saying the Shakespearean words and sounding like you are conveying the modern words.

CREATIVE INQUIRY   *CI*   DATE:

Think about a loved one from your real life to talk to. Play yourself. Establish CWOW. Make notes on 1.) To whom are you talking? 2.) What do you want and what is your objective? 3.) Where are you placing yourself and your implied other character and what is your location? 4.) What tactics are you using in the sonnet? 5.) What pantomime action are you doing while you are expressing the emotions of the sonnet to your implied partner? and 6.) Do you achieve your objective by the end of the sonnet?

Working on Shakespearean sonnets and plays will develop your vocal capabilities. Improving your vocal and physical skills are ways you can prepare for any audition and performance. Your vocal rehearsal routine can be a continuous process to create flexibility, stamina, and projection. If you can be heard and understood in each audition and performance, then you are ahead of many emerging actors.

Closure for Chapter Four: Vocal Work

ASSIGNMENT Closure   DATE:

As a culmination of the vocal work that you just experienced, choose ten vocal terms from this chapter to add to your vocal warm-up routine. Which ten Vocal Vocabulary and Assignments will you include in your vocal warm-up routine?

1.

2.

3.

4.

5.

6.

7.

8.

9.

10.

A defective voice will always preclude an artist from achieving the complete development of his art, however intelligent he may be …. The voice is an instrument which the artist must learn to use with suppleness and sureness, as if it were a limb.

Sarah Bernhardt, early film actress

The next chapter introduces improvisation for the actor. You will utilize your positive attitude, your developed creativity, your flexible body, and your expressive voice to create, rehearse and perform in improvisations.

CHAPTER FIVE: IMPROVISATION

Introduction to Improvisation

You may have heard the following phrases, "Let's play it by ear," "Take it as it comes," and "Make it up as we go along." These sayings come from improvisational experiences and are used in day-to-day life. You usually don't get up each morning and plan exactly what you will say and how you will react to each event that happens during the day. Sometimes you might practice what you will say to prepare for a situation, but you have to adjust the scenarios based on what others say or do. In daily life you are involved in some kinds of improvisation that require you to listen, take inventory of your thoughts and feelings, think on your feet, make adjustments, act, and respond. You adjust to what is happening in life.

Definition of Improvisation

Improvisation is known as Improv, which is the playing of a scene or scenes for which no script is written. It incorporates the skills of listening, reacting, and then acting. You as an actor are in the moment, creating and responding to a stimulus that you have not planned for.

During an improvisation which is considered a rehearsal and a performance event, your concentration is focused on what is said and done onstage and how each character reacts. There is no script, so actors have to rely on playing objectives, using tactics, and making adjustments to invented lines and scenarios. Nothing that happens in an improvisation is planned in advance.

So how can you practice for an improvisation? Think of it as being ready when the starter pistol is fired to signify the beginning of a race. The runner has practiced, so when the starter pistol is fired, the athlete knows precisely what to do next. Improv actors are ready to respond, because they have practiced.

Make some notes on an improvised situation you saw on stage and any improvised performance, such as Second City, ComedySportz or Theatre Sports shows.

What observation did you make about the acting in an improvisation?

History of Improvisation

Improvisation can be traced to Commedia dell 'Arte of the sixteenth century. The actors utilized universal characters with familiar stage business and well-known plots. The actors' lines were created on the spur of the moment and progressed the story lines.

~ **Konstantin Stanislavski**, the Russian director, and the French dramatist Jacques Copeau founded two major theories of acting; each theory incorporated improvisations to obtain depths of emotion without scripted lines.
~ **Winifred Ward** used improvisation with creative dramatics study, in which participants are guided by a leader to enact situations.
~ **Dorothy Heathcoate** devised similar work in England.
~ **Viola Spolin** created theater games that involved improvisation, in the 1940s. Spolin's techniques were innovative and proved to be a major influence on improvisational Theatre, Theatre education, and acting in general. Her son, Paul Sills, originated *The Second City,* an improv company, which began in Chicago in the 1950s. Many of its

graduates are noted for their work on the television show *Saturday Night Live*.

~ **Keith Johnston** originated Theatresports with competitive games judged by the audience.
~ **Dick Chudnow** founded ComedySportz in Milwaukee in the 1980s. Teams performed rehearsed, formatted games for comedy. They are given suggestions from the family-friendly audience.

There are serious forms of political improvisational work that were founded by Jerzy Grotowski in Poland in the 1950s and Augusto Boal's in South America "Forum Theatre" in the 1970s.

Why an Actor Studies Improvisation

The following qualities are needed for improvising: your confidence, creativity, imagination, intuition, relaxed body, and expressive voice assures that you will make appropriate choices to progress the story. Your improv work appears to be created "on the spot." You need to trust yourself to think freely, without judging, and make courageous choices. In solo improv, once you establish an improv character, you interact with an implied or invisible partner. Or if your character chooses, he/she can talk to him/herself without any implied character. Your character works toward your objective. You create a location for your character and then you invent stage business and mime action that you integrate with your lines while doing your improvisation story. Your character is given endowments and suggestions that give your character definition.

Vocabulary Used in the Study of Improvisation

If you are working with Improvisation, which is also called Improv, you need to be acquainted with the following terms:

~ **Believability**—The ability to convince the audience of the actor's character and spontaneity. The impression must be so strong that it seems real and in the moment.
~ **Blocking**—The rejection or denial of an offer or suggestion whether of your own creation or an acting partner's creation. The definition

for blocking in an improvisation differs from the Vocabulary for the Actor.

- **Character**—A created personality. The definition for Character in an improvisation differs from the Vocabulary for the Actor.
- **Conflict**—Opposing objectives. A strong conflict can provide the foundation for an improvisation.
- **Endowment**—A suggestion that gives characters definition and gives the environment specifics, such as size, attitude, weather, or unusual circumstances.
- **Focus or point of focus**—The point of attention on stage or in the story at any moment on which the performers and audience focus. The definition for Focus in an improvisation differs from the Vocabulary for the Actor.
- **Freeze**—The act of remaining motionless, a complete stop of action, a tableau composed of a stationary actor or actors.
- **Game or performance games**—The scene format that actors play in front of an audience.
- **Genre**—A type of literary form or style, such as comedy or tragedy. Other genres can include mystery, musical Theatre, children's literature, Greek tragedy, and melodrama. An Improv can be performed in any genre.
- **Gibberish**—A created speech using meaningless sounds in the form of a made-up language with different pitches, accents, and inflections.
- **Label line**—The first sentences of any improvisation, which establishes CWOW.
- **Long form improvisation**—One or more scenes connected by a story or theme.
- **Narrative**—A story or the telling of events. The events can be true or fictitious.
- **Objective**—What the character wants to happen. Keeping your character's objective in mind at all times during an improvisation keeps the improv on target. Everything you say or do must be directed to the accomplishment of your character's objective.
- **Obstacles**—The challenges created by the performers, to keep a character from achieving his or her objective. The obstacles can be humorous or serious to the audience. Whether the obstacle is physical or psychological, the character considers it a very important obstacle to overcome or conquer to achieve an objective.

- **Short form improv**—A series of games with no connection to one another, having no common theme.
- **Side coaching**—A guide, a hint, a phrase to remind the actor to stay focused.
- **Solo improvisation**—One actor on stage creating lines and action to advance an objective. Often, the character speaks to him or herself or an implied partner.
- **Spontaneity**—The action of proceeding from one's natural feeling without constraint. Spontaneity arises from a momentary impulse.
- **Status**—The hierarchy of characters within a scene.
- **Subtext**—The unspoken meaning that is underneath the dialogue. It is what a character is really thinking or desires, but does not say.
- **Tactic**—A technique used to achieve a successful objective. Tactics make up the character's strategy.
- **Task**—The action for the actor to do in the improvised scene.
- **Theatre games**—The activities that can be used in the classroom or rehearsal hall in which each participant is included. Theatre games are used for warm-ups, focus, and relaxation. The actors work individually or together to achieve a goal.

Difference between Giving a Speech and Solo Improvisation Performance

Giving a speech involves talking about a topic. The speech maker usually stands still and talks directly to an audience. Acting in a solo improv involves performing and doing some kind of staged business while playing a character. The actor establishes a fourth wall, a character who works toward an objective, and a story.

Difference between Ad Lib and Improvisation

Ad lib or ad-lib is a term which means a momentary invention of dialogue to cover a mistake in lines, action, or technical aspects of a performance. It is unscripted material, which hides errors. When the entire performance is a process that involves no written lines, the product is called an improvisation.

... improvising is wonderful. But, the thing is that you cannot improvise unless you know exactly what you're doing.

Christopher Walken, actor

How an Actor Uses Improvisation

While the study of improvisation may lead to a career in improvisational Theatre, its major use in Theatre rehearsals is to discover how to explore emotional responses to situations in a script. In an improv experience, without lines to constrict you have freer rein in character development.

Improv teaches acting skills without any concern for script and memorization. You utilize concentration, a willingness to play—which incorporates spontaneity—and responding in the moment. Being able to improvise is enormously helpful for anyone wanting to be a performer. You will find Improvisation a very important tool in your skill box as a way to create bold characters.

Improv sets up a sequential set of exercises that foster creativity and spontaneity of character. Actors utilize concentration, a willingness to play—which incorporates spontaneity, and responding in the moment.

Improvisation is great fun to do as well as being challenging and one of the best means of finding your way through a scene or into the head of a character. Many actors who work with scripts use improvisation in their rehearsal process to create emotional beats or to keep the work fresh. Improvisation may be used in many stages of the rehearsal process, beginning before you as the actor look at the script. It can be used to help you investigate the character's past—back story—and understand his/her immediate and overarching objectives. You can explore his/her character's personality traits. You can focus on the moods, attitudes, and emotions of the scripted character. It is important to understand what a character did prior to the action of the play to understand why the character thinks, speaks and acts in a certain manner. The actor can explore what might take place off stage before an entrance or what happens after he/she exits before another entrance.

Improv requires discovery and for you to be engaged in the moment. It requires that you listen and respond spontaneously without preconceived scene endings in mind.

Basic Principles of Improvisation

~ Say Yes. Never deny an offer or idea. The spontaneity is stopped with a denial or the blocking of creative work.
~ Make statements. Avoid "yes" and "no" questions.
~ Be sincere. Don't try to be funny.
~ Think quickly.
~ Establish CWOW.
~ Create a specific character.
~ Change. The character/s in a scene must experience some kind of change.
~ Play the character's objective.
~ Call your implied partner or real improv acting partner by character name, so that the audience and/or improv partner knows immediately who he/she is.
~ Focus on actions.
~ Express emotions.
~ Use mime unless you have some props.
~ Keep the scene advancing to tell a story.
~ Build the improv story to a climax.
~ Have a resolution to the improvised monologue or scene.
~ Keep it clean. Raise the status of your work, eliminating negativity or cheap laughs at someone's expense.

Side Coaching

In improvisation, it is helpful to have a supporter who is a guide, an assistant, or to have your own inner voice that helps you stay focused. Side coaching is a message to aid you, to keep you on task. You can become your own side coach to instruct yourself when needed. If you feel disconnected or distracted, you can create hints for yourself to apply when you recognize that you are off your game.

In improv, staying focused helps you be in the moment and work toward an objective. So side coaching phrases, such as "act," "trust yourself," "go for it," "add action," "what would the character do?" or "CWOW" will spur you along.

Warm-Ups for Improvisations

The exercises described below invite you to work on situations without the support of a written text. It allows the free exploration of ideas for rehearsal and experimentation. You can explore fully how improvisation works for you as an actor, what the techniques are, how to develop from a starting point, and how not to come to a grinding halt because of being blocked from ideas. You will experience an array of methods that you can use to hone improvisation skills. The more improvs you do, the more experienced you become.

You are now aware of the need for warm-ups for your body, voice and imagination. Following are numerous warm-ups to prepare for improvisation.

ASSIGNMENT Sound Ball Experience   DATE:

Pick up an imaginary ball, the size of a volley ball.

Toss it up and catch it three times; each time add a sound. Change your sound each time you throw it.

Change to a ping pong ball. Your sounds will change with the weight and size of the ball.

Increase the speed of the toss and catch.

Change to a basketball. Create more sounds.

Change to a heavy, oversized giant balloon ball. Let the weight and size of the balloon ball suggest sounds.

ASSIGNMENT Imaginary Hats 1   DATE:

Take a pantomime hat from an invisible shelf. Create what kind of hat you have taken off the shelf.

Place the hat on your head.

Stand in front of an imaginary full-length mirror.

Establish a character stance and movements suggested by the hat.

Establish CWOW for the hatted character.

Talk out loud to yourself and your mirror reflection.

Say three improvisation lines, using animated voice and actions.

Take off the hat, placing it back on the shelf.

Return to neutral stance.

Search the invisible shelf for another hat.

Repeat the procedure for three (3) more hats.

ASSIGNMENT Imaginary Hats 2   DATE:

Use your video camera and video your rehearsal of taking the three pantomime hats and establishing CWOW lines.

CREATIVE INQUIRY   DATE:

Revisit your rehearsal. Make some notes on three different hats and three creative CWOWs.

Hat	Character	Where are you?	Objective	To Whom Are You Talking?
1.				
2.				
3.				

ASSIGNMENT Spontaneous Talking   DATE:

Answer the following questions with the first thing that comes to your mind. Have confidence that you will contribute imaginative answers. You may create answers that are not based in fact.

1. I was named..........after...............because....

2. My unusual imaginative pet was....

3. My cheapest childhood toy was....

4. The funniest joke I remember is....

5. My favorite childhood activity was....

6. My first crush was....

7. One holiday I remember was....

8. My least useful present I ever received was....

9. A celebrity I would like to meet is.......... I would like to say the following to this celebrity...

ASSIGNMENT First Response　　　　　　　　DATE:

Complete the sentences below with creative, spontaneous answers.

Suddenly last summer I discovered....

When the door opened, Martha screamed, "....

Remember the time I....

Help....

If I were a rabbit, I would....

One time I....

Remember the time we landed....

Finally I was able....

ASSIGNMENT Endowments   DATE:

Part of performing an improvisation involves creating a character with endowments. Remember you can add interesting sizes, attitudes, relationships, or unusual circumstances.

Now count 1–10 using the following endowments:

A soft, shy voice and with something scratching your neck.

A loud voice feeling a need to get out of the room as soon as possible.

A sweet, sympathetic voice trying not to cry.

ASSIGNMENT Nursery Rhyme with Endowments   DATE:

Think of a familiar nursery rhyme or short story, which you have committed to memory.

Perform a familiar nursery rhyme and a character with a physical irritation, such as tight collar, food caught in teeth, fly buzzing, or sweaty hands.

Keep your concentration on the rhyme or story.

Make the irritation affect the way you say the nursery rhyme or story.

Your objective is to say the nursery rhyme or story; your obstacle, what prevents you achieving your objective, is the endowment.

Your tactic is to deal with the endowment so that it does not stop you from your objective.

ASSIGNMENT What Are You Doing? For the Solo Actor   DATE:

Begin a repetitive, non-auditory gesture. A repetitive gesture is an action with your hand, arm, head, face and/or body that you can do for approximately one minute.

Ask yourself the question, "What are you doing?"

Answer with an "ing" verb tied to some action you are not doing.

This is an illustration of "What Are You Doing?" for the Solo Actor:

Do a repetitive action moving your arms up and down.

Ask yourself "What are you doing?"

Answer with an "ing" verb tied to some action you are not doing; for example, "walking on the moon."

Begin a motion that looks like you are walking on the moon.

Ask yourself "What are you doing?" Answer with the first idea you have that you are not doing, such as "eating a balloon."

Keep doing new actions and responses for one minute.

~~~~~~
REFLECTIVE INQUIRY **RI**   DATE:
~~~~~~

Recall how you felt completing the assignment above. Make some notes on
1.) How quickly you created the "ing" phrases, and 2.) Whether you use stall techniques,
such as I am.

~~~~~~
ASSIGNMENT Solo Prompts and Opening Line   DATE:
~~~~~~

Develop a creative opening line in response to each of the prompts below. A prompt is
something said to you by an implied partner or something that happens that causes a
verbal response. Create CWOW before you respond and make some notes under each
prompt.

You just won the lottery.

You discovered you just dropped your ice cream cone in the dirt.

Someone famous asked you who your favorite celebrity is.

You just found out that a friend lied.

You delivered a love letter to the wrong person.

You were called to principal's office.

Well, you are about to start the greatest improvisation of all. With no script. No idea what's going to happen, often with people and places you have never seen before. And you are not in control. So say "yes." And if you're lucky, you'll find people who will say "yes" back.

Stephen Colbert, television humorist

Solo Improvisation

For the next pages there are numerous improvisation experiences for the solo actor. Once you try the experience, you will increase in confidence by rehearing and rehearsing with more creative ideas. To prepare for improvisation performances, you can assess your solo work. Use the following Guidelines for Assessing a Solo Improvisation.

Guidelines for Assessing a Solo Improvisation

- ~ Could you hear, understand and believe each spoken word?
- ~ Could you see your facial expressions?
- ~ Was there action and stage business?
- ~ Were you acting instead of performing a speech?
- ~ Did you establish CWOW?
- ~ How closely did you stick to your objective?
- ~ What tactics did you use to achieve your objective?
- ~ Did you as the solo actor appear to be really talking to yourself and/or implied acting partner?
- ~ If you are viewing an improvised monologue, did the monologue build to a vocal and physical climax?
- ~ Did you hold the final moment, tag look, then relax and smile?
- ~ Did you keep concentration and not break character?
- ~ Was there too much talk and too little action?
- ~ Did you use bold, creative choices?

Improv Experiences for the Solo Actor

Solo improvisation gives you an opportunity to practice spontaneous, creative skills without being concerned with a partner. You create for you and an implied acting partner, if you choose to incorporate an invisible character to whom you are talking. You may also indicate that you are talking to yourself, verbalizing your thoughts and feelings out loud.

ASSIGNMENT Improv Experiences for the Solo Actor   DATE:

Look at the Solo Actor Improv Planning Sheet below. Establish CWOW (the W for the Where is provided in the Solo Actor Improv Planning Sheet below).

Create your character that might be in the location

Decide your character's Objective.

Select who your character is talking to, your implied partner or yourself.

Construct business or action you might be doing in the location. What can your character be doing?

Solo Actor Improv Planning Sheet

Character	Who are you talking to? Implied Partner or Yourself?	Objective	Where? Location	Business
			Museum	
			Dentist Office	
			Zoo	

			In a movie line for a scary movie	

Physical Starting Position Improv

Using body language, establishing the way you sit, stand and move can reveal attitudes and emotions and be the starting point for a solo improvisation. The opening stances in the chart below are poses to stimulate the aspects of an improvisation. The character choices and conflicts are determined by the way you as a character are positioned in the beginning.

ASSIGNMENT Physical Starting Position Improv 1   DATE:

Look at the Physical Starting Position Improv Planning Sheet chart below.

Read the Column headed Opening Stance and brainstorm CWOW.

Establish your character—who might have that stance? Let the opening stance stimulate CWOW.

Decide to whom you will be talking—your Implied Partner or if you will talk to yourself?

Create your character's objective—what you want from the implied partner, if anything.

Form a Location based on your opening stance—a place where the improv takes place.

Craft business that you will do based on your opening stance—an action the character does while performing the improvisation.

Make up the unheard prompt line to which you will respond. Remember your opening stance.

Write your first line.

Physical Starting Position Improv Planning Sheet

Opening stance	Your character	Implied partner or yourself	Your objective	Location	Business	Unheard prompt line to which you respond	Your first line
Hands over your head							
Full back to the audience with one hand to the side							
Standing on one foot							

ASSIGNMENT Physical Starting Position Improv 2   DATE:

Set up your video camera.

Take the stage or playing area; face the camera with your neutral stance.

Establish your starting physical position.

Hear the imaginary prompt line to which you respond with your first line.

Continue the improvisation for approximately two minutes, verbalizing your improv lines out loud and doing your business until the solo improv, which is called an improvised monologue, builds to a climax and resolution. At the end of the improv, hold the final moment showing your facial reaction as a tag look, then relax, return to neutral stance, and smile.

Watch the Video.

REFLECTIVE INQUIRY DATE:

Recall how you felt when you performed in the video. How well did you let the physical starting position stimulate the improvisation?

ASSIGNMENT The Expert Improvisation DATE:

Create a character who is the expert on a specific topic. Think of a fun topic. Your endowment is to be very confident and present material as if what you are saying is the most important talk ever presented on this topic. Your objective is to convince your listener that you are the world expert on this topic. Choose an implied character who you are trying to convince.

Some examples of expert topics might include: Eating an Ice Cream Cone Before It Melts; Walking as Slowly as Possible When You Don't Want to Do Something; Keeping a Messy Room.

Imagine you are talking about the topic as you demonstrate the action.

REFLECTIVE INQUIRY DATE:

Recall how it felt to be the expert? Make some notes on this below.

ASSIGNMENT Solo Telephone Call Improvisation DATE:

An imaginary phone rings. Answer the phone, and with your improvised sentences, establish CWOW: who you are, to whom you are speaking, where are you taking this call, what the other person wants, and how the phone conversation ends. Stand like a character who is taking a call. Video your Solo Telephone Call Improvisation.

REFLECTIVE INQUIRY **RI**

DATE:

Revisit your phone call. Make some notes about what you observed.

How do you feel about your performance?

What was your CWOW?

What information was clear?

Did you sound as if you were making this up on the spot?

Were you committed to your character's objective?

Did your character achieve his/her objective?

CREATIVE INQUIRY **CI**

DATE:

Think about a second Solo Telephone Call Improvisation. What three changes will you make?

1.

2.

3.

ASSIGNMENT One-Minute Movie Improvisation   DATE:

Recall your favorite movie. Think about all of the main characters. Act out every character's lines and action. Perform the entire movie in a version lasting one minute. Talk and act in fast-forward motion. Use animated voices and actions. Video your One-Minute Movie Improvisation.

REFLECTIVE INQUIRY   DATE:

Revisit your movie. Make notes on the making of your movie.

1. How physically detailed was your movie?

2. Could you tell the difference vocally between the characters?

3. Did you perform the entire movie in approximately one minute?

ASSIGNMENT Gibberish Sales Pitch Improvisation   DATE:

Revisit your experience with Gibberish. If you need a reminder, look back for an explanation of Gibberish. Decide on a product you want to sell. Your character is a television sales person. You have a product to sell and must demonstrate how it works. You are talking to a television audience. Your objective is to sell your product. Establish what the selling price is and how the television viewers can purchase the product.

Now with gibberish made-up language, show the product, demonstrate how the product works, the price and how to purchase it. Your Gibberish commercial should be one minute in length. Video record this pitch and watch it.

REFLECTIVE INQUIRY   RI

DATE:

Revisit your pitch. Answer the questions below.

1. How clear were the actions?

2. Could you tell what your product was and how it works, by your actions?

3. How excited did your voice get when telling the virtues of the product?

4. Was it clear how to purchase and what the selling price was?

ASSIGNMENT Sock Puppet Improvisation   A

DATE:

Find two socks. They can be mismatched.

Devise a character for each sock.

Establish CWOW for your sock improvisation.

Create a scene with your two sock puppets that involves two distinct voices for dialogue and movements. Establish what each sock puppet wants from the other sock puppet. The scene needs to have a beginning, middle, climax and end. Have your puppets take bows.

ASSIGNMENT Confessions Improvisation   A

DATE:

Develop CWOW for each of the following characters. The confession can be humorous in nature, but to your character it is very serious. Your character's objective is to confess.

Your Character	To Whom are you confessing?	What is it you are confessing?	What is your location?	What is your stage business?
A five-year-old child				
A person who got caught taking candy				
Someone coming in late				

ASSIGNMENT ABCD . . . Z Solo Improvisation DATE:

Read the CWOW scenario below. Portray each character below doing the stage business suggested and talking to the implied other, trying to achieve the objective of your character. Each sentence begins with the next letter of the alphabet in order. There are twenty-six letters, so you will have twenty-six sentences. Your twenty-six sentences will make up a monologue.

CWOW

You are a new employee at a fast food restaurant.

You are talking to a customer who is ordering. You can imagine the implied, invisible person to whom you are talking says something to you, so you can pause to listen.

Your objective is to get the order correct.

Your conflict is that you are having trouble getting the order correct.

Your improvised monologue is to end with a sentence beginning with the letter "Z."

Try to do the improv without writing ideas down. Create spontaneously. Say the lines out loud.

Example of some sentences for a new employee at a fast food restaurant:

"A special today at (name of fast food restaurant) is ....

By the way, may I offer you a discount if you order ...

Can't take all of your order that fast ...

Didn't get that ...

Enough ... (Finish the scene for your portrayal of a new employee at a fast food restaurant.)

F

G

H

I

J

K

L

M

N

O

P

Quite okay

R

S

T

U

V

W

X marks the spot where I will indicate what your order is

Y

Zounds I finally got the order right. Zounds.

REFLECTIVE INQUIRY   DATE:

Revisit all your sentences from the ABCD ... Z Solo Improvisation. Make some notes on how much sense your sentences made.

Practice the ABCD ... Z Solo Improvisation periodically. Create different CWOWs.

Serious Improvisation

Developing an improvisation with a serious subject matter can help you access and explore serious emotions. In order to explore the full range of emotions for improvisations, you practice exploring solemn subjects, along with fun and light topics.

Read the Obituary Section of a newspaper. Develop a one-person solo improvisation, recounting the life of a person who has died. Speak in the first person, using the facts you learned from the person's obituary. Imagine how the person spoke, of what the person was proud, on what topic the person felt he/she was an expert, and give any words of advice from the person's perspective. You can communicate the facts and details of the person's life or use the facts to create a character based on the obituary that you read.

With your experiences of working with humorous and serious improvisations you have added to your acting practice.

Closure for Chapter Five: Improvisation

It is time to reflect on what you have learned, looking back at your progress in the study of acting. Checking your development asks that you give feedback regarding what you remember about a topic.

ASSIGNMENT Closure   DATE:

What skill from day-to-day life can you use in your improvisational experiences?

How does an actor practice improvisation?

Look back at the History of Improvisation. List two names of improvisation teachers who you might like to research.

Name two reasons why an actor studies improvisation.

Look at the Vocabulary Used in the Study of improvisation. List twelve words that you think are the most important for an improvisation student to know.

1.

2.

3.

4.

5.

6.

7.

8.

9.

10.

11.

12.

Explain the difference between giving a speech and a solo improvisation performance.

Explain the difference between an ad lib and improvisation.

Explain one way that an actor uses improvisaton.

Look at the Basic Principles of Improvisation. List the three that you think are the most important. Explain why you chose those three principles.

Principle	Why You Chose This Principle

1.

2.

3.

Explain side coaching.

Why is it important for an actor to warm-up before doing an improvisation?

Now look back at the various warm-up for improvisations and Assignments. List three warm-ups that were fun to try.

1.

2.

3.

Which warm-up was challenging?

Which warm-up required fast thinking?

Which warm-up did you feel comfortable rehearsing?

For each of the experiences for Solo Improvisation listed below, write one thing that you will work on or change for the next time you experiment with the Improv Experience.

Solo Actor Improv Planning Sheet

Physical Starting Position Improv

The Expert Improvisation

Solo Telephone Call Improvisation

One-Minute Movie Improvisation

Gibberish Sales Pitch Improvisation

Confessions Improvisation

ABCD . . . Z Solo Improvisation

Serious Improvisations

Why is it important for an actor to act in serious improvisations?

Improvisation is a tool for developing your acting skills. It requires that you focus on creating characters, pursuing objectives, establishing action, responding impulsively with honesty in an authentic manner, and thinking creatively. The skills you learned in this section work along with your confidence, relaxed body, and expressive voice to help you in your study of acting.

Having rehearsed techniques of mime, movement, vocal work, and solo improvisation, you are ready to study acting in more depth, analyze play scripts, and create a character monologue from a script. You are adding more tools on your road to becoming an emerging actor.

CHAPTER SIX: ACTING AND SCRIPT STUDY

One went to school, one wanted to act, one started to act, and one is still acting.

Maggie Smith, actor

Introduction to Acting

You are an emerging actor or a working actor. Acting is an art and a craft. Do you think of yourself as an artist? Or a craftsman? The distinction between acting as an art or acting as a craft has been debated for a long time. The difference addresses the art of a dramatic work, and the craft of actors who deliver the product. A useful way of determining the difference between the art and the craft is to consider that a craft is something that you can learn. You can learn methods and techniques and put these principles into practice as an artist. What is agreed upon is that there is no art without craft. Learning the craft is the beginning to the path of artistry. Art can be thought of as the quality that gifted actors possess; this is sometimes called innate talent. Whether you have innate talent or not, studying the craft of acting can lead to acting artistry. This book proposes that someone who studies the craft and adds something that is uniquely his/her own is an artist.

Acting is bringing the life of the story to the stage. Acting is expressing emotions. Acting is connecting the interpretation of your role with the playwright's words. Acting is creating a physical picture for the audience through your knowledge of the character's psychological workings. Acting is the understanding of what the character is saying, thinking, and feeling, thereby creating a convincing character based on the playwright's text.

Creating compelling characters is your actor's goal. Bold character choices help an actor to audition successfully and to gain audience appreciation in performances. Effective character development is more than just reading a script. The text study tells you how to create a character using movement, thoughts, and emotions. Crafting the character's physical stance, movement, and voice are your challenges. You analyze a script to give personality to a playwright's creation. You look for a story arc in order to trace the character's journey and to discover from the script, the role's objectives. It is your job to infuse the character with thoughts and feelings, and give physical life to the playwright's creation. The scriptwriter's text lets the actor discover the character's objective, obstacles, and tactics. The physical, vocal, and emotional creation is part of your work in crafting characters.

Your craftsmanship includes a set of tips and tools that you have at your disposal to create effective characters. The acting guidelines in this chapter help you to devise your own techniques and develop your set of tools. You are continually developing your craft. Your technique is established using many tools that you have refined through study. The study of acting presents several approaches to use in your craft. The varied acting theories are described in this chapter.

History of Acting: Mechanical to Method

The history of acting is closely intertwined with Theatre history. In this chapter the modern acting teachers and their theories are briefly presented. Further study is recommended for the serious actor. As an emerging actor, you can become familiar with two styles of acting that have affected the modern actor's work. The mechanical style of Delsarte was known as Aesthetic Gymnastics for Actors. In the 1890s James-Lange presented the theory of creating a character from the outside in, using poses. Body positions were assumed by the actor with the instruction that corresponding emotions would automatically appear. Actors studied in front of mirrors to perfect the correct body postures to convey a range of emotions, such as Joy, Love, Pity, Anxiety, Fear, Modesty, and Shame. To portray Joy, the actor displayed an open countenance, while clapping hands, raising eyes toward the heavens, with the body, demonstrating a spring. The outside-in approach of the by-gone time evolved into modern acting approaches.

The farthest point on the acting continuum from Delsarte's Aesthetic Gymnastics is The Method, which was created by Konstantin Stanislavski, and became known as the Stanislavski System. One of Stanislavski's main concepts was that the actor uses memory to recall experiences from real life. These life experiences generate feelings similar to those which the character is experiencing, resulting in a very truthful, emotional believability. The actor comprehends the inner feelings of the character and develops vocal and bodily manifestations from that understanding. The word *if* or *as if* or *what if* is important to the Method actor. If the events were really happening, how would you as the character feel? This approach asks for the actor's involvement with personal experiences. This is known as the inside-out tactic of acting.

Master Acting Teachers

Growth as an actor and as a human being are synonymous.

Stella Adler, actress, acting teacher

In your study of acting, you discover that if you practice theories presented by acting teachers, your skills will progress. Sometimes actors become devotees of one of the master acting teachers; others use eclectic techniques, which incorporate several theories. Studying books and resources written by these masters aids progress in your journey. The ideas of these teachers are referenced and practiced in many acting classes. The following chronological list of acting teachers recognizes those whose work has had lasting influence on the modern acting styles. The list is organized by birth dates of acting teachers. The list does not include all known acting teachers.

- ~ **Aristotle**—(384 BC–322 BC)—A Greek philosopher and writer who wrote *The Poetics*, the earliest known work of dramatic theory.
- ~ **James-Lange**—(1811–1871)—See the section entitled History of Acting: Mechanical to Method
- ~ **Konstantin Stanislavski**—(1863–1938)—A Russian director and acting teacher whose system included concentration, voice, physical skills, emotion memory, observation, and dramatic analysis. It became known as The Method.
- ~ **Michael Chekhov**—(1891–1955)—A Russian-American director and Theatre teacher, who developed Psychological Gesture.
- ~ **Lee Strasberg**—(1901–1982)—An American teacher who is considered the father of The Method acting in America, whose teaching emphasized affective memory and improvisation.

- **Stella Adler**—(1901–1992)—An American actress and acting teacher whose technique was based on a combination of imagination and memory and included physical embodiment of the character.
- **Sanford Meisner**—(1905–1997)—An American actor and acting teacher who developed a form of The Method acting known as the Meisner technique. The Meisner principles emphasized the actor's living truthfully under imaginary circumstances.
- **Viola Spolin**—(1906–1994)—An American Theatre innovator who created directorial techniques based on improvisation known as Theater Games. Spolin developed a way to teach acting principles by improvisation.
- **Robert (Bobby) Lewis**—(1909–1997)—An American acting teacher, director, and writer who focused on the use of the imagination to stimulate emotion.
- **Uta Hagan**—(1919–2004)—A German-American actress and teacher, whose practice promoted realistic acting.
- **Jerzy Grotowski**—(1933–1999)—A Polish Theatre director who formulated techniques of the mind working with the body techniques.
- **Robert Cohen**—(1938–)—An American Theatre director and professor, whose books present a system of acting called GOTE: goal, objectives, techniques, expectations.
- **David Mamet**—(1947–)—An American playwright and teacher, who advises actors on topics such as judging a role, approaching the part, working with the playwright, undertaking auditions, and handling show business.
- **Anne Bogart**—(1951–)—An American Theatre director, who founded improvisational, ensemble-building techniques, known as Viewpoints.
- **Eric Morris**—(1977–)—An American acting teacher who formulated his own theory, based on seven obligations to material: 1) Time and Place, 2) Relationship, 3) Emotional Obligation, 4) Character Obligation, 5) Historic Obligation, 6) Thematic Obligation, 7) Directorial Obligation.

The actor is onstage to communicate the play to the audience.

David Mamet, playwright, director, author, acting teacher

ASSIGNMENT Master Acting Teachers   DATE:

Each week choose one acting teacher to read and research. Make notes about the teacher's principles.

Which teacher will you study first?

Why did you choose that teacher?

As you read each teacher's theories, keep a journal of notes about the teacher's chief principles.

What question would you like to ask one of the master acting teachers?

Acting Vocabulary

In order to take part intelligently in the acting process, you must learn vocabulary terms that you will need in order to analyze characters, to analyze scripts, and to write original monologues. Just as any profession has its own terminology, acting does also. Below is a list of some key acting vocabulary terms.

ASSIGNMENT Acting Vocabulary   DATE:

Study the list of vocabulary below. If a blank space follows the definition then it means the word was defined in an earlier chapter. Write in the vocabulary definition using your own words. Look back at previous chapters to check your work. If the word is defined in the list below, you need to become familiar with the term as an actor.

Action—The complete story, consisting of a beginning, middle, and an end.

Affective memory—The memory of details, also known as emotional memory, that Stanislavski's system used.

Antagonist—A person, group, or force that opposes the protagonist's goals or objectives.

Arc

Back story—The life of the character that the actor creates from the text. The back story is not explicitly acted out for the audience, but is essential to the actor's success in creating his/her role.

Beat—The silence between words, speeches or actions. During a beat, an actor may convey a change of topic, emotion, mood, objective, thought, and/or tactic.

Bit, bit part—A small role with very few lines and/or a brief appearance on stage.

Blocking

Business/stage business

Cast

Character

Climax

Conflict

Crisis

Cue

Curtain line

Denouement—The final resolution of the play's plot. The denouement follows the climax of the story.

Dialogue or dialog

Dramatis personae

Fourth wall

French scene

Given circumstances

Gesture

Hero, heroine

Intention—The objective of the character. Tactics are employed to achieve the intention.

Indicating—The acting term that signifies stereotypical behavior which is poorly connected to the character's emotion.

Leading roles

Lines

Magic if, what if, or as if—A tool to help the actor make choices based on what he/she would do if his/her character were in the situation of the scene or play.

Melodrama—The dramatic form that emphasizes plot and catastrophe and has a moralistic tone.

Monologue

Motivation—A character's reason for feeling, for speaking, or for performing an action.

Objective

Obstacle

One-act play

Organic acting—The acting technique that has the actor immerse himself/herself into the mind and body of the character. The actor allows the character to dictate style, movements and speech.

Physical action—All the things the actor does on stage. Action includes movement and stage business

Plot

Pick up cues—An acting technique of saying the lines of a monologue, scene, or play so there are no pauses between lines.

Point of attack

Point of focus

Portfolio

Precast—The casting of some roles before open auditions.

Principals

Principles—The teaching that serves as the foundation for a system.

Process—The rehearsal period before the production.

Protagonist

Prompt book

Psychological gesture—The character's move or activity that shows his/her motives.

Public Domain—A script that is either ineligible for copyright protection or has an expired copyright. No permission is needed to copy or use the public domain script.

Realistic acting—The Stanislavski style of natural acting in which actors become emotionally and psychologically involved with their roles.

Repertory or repertoire

Resolution

Role

Royalty

Setting—The location of a play's action.

Scoring a role

Script

Slate—The introduction to an audition. It consists of a greeting, your name, title, and character name.

Soliloquy—The lines of one character standing onstage alone talking to himself/herself, speaking thought aloud.

Speeches—The actor's lines.

Stage directions

Stakes—The strong commitment to wanting your objective.

Standby—An actor who is ready to replace another actor in a performance.

Stock characters—The characters who represent particular personality types that are universally recognizable by the audience.

Strategy—A plan or technique a character uses to get what he/she wants. Tactics are part of strategy.

Subtext—The character's thoughts and feelings that are implied but never stated. Subtext can be thought of as your character's inner monologue.

Superobjective—The term utilized in Stanislavski's The Method. The superobjective is the character's continuing goal.

Supporting role—The minor character who supports the principal characters.

Tactic—A technique used to achieve a successful objective. Tactics make up the character's strategy.

Tag line

Text

Theme

Villain

We speak not to express our desires. We speak to accomplish our desires.

David Mamet, playwright, director, author, acting teacher

Reading and Analyzing a Script from an Actor's Point of View

In this chapter you concentrate on script analysis from the point of view of an actor who wants to construct a monologue from a script. You experience the techniques of how to read a play as an actor, how to analyze a monologue, how to stage a monologue, and how to write a monologue. In order to act a role, create a monologue from a script, or write a monologue, you need to understand how to read and examine a play from your actor's perspective.

Reading plays was introduced in the Prologue of this book. Reading a play is the beginning of the actor's analysis process. Script inquiry is the discovery of the play's story, the central conflict, the theme, the character's relationship to the story and to the conflict, the character's purpose in the script, the character's objective, and the achievement of the character's objective by overcoming obstacles. Analysis is a significant part of the actor's craft. Exploration leads to your making choices that guide you to a strong performance. When you use the tools of play analysis, you are looking at the story from a character's point of view.

The study keeps the actor on course to discover the playwright's intentions. This is a practical, academic exercise. It is a tool that helps you make confident choices. Referring to the text is needed to get answers for your character's creation. Script analysis is like a road map to understanding the script and creating a character's journey.

The play's the thing wherein I'll catch the conscience of the king.

Hamlet by Shakespeare

Reading and Analyzing a Script: Overtones

Below is the rest of the play *Overtones.* Please read the play and then move to the assignment section, where there are some questions for you to answer and think about. The play has a cast of four females. Following the play *Overtones* is a play *The Boy,* which has two male characters.

Some of the answers can be found in the script text; others require you to use your imagination. For some answers you will need to use your thoughts and create an appropriate response based on what you have read to that point. Some questions ask you to give your opinion.

When answering the questions, make a choice based on what you know or feel.

Overtones

A play in one-act by Alice Gerstenberg

This is reprinted from *Washington Square Plays*. Ed. Edward Goodman. New York: Doubleday, Page & Co., 1916. It is now in the public domain and may therefore be performed without royalties.

CHARACTERS

Dramatis Personae

HARRIET, a cultured woman

HETTY, her primitive self

MARGARET, a cultured woman

MAGGIE, her primitive self

HARRIET'S fashionable living room. The door at the back leads to the hall. In the centre a tea table with a chair either side.

At the back a cabinet. HARRIET'S gown is a light, "jealous" green. Her counterpart, HETTY, wears a gown of the same design but in a darker shade. MARGARET wears a gown of lavender chiffon while her counterpart, MAGGIE, wears a gown of the same design in purple, a purple scarf veiling her face. Chiffon is used to give a sheer effect, suggesting a possibility of primitive and cultured selves merging into one woman.

The primitive and cultured selves never come into actual physical contact but try to sustain the impression of mental conflict. HARRIET never sees HETTY, never talks to her but rather thinks aloud looking into space. HETTY, however, looks at HARRIET, talks intently and shadows her continually. The same is true of MARGARET and MAGGIE. The voices of the cultured women are affected and lingering, the voices of the primitive impulsive and more or less staccato.

[When the curtain rises HARRIET is seated right of tea table, busying herself with the tea things.]

HETTY: Harriet. *[There is no answer.]* Harriet, my other self.
            [There is no answer.] My trained self.

HARRIET: *[listens intently]* Yes?

[From behind HARRIET'S chair HETTY rises slowly.]

HETTY: I want to talk to you.

HARRIET: Well?

HETTY: *[looking at HARRIET admiringly]* Oh, Harriet, you are
            beautiful today.

HARRIET: Am I presentable, Hetty?

HETTY: Suits me.

HARRIET: I've tried to make the best of the good points.

HETTY: My passions are deeper than yours. I can't keep on
            the mask as you do. I'm crude and real, you are my
            appearance in the world.

HARRIET: I am what you wish the world to believe you are.

HETTY: You are the part of me that has been trained.

HARRIET: I am your educated self.

HETTY: I am the rushing river; you are the ice over the current.

HARRIET: I am your subtle overtones.

HETTY: But together we are one woman, the wife of Charles Goodrich.

HARRIET: There I disagree with you, Hetty, I alone am his wife.

HETTY: *[indignantly]* Harriet, how can you say such a thing!

HARRIET: Certainly. I am the one who flatters him. I have to be the one who talks to him. If I gave you a chance you would tell him at once that you dislike him.

HETTY: *[moving away]* I don't love him, that's certain.

HARRIET: You leave all the fibbing to me. He doesn't suspect that my calm, suave manner hides your hatred. Considering the amount of scheming it causes me it can safely be said that he is my husband.

HETTY: Oh, if you love him--

HARRIET: I? I haven't any feelings. It isn't my business to love anybody.

HETTY: Then why need you object to calling him my husband?

HARRIET: I resent your appropriation of a man who is managed only through the cleverness of my artifice.

HETTY: You may be clever enough to deceive him, Harriet, but I am still the one who suffers. I can't forget he is my husband. I can't forget that I might have married John Caldwell.

HARRIET: How foolish of you to remember John, just because we met his wife by chance.

HETTY: That's what I want to talk to you about. She may be here at any moment. I want to advise you about what to say to her this afternoon.

HARRIET: By all means tell me now and don't interrupt while she is here. You have a most annoying habit of talking to me when people are present. Sometimes it is all I can do to keep my poise and appear not to be listening to you.

HETTY: Impress her.

HARRIET: Hetty, dear, is it not my custom to impress people?

HETTY: I hate her.

HARRIET: I can't let her see that.

HETTY: I hate her because she married John.

HARRIET: Only after you had refused him.

HETTY: [turning on HARRIET] Was it my fault that I refused him?

HARRIET: That's right, blame me.

HETTY: It was your fault. You told me he was too poor and never would be able to do anything in painting. Look at him now, known in Europe, just returned from eight years in Paris, famous.

HARRIET: It was too poor a gamble at the time. It was much safer to accept Charles's money and position.

HETTY: And then John married Margaret within the year.

HARRIET: Out of spite.

HETTY: Freckled, gawky-looking thing she was, too.

HARRIET: *[a little sadly]* Europe improved her. She was stunning the other morning.

HETTY: Make her jealous today.

HARRIET: Shall I be haughty or cordial or caustic or—

HETTY: Above all else you must let her know that we are rich.

HARRIET: Oh, yes, I do that quite easily now.

HETTY: You must put it on a bit.

HARRIET: Never fear.

HETTY: Tell her I love my husband.

HARRIET: My husband—

HETTY: Are you going to quarrel with me?

HARRIET: *[moves away]* No, I have no desire to quarrel with you. It is quite too uncomfortable. I couldn't get away from you if I tried.

HETTY: *[stamping her foot and following HARRIET]* You were a stupid fool to make me refuse John, I'll never forgive you —never—

HARRIET: *[stopping and holding up her hand]* Don't get me all excited. I'll be in no condition to meet her properly this afternoon.

HETTY: *[passionately]* I could choke you for robbing me of John.

HARRIET: *[retreating]* Don't muss me!

HETTY: You don't know how you have made me suffer.

HARRIET: *[beginning to feel the strength of HETTY'S emotion surge through her and trying to conquer it]* It is not my business to have heartaches.

HETTY: You're bloodless. Nothing but sham—sham—while I—

HARRIET: *[emotionally]* Be quiet! I can't let her see that I have been fighting with my inner self.

HETTY: And now after all my suffering you say it has cost you more than it has cost me to be married to Charles. But it's the pain here in my heart—I've paid the price—I've paid — Charles is not your husband!

HARRIET: *[trying to conquer emotion]* He is.

HETTY: *[follows HARRIET]* He isn't.

HARRIET: *[weakly]* He is.

HETTY: *[towering over HARRIET]* He isn't! I'll kill you!

HARRIET: *[overpowered, sinks into a chair]* Don't—don't—you're stronger than I—you're—

HETTY: Say he's mine.

HARRIET: He's ours.

HETTY: *[the telephone rings]* There she is now.

[HETTY hurries to phone but HARRIET regains her supremacy.]

HETTY: *[authoritatively]* Wait! I can't let the telephone girl down there hear my real self. It isn't proper. *[into the phone]* Show Mrs. Caldwell up.

HETTY: I'm so excited, my heart's in my mouth.

HARRIET: *[at the mirror]* A nice state you've put my nerves into.

HETTY: Don't let her see you're nervous.

HARRIET: Quick, put the veil on, or she'll see you shining through me.

[HARRIET takes a scarf of chiffon that has been lying over the back of a chair and drapes it on HETTY, covering her face. The chiffon is the same color of their gowns but paler in shade so that it pales HETTY'S darker gown to match HARRIET'S lighter one. As HETTY moves in the following scene the chiffon falls away revealing now and then the gown of deeper dye underneath.]

HETTY: Tell her Charles is rich and fascinating—boast of our friends, make her feel she needs us.

HARRIET: I'll make her ask John to paint us.

HETTY: That's just my thought—if John paints our portrait—

HARRIET: We can wear an exquisite gown—

HETTY: And make him fall in love again and—

HARRIET: *[schemingly]* Yes.

[MARGARET parts the portieres back centre and extends her hand. MARGARET is followed by her counterpart MAGGIE.]

HARRIET: Oh, Margaret, I'm so glad to see you!

HETTY: *[to MAGGIE]* That's a lie.

MARGARET: *[in superficial voice throughout]* It's enchanting to see you, Harriet.

MAGGIE: *[in emotional voice throughout]* I'd bite you, if I dared.

HARRIET: *[to MARGARET]* Wasn't our meeting a stroke of luck?

MARGARET: *[coming down left of table]* I've thought of you so often, Harriet; and to come back and find you living in New York.

HARRIET: *[coming down right of table]* Mr. Goodrich has many interests here.

MAGGIE: *[to MARGARET]* Flatter her.

MARGARET: I know, Mr. Goodrich is so successful.

HETTY: *[to HARRIET]* Tell her we're rich.

HARRIET: *[to MARGARET]* Won't you sit down?

MARGARET: *[takes a chair]* What a beautiful lamp!

HARRIET: Do you like it? I'm afraid Charles paid an extravagant price.

MAGGIE: *[to HETTY]* I don't believe it.

MARGARET: *[sitting down. To HARRIET]* I am sure he must have.

HARRIET: *[sitting down]* How well you are looking, Margaret.

HETTY: Yes, you are not. There are circles under your eyes.

MAGGIE: *[to HETTY]* I haven't eaten since breakfast and I'm hungry.

MARGARET: *[to HARRIET]* How well you are looking, too.

MAGGIE: *[to HETTY]* You have hard lines about your lips, are you happy?

HETTY: *[to HARRIET]* Don't let her know that I'm unhappy.

HARRIET: *[to MARGARET]* Why shouldn't I look well? My life is full, happy, complete—

MAGGIE: I wonder.

HETTY: *[in HARRIET'S ear]* Tell her we have an automobile.

MARGARET: *[to HARRIET]* My life is complete, too.

MAGGIE: My heart is torn with sorrow; my husband cannot make a living. He will kill himself if he does not get an order for a painting.

MARGARET: *[laughs]* You must come and see us in our studio. John has been doing some excellent portraits. He cannot begin to fill his orders.

HETTY: *[to HARRIET]* Tell her we have an automobile.

HARRIET: *[to MARGARET]* Do you take lemon in your tea?

MAGGIE: Take cream. It's more filling.

MARGARET: *[looking nonchalantly at tea things]* No, cream, if you please. How cozy!

MAGGIE: *[glaring at tea things]* Only cakes! I could eat them all!

HARRIET: *[to MARGARET]* How many lumps?

MAGGIE: *[to MARGARET]* Sugar is nourishing.

MARGARET: *[to HARRIET]* Three, please. I used to drink very sweet coffee in Turkey and ever since I've—

HETTY: I don't believe you were ever in Turkey.

MAGGIE: I wasn't, but it is none of your business.

HARRIET: *[pouring tea]* Have you been in Turkey, do tell me about it.

MAGGIE: *[to MARGARET]* Change the subject.

MARGARET: *[to HARRIET]* You must go there. You have so much taste in dress you would enjoy seeing their costumes.

MAGGIE: Isn't she going to pass the cake?

MARGARET: *[to HARRIET]* John painted several portraits there.

HETTY: *[to HARRIET]* Why don't you stop her bragging and tell her we have an automobile?

HARRIET: *[offers cake across the table to MARGARET]* Cake?

MAGGIE: *[stands back of MARGARET, shadowing her as HETTY shadows HARRIET. MAGGIE reaches claws out for the cake and groans with joy]* At last! *[But her claws do not touch the cake]*

MARGARET: *[with a graceful, nonchalant hand places cake upon her plate and bites at it slowly and delicately]* Thank you.

HETTY: *[to HARRIET]* Automobile!

MAGGIE: *[to MARGARET]* Follow up the costumes with the suggestion that she would make a good model for John. It isn't too early to begin getting what you came for.

MARGARET: *[ignoring MAGGIE]* What delicious cake.

HETTY: *[excitedly to HARRIET]* There's your chance for the auto.

HARRIET: *[nonchalantly to MARGARET]* Yes, it is good cake, isn't it? There are always a great many people buying it at Harper's. I sat in my automobile fifteen minutes this morning waiting for my chauffeur to get it.

MAGGIE: *[to MARGARET]* Make her order a portrait.

MARGARET: *[to HARRIET]* If you stopped at Harper's you must have noticed the new gowns at Henderson's. Aren't the shop windows alluring these days?

HARRIET: Even my chauffeur notices them.

MAGGIE: I know you have an automobile, I heard you the first time.

MARGARET: I notice gowns now with an artist's eye as John does. The one you have on, my dear, is very paintable.

HETTY: Don't let her see you're anxious to be painted.

HARRIET: *[nonchalantly]* Oh, it's just a little model.

MAGGIE: *[to MARGARET]* Don't seem anxious to get the order.

MARGARET: *[nonchalantly]* Perhaps it isn't the gown itself but the way you wear it that pleases the eye. Some people can wear anything with grace.

HETTY: Yes, I'm very graceful.

HARRIET: *[to MARGARET]* You flatter me, my dear.

MARGARET: On the contrary, Harriet, I have an intense admiration for you. I remember how beautiful you were—as a girl. In fact, I was quite jealous when John was paying you so much attention.

HETTY: She is gloating because I lost him.

HARRIET: Those were childhood days in a country town.

MAGGIE: *[to MARGARET]* She's trying to make you feel that John was only a country boy.

MARGARET: Most great men have come from the country. There is a fair chance that John will be added to the list.

HETTY: I know it and I am bitterly jealous of you.

HARRIET: Undoubtedly he owes much of his success to you, Margaret, your experience in economy and your ability to endure hardship. Those first few years in Paris must have been a struggle.

MAGGIE: She is sneering at your poverty.

MARGARET: Yes, we did find life difficult at first, not the luxurious start a girl has who marries wealth.

HETTY: [to HARRIET] Deny that you married Charles for his money.

[HARRIET deems it wise to ignore HETTY'S advice.]

MARGARET: But John and I are so congenial in our tastes, that we were impervious to hardship or unhappiness.

HETTY: [in anguish] Do you love each other? Is it really true?

HARRIET: [sweetly] Did you have all the romance of starving for his art?

MAGGIE: [to MARGARET] She's taunting you. Get even with her.

MARGARET: Not for long. Prince Rier soon discovered John's genius, and introduced him royally to wealthy Parisians who gave him many orders.

HETTY: [to MAGGIE] Are you telling the truth or are you lying?

HARRIET: If he had so many opportunities there, you must have had great inducements to come back to the States.

MAGGIE: [to HETTY] We did, but not the kind you think.

MARGARET: John became the rage among Americans travelling in France, too, and they simply insisted upon his coming here.

HARRIET: Whom is he going to paint here?

MAGGIE: [frightened] What names dare I make up?

MARGARET: [calmly] Just at present Miss Dorothy Ainsworth of Oregon is posing. You may not know the name, but she is the daughter of a wealthy miner who found gold in Alaska.

HARRIET: I dare say there are many Western people we have never heard of.

MARGARET: You must have found social life in New York very interesting, Harriet, after the simplicity of our home town.

HETTY: *[to MAGGIE]* There's no need to remind us that our beginnings were the same.

HARRIET: Of course Charles's family made everything delightful for me. They are so well connected.

MAGGIE: *[to MARGARET]* Flatter her.

MARGARET: I heard it mentioned yesterday that you had made yourself very popular. Someone said you were very clever!

HARRIET: *[pleased]* Who told you that?

MAGGIE: Nobody!

MARGARET: *[pleasantly]* Oh, confidences should be suspected— respected, I mean. They said, too, that you are gaining some reputation as a critic of art.

HARRIET: I make no pretenses.

MARGARET: Are you and Mr. Goodrich interested in the same things, too?

HETTY: No!

HARRIET: Yes, indeed, Charles and I are inseparable.

MAGGIE: I wonder.

HARRIET: Do have another cake.

MAGGIE: *[in relief]* Oh, yes. *[Again her claws extend but do not touch the cake.]*

MARGARET: *[takes cake delicately]* I really shouldn't—after my big luncheon. John took me to the Ritz and we are invited to the Bedfords' for dinner—they have such a magnificent house near the drive—I really shouldn't, but the cakes are so good.

MAGGIE: Starving!

HARRIET: *[to MARGARET]* More tea?

MAGGIE: Yes!

MARGARET: No, thank you. How wonderfully life has arranged itself for you. Wealth, position, a happy marriage, every opportunity to enjoy all pleasures; beauty, art—how happy you must be.

HETTY: *[in anguish]*. Don't call me happy. I've never been happy since I gave up John. All these years without him—a future without him—no—no—I shall win him back—away from you—away from you—

HARRIET: *[does not see MAGGIE pointing to cream and MARGARET stealing some]* I sometimes think it is unfair for anyone to be as happy as I am. Charles and I are just as much in love now as when we married. To me he is just the dearest man in the world.

MAGGIE: *[passionately]* My John is. I love him so much I could die for him. I'm going through hunger and want to make him great and he loves me. He worships me!

MARGARET: *[leisurely to HARRIET]* I should like to meet Mr. Goodrich. Bring him to our studio. John has some sketches to show. Not many, because all the portraits have been purchased by the subjects. He gets as much as four thousand dollars now.

HETTY: *[to HARRIET]* Don't pay that much.

HARRIET: *[to MARGARET]* As much as that?

MARGARET: It is not really too much when one considers that John is in the foremost rank of artists to-day. A picture painted by him now will double and treble in value.

MAGGIE: It's all a lie. He is growing weak with despair.

HARRIET: Does he paint all day long?

MAGGIE: No, he draws advertisements for our bread.

MARGARET: *[to HARRIET]* When you and your husband come to see us, telephone first—

MAGGIE: Yes, so he can get the advertisements out of the way.

MARGARET: Otherwise you might arrive while he has a sitter, and John refuses to let me disturb him then.

HETTY: Make her ask for an order.

HARRIET: *[to MARGARET]* Le Grange offered to paint me for a thousand.

MARGARET: Louis Le Grange's reputation isn't worth more than that.

HARRIET: Well, I've heard his work well mentioned.

MAGGIE: Yes, he is doing splendid work.

MARGARET: Oh, dear me, no. He is only praised by the masses. He is accepted not at all by artists themselves.

HETTY: *[anxiously]* Must I really pay the full price?

HARRIET: Le Grange thought I would make a good subject.

MAGGIE: *[to MARGARET]* Let her fish for it.

MARGARET: Of course you would. Why don't you let Le Grange paint you, if you trust him?

HETTY: She doesn't seem anxious to have John do it.

HARRIET: But if Le Grange isn't accepted by artists, it would be a waste of time to pose for him, wouldn't it?

MARGARET: Yes, I think it would.

MAGGIE: *[passionately to HETTY across back of table]* Give us the order. John is so despondent he can't endure much longer. Help us! Help me! Save us!

HETTY: *[to HARRIET]* Don't seem too eager.

HARRIET: And yet if he charges only a thousand one might consider it.

MARGARET: If you really wish to be painted, why don't you give a little more and have a portrait really worthwhile? John might be induced to do you for a little below his usual price considering that you used to be such good friends.

HETTY: *[in glee]* Hurrah!

HARRIET: *[quietly to MARGARET]* That's very nice of you to suggest —of course I don't know—

MAGGIE: *[in fear]* For God's sake, say yes.

MARGARET: *[quietly to HARRIET]* Of course, I don't know whether John would. He is very peculiar in these matters. He sets his value on his work and thinks it beneath him to discuss price.

HETTY: *[to MAGGIE]* You needn't try to make us feel small.

MARGARET: Still, I might quite delicately mention to him that inasmuch as you have many influential friends you would be very glad to—to—

MAGGIE: *[to HETTY]* Finish what I don't want to say.

HETTY: *[to HARRIET]* Help her out.

HARRIET: Oh, yes, introductions will follow the exhibition of my portrait. No doubt I—

HETTY: *[to HARRIET]* Be patronizing.

HARRIET: No doubt I shall be able to introduce your husband to his advantage.

MAGGIE: *[relieved]* Saved.

MARGARET: If I find John in a propitious mood I shall take pleasure, for your sake, in telling him about your beauty. Just as you are sitting now would be a lovely pose.

MAGGIE: *[to MARGARET]* We can go now.

HETTY: *[to HARRIET]* Don't let her think she is doing us a favor.

HARRIET: It will give me pleasure to add my name to your husband's list of patronesses.

MAGGIE: *[excitedly to MARGARET]* Run home and tell John the good news.

MARGARET: *[leisurely to HARRIET]* I little guessed when I came for a pleasant chat about old times that it would develop into business arrangements. I had no idea, Harriet, that you had any intention of being painted. By Le Grange, too. Well, I came just in time to rescue you.

MAGGIE: *[to MARGARET]* Run home and tell John. Hurry, hurry!

HETTY: *[to HARRIET]* You managed the order very neatly. She doesn't suspect that you wanted it.

HARRIET: Now if I am not satisfied with my portrait I shall blame you, Margaret, dear. I am relying upon your opinion of John's talent.

MAGGIE: *[to MARGARET]* She doesn't suspect what you came for. Run home and tell John!

HARRIET: You always had a brilliant mind, Margaret.

MARGARET: Ah, it is you who flatter, now.

MAGGIE: *[to MARGARET]* You don't have to stay so long. Hurry home!

HARRIET: Ah, one does not flatter when one tells the truth.

MARGARET: *[smiles]* I must be going or you will have me completely under your spell.

HETTY: *[looks at clock]* Yes, do go. I have to dress for dinner.

HARRIET: *[to MARGARET]* Oh, don't hurry.

MAGGIE: *[to HETTY]* I hate you!

MARGARET: *[to HARRIET]* No, really I must, but I hope we shall see each other often at the studio. I find you so stimulating.

HETTY: *[to MAGGIE]* I hate you!

HARRIET: *[to MARGARET]* It is indeed gratifying to find a kindred spirit.

MAGGIE: *[to HETTY]* I came for your gold.

MARGARET: *[to HARRIET]* How delightful it is to know you again.

HETTY: *[to MAGGIE]* I am going to make you and your husband suffer.

HARRIET: My kind regards to John.

MAGGIE: *[to HETTY]* He has forgotten all about you.

MARGARET: *[rises]* He will be so happy to receive them.

HETTY: *[to MAGGIE]* I can hardly wait to talk to him again.

HARRIET: I shall wait, then, until you send me word?

MARGARET: *[offering her hand]* I'll speak to John about it as soon as I can and tell you when to come.

[HARRIET takes MARGARET'S hand affectionately. HETTY and MAGGIE rush at each other, throw back their veils, and fling their speeches fiercely at each other.]

HETTY: I love him—I love him—

MAGGIE: He's starving—I'm starving—

HETTY: I'm going to take him away from you—

MAGGIE: I want your money—and your influence.

HETTY and MAGGIE: I'm going to rob you—rob you.

[There is a cymbal crash, the lights go out and come up again slowly, leaving only MARGARET and HARRIET visible.]

MARGARET: *[quietly to HARRIET]* I've had such a delightful afternoon.

HARRIET: *[offering her hand]* It has been a joy to see you.

MARGARET: *[sweetly to HARRIET]* Good-bye.

HARRIET: *[sweetly to MARGARET as she kisses her]* Good-bye, my dear.

END OF PLAY

ASSIGNMENT Reading and Analyzing a Script from an Actor's Point of View   DATE:

In the Prologue you read part of a script entitled *Overtones* and began to analyze the play. Now, the following assignment to read the entire script includes looking for the following aspects and making notes about your discoveries.

Notice any directions, settings, notes that the playwright gives at the beginning of the play.

Make a note of the time period for which the play was written.

Read the cast list. Get a feeling for the characters and why you think the playwright used the specific names.

Decide who the protagonist and antagonist are.

Look at how the characters work toward their objectives.

Read the play rapidly to get the story line and the arc of the story.

Read the stage directions, the italicized directions in parenthesis. Let the stage directions tell you what stage business the character is doing.

Recall the overall action of the play. What is the central conflict?

Finish the sentence, "This play is about people who ...."

Be aware of beats and the objectives of each character.

Remember CWOW.

Decide what obstacles stand in each character's way.

Specify which characters cause conflict.

Identify the strategy the character uses to achieve her objective.

Locate the tactics the character uses to achieve her objective.

Decide if the character is successful in achieving the objective.

Decide if the character changes her objective during the course of the play.

Notice what the climax of the plot is.

Tell the story in three sentences.

Be aware of the denouement of the story with exposition, inciting incident, rising action, climax, falling action, resolution, and conclusion.

Ask, what happens next every once in a while. How does the play move forward? How does the character develop?

Make a note how the play ends.

Cast famous people in the roles of Harriet, Hetty, Margaret, and Maggie. Think about someone whose public persona or acting roles are like the four characters in the play.

Notice any props, and stage business that the playwright has indicated.

Visualize the costume colors that each character is wearing. Each character's colors should suggest her personality type.

Imagine the time period of the set and props, the style and the colors.

Ask what the main character learns?

Brainstorm about what the theme of the play is. Finish the sentence, "This play is about …

Try to phrase the theme without using the word, "people."

ASSIGNMENT Script analysis of Overtones   DATE:

What do you think the title *Overtones* means?

What time period do you think will work for this production?

How do you see these characters dressed to show status? Take your clues from the Dramatis Personae, which includes a description of the characters.

What kind of man do you think Charles Goodrich is?

Describe the tone of voice the actor playing Harriet uses to say, "I haven't any feelings."

Define the word "artifice."

What kind of man might John Caldwell be?

Where do you think Harriet might have met John and his wife?

How did John's wife get invited to come to Harriet's house?

What is John's occupation?

What do you imagine Charles's job is?

What does Hetty's line, "Freckled, gawky-looking thing she was, too", tell the director about the casting of the role of Hetty?

What do you think the line "I couldn't get away from you if I tried," means?

How does Harriet feel about not getting away from Hetty?

Does Hetty mean that she really could choke Harriet? What would happen to the plot if she did choke her?

If you were playing the role of Harriet, how would you say the line, "It is not my business to have heartaches," and show the feelings describe in the parenthesis?

Do you think that Harriet will be "killed" by Hetty before the play is completed? Why or why not? What would happen to the rest of the play if Hetty killed Harriet?

The moment when Hetty overpowers Harriet and Harriet is forced to sink into the chair is an exciting high point of this scene. What kind of voice would you use if you were portraying Hetty? And what kind of voice would you use if you were portraying Harriet?

What does Harriet mean when she says, "I can't let the telephone girl down there hear my real self"?

The scarf of chiffon is a prop that must match the costume. How must it be constructed and worn, so that the actor can see and move?

Why do you think it is so important for Margaret to hear how rich and fascinating Charles is?

Is Harriet's objective to make John fall in love with her again?

Where do you see Hetty and Maggie standing on stage in relationship to Harriet and Margaret?

In the scene between Hetty, Maggie, Harriet and Margaret, Hetty and Maggie are speaking the subtext out loud. What vocal qualities would you have them use so that the audience can hear them, while appearing not to be as powerful as Harriet and Margaret?

Why does Harriet ignore Hetty when she asks Margaret to sit down?

Margaret's line about the beautiful lamp indicates a prop for the set decoration. What kind of lamp is needed?

Why does Harriet change topics by telling Margaret how well she looks when Margaret had been commenting on the price of the lamp? This is a beat.

In this scene Hetty and Maggie hear and react to each other. Harriet and Margaret hear and react to each other. Harriet hears Hetty. Margaret hears Maggie. Does Harriet hear Maggie? Does Margaret hear Hetty?

Why is having an automobile so important in 1916?

Why does Harriet ignore Hetty when she says, "Tell her we have an automobile"?

Why does Margaret ignore Maggie's suggestion to "Take more cream"?

How is Maggie feeling when she says, "Isn't she going to pass the cake?" How is Margaret feeling when Maggie says this.

Based on Maggie's line "It isn't too early to begin getting what you came for," what is Margaret's objective in coming to the gathering?

Who or what do you think Harper's is?

Notice how Maggie's and Hetty's lines are coaching Margaret and Harriet on how to say their lines when they say,' Don't let her see you're anxious to be painted' and "Don't seem anxious to get the order". If you were portraying Margaret, how would you say the lines to indicate that you heard Maggie's direction?

Look at the section beginning "You flatter me, my dear." At this point which characters are really telling the truth?

Does Harriet ever look at Hetty?

What does Margaret mean about "being impervious to hardship or unhappiness?" Is that a true statement?

When Margaret talks about Prince Rier is she telling the truth, or lying?

The name Miss Dorothy Ainsworth gives a feeling that she is rich. Who from famous people nowadays would you think might be equal to Miss Dorothy Ainsworth?

Did Margaret and Harriet know each other as children? And if so, were they friends?

Is Margaret lying when she says "Someone said you were very clever?"

Is Harriet telling the truth when she says, "Charles and I are inseparable"? If not, how does the actor indicate that she is lying using her voice and body?

How does Harriet react with her face when she hears, "how happy you must be?"

What do you think the phrase "treble in value," means?

Should the actor playing Harriet be a pretty lady? Explain why or why not.

Notice that Maggie and Hetty are silent during Margaret and Harriet's exchange about Louis de Grange. Why do you think Hetty and Maggie do not comment on Louis Le Grange?

Why does Maggie plead directly to Hetty saying, "Help us! Help me! Save us!"?

Why does Margaret say, "Of course, I don't know whether John would" and express doubt that John would paint Harriet's portrait after pushing so hard for Harriet to agree to this.

As the actor playing Margaret, you need to know what the word "propitious" means. What is the definition of "propitious?"

What social game are Harriet and Margaret playing with each other when they discuss the portrait in more detail?

Why is Maggie so anxious to leave following the discussion of the portrait?

When Maggie tells Hetty that she hates her for the first time we begin to move towards the climax of the play. The pace will build. How will you use your voice to show that the play is moving to the climax?

What do Margaret and Harriet do while Hetty and Maggie throw back their veils and begin to fight?

Where do Maggie and Hetty go after the lights come up?

Why do you think the playwright has Maggie and Hetty disappear?

Do you think Margaret and Harriet are being honest with their statements about "a delightful afternoon" and "joy to see you?" Why or why not?

Was the ending a surprise to you?

How else might this play have ended?

Reading a Script: Backwards and Forwards

To understand the dramatic relationships, you can gain new insights by reading the play not only forward, but also backward, from the last line to the first line. You know how it ends, so reading it from the last line to the first allows you to see how the playwright unfolds the story and develops relationships. Pay attention to any new discoveries that you did not realize during the initial reading.

REFLECTIVE INQUIRY   DATE:

Revisit the play again. Make any notes about the play that seem to stand out from the last line to the first line.

CREATIVE INQUIRY Analyzing Overtones   DATE:

Think about your experience of reading *Overtones*, and answer the following questions based on that experience.

Who do you think is the main character? Which character in "Overtones" has to appear in the play in order for the play to happen? Is there more than one main character in this play?

How does/do the main character/s change during the act? How does/do the main character/s change by the last line?

What is the theme of the play? What did the main character/s learn? What lesson does the playwright want the audience to take from the play?

Read the playwright's stage directions, which are enclosed in parentheses. List any that are important for an actor to note if she were studying a role in the play.

What is the climax of the play? Remember that the story's climax is defined as the most intense part of the play and the turning point in the conflict. It appears near the end of the play.

With which character or characters do you identify? Why did you choose that character?

What is your feeling after the final line of the play?

Later in this chapter, if you are a female, you will continue to work with *Overtones* to create a monologue for Harriet. So it is important that you continue to think about the role of Margaret. I have also included the script *The Genius*, which has an all-male cast, so that guys can do script analysis for a play with two males.

Reading and Analyzing a Script: *The Genius*
Before you read the following play, *The Genius,* turn forward to past the end of the play to look at the Script Analysis questions. Read the play, *The Genius*, implementing what you learned by analyzing *Overtones*. Make any notes on the script as you read, and mark any line which provides insight to the two characters.

The Genius

A play in one act by Horace Holley

It is reprinted from *Read-aloud Plays*. Horace Holley. New York: Mitchell Kennerley, 1916. It is now in the public domain and may therefore be performed without royalties.

CHARACTERS

THE BOY

THE MAN

[The front porch of a small farmhouse in New England. Stone flags lead to the road; the yard is a careless, comfortable lawn with two or three old maples. It is autumn.]

[A BOY of sixteen or so, carrying a paper parcel, stops hesitatingly, looks in a moment and then walks to the porch. As he stands there a MAN comes out of the house. The man is in his early forties, he stoops a little, but not from weakness; his expression is one of deep calm.]

THE MAN:	I wonder if you have seen my dog? I was going for a walk, but Rex seems to have grown tired of waiting.
THE BOY:	Your dog? No, sir, I haven't seen him. Shall I go look?
THE MAN:	No, never mind. He'll come back. Rex and I understand each other. He has his little moods, like me.
THE BOY:	If you were going for a walk—?
THE MAN:	It doesn't matter at all. I can go any time. You don't live in this country?
THE BOY:	No, sir. I live in New York. I wish I did. It's beautiful here, isn't it?

THE MAN: It's very beautiful to me. I love it. You may have come a long road this morning, let's sit down.

THE BOY: Thank you. I'm not interfering with anything?

THE MAN: Bless your heart! No indeed. What is there to interfere with? All we have is life, and this is part of it.

THE BOY: I like to sit under these trees. It makes me think of the Old Testament.

THE MAN: That's interesting. How?

THE BOY: Well, maybe I'm wrong, but whenever I think of the Old Testament I see an old man under a tree—

THE MAN: Yes?

THE BOY: A man who has lived it all through, you know, and found out something real about it; and he sits there calm and strong, something like a tree himself; and every once in a while somebody comes along—a boy, you know,—and the boy talks to him all about himself, just as we imagine we'd like to with our fathers, if they weren't so busy, or our teachers, if they didn't depend so much upon books, or our ministers, if we thought they would really understand,—and the old man doesn't say much maybe, but the boy goes away much stronger and happier....

THE MAN: Yes, yes, I understand. The Old Testament.... They did get hold of things, didn't they?

THE BOY: What I can't understand is how nowadays people seem more grown up and competent than those men were, in a way, and we do such wonderful things—skyscrapers and aeroplanes—and yet we aren't half so wonderful as they were in the Old Testament with their jugs and their wooden plows. I mean, we aren't near so big as the things we do, while those old fellows were so much bigger. We smile at them, but if some day one of our machines fell over on us what would we do about it?

THE MAN: I wonder.

THE BOY: I went through a big factory just last week. One of my friends' father is the manager, and all I could think of was what could a fellow do who didn't like it, who didn't fit in. . . Nowadays most everybody seems competent about factories or business or something like that—you know—and they've got hold of everything, so a fellow's got to do the same thing or where is he?

THE MAN: That's the first question, certainly: where is he? But where is he if he does do the same thing?

THE BOY: Why, he's with the rest. And they don't ask that question...

THE MAN: I'm afraid they don't. It would be interesting to be there if they should begin to ask it, wouldn't it?

THE BOY: Yes. . . I'd like to be there when some I know ask themselves! But they never will. Why should they?

THE MAN: Don't you mean how can they?

THE BOY: Yes, of course. They don't ask the question because the big thing they are doing seems to be the answer beforehand. But it isn't! Not compared with the Old Testament. So we have to ask it for ourselves. And that's why I came here...

THE MAN: Oh. You want to know where they are, with their power, or where you will be without it?

THE BOY: Where I'll be. I hate it! But what else is there today?

THE MAN: Why, there's you.

THE BOY: But that's just it! What am I for if I can't join in? I came to you. . .You don't mind my talking, do you?

THE MAN: On the contrary.

THE BOY: Well, everybody I know is a part of it, so how could they tell me what to do outside of it? I've been wondering about that for a year. Before then, when I was just a boy, the world seemed full of everything, but now it seems to have only one thing. That or nothing. Then one day I saw a photograph somebody had cut out of a Sunday paper, and I thought to myself there's a man who seems outside, entirely outside, and yet he has something. It wasn't all or nothing for him . . . and I wondered who it was. Then I found your book, with the same picture in it. You bet I read it right off! It was the first time in my life I had ever felt power as great as skyscrapers and railroads and yet apart from them. Outside of all they mean. Like the Old Testament. Those poems!

THE MAN: You liked them?

THE BOY: It was more than that. How can a fellow like the ocean, or a snow storm?

THE MAN: Is that what you thought they were like?

THE BOY: Why, they went off like a fourteen inch gun! Not a whine about life in them—not a single regret for anything. They were wonderful! They seemed to pick up mountains and cities and toss them all about like toys. They made me feel that what I was looking for was able to conquer what I didn't like.... I said to myself I don't care if he does laugh at me, I'll go and ask him where all that power is! And so I came....

THE MAN: There's Rex now—over across the road. He's wondering who you are. He sees we are friends, and he's pretending to be jealous. Dogs are funny, aren't they? But you were speaking about my poems. It's odd that their first criticism should come from you like this. You must be about the same age I was when I began writing—when I wanted above anything to write a book like that, and when such a book seemed the most impossible thing I could do. Like trying to swim the Atlantic, or live forever.

THE BOY: It seemed impossible? I should think it would be the most natural thing in the world, for you—like eating dinner.

THE MAN: That's the wonderful thing—not the book, but that I should have come to write it!

THE BOY: But who else could write it?

THE MAN: At your age I thought anybody could—anybody and everybody except myself.

THE BOY: Really?

THE MAN: Really and truly. You've no idea what a useless misfit I was.

THE BOY: But I read somewhere you had always been brilliant, even as a boy.

THE MAN: Unfortunately . . . yes. That was what made it so hard for me. Shall I tell you about it?

THE BOY: I wish you would!

THE MAN: Brilliance—I'll tell you what that was, at least for me. I wrote several things that people called "brilliant." One in particular, a little play of decadent epigram. It was acted by amateurs before an admiring "select" audience. That was when I was twenty-one. From about sixteen on I had been acutely miserable—physically miserable. I never knew when I wouldn't actually cave in. I felt like a bankrupt living on borrowed money. Of course, it's plain enough now—the revolt of starved nerves. I cared only for my mind, grew only in that, and the rest of me withered up like a stalk in dry soil. So the flower drooped too—in decadent epigram. But nobody pointed out the truth of it all to me, and I scorned to give my body a thought. People predicted a brilliant future—for me, crying inside! Then I married. I married the girl who had taken the star part in the play. According to the logic of the situation, it was inevitable. Everybody remarked how inevitable it was. A decorative girl, you know. She wanted to be the wife of a great man. . . Well, we didn't get along. There was an honest streak in me somewhere which hated deception. I couldn't play the part of "brilliant" young poet with any success. She was at me all the while to write more of the same thing. And I didn't want to. The difference between the "great" man I was supposed to be and the sick child I really was, began to torture. I knew I oughtn't to go on any further if I wanted to do anything real. Then one night we had an "artistic" dinner. My wife had gotten hold of a famous English poet, and through him a publisher. The publisher was her real game. I drank champagne before dinner so as to be "brilliant." I was. And before I realized it, Norah had secured a promise from the publisher to bring out a book of plays. I remember she said it was practically finished. But it wasn't, only the one, and I hated that. But I sat down conscientiously to write the book that she, and apparently all the world that counted, expected me to write. Well, I couldn't write it. Not a blessed word! Something inside me refused to work. And there I was. In a month or so she began to ask about it. Norah thought I ought to turn them out while she waited. I walked up and down the park one afternoon wondering what to tell her. . . And when I realized that either she would never understand or would despise me, I grew desperate. I wrote her a note, full of fine phrases about "incompatibility," her "unapproachable ideals," the "soul's need of freedom"— things she would understand and wear a heroic attitude about—and fled. I came here....

THE BOY: Of course. But didn't she follow you? Didn't they bother you?

THE MAN: Not a bit. Norah preferred her lonely heroism. In a few months I was quite forgotten. That was one of the healthful things I learned. Well, I was a wreck when I came here, I wanted only to lie down under a tree. . . And there it was, under that tree yonder, my salvation came.

THE BOY: Your salvation?

THE MAN: Hunger. That was my salvation. Simple, elemental, inescapable appetite. You see I had no servant, no one at all. So I had to get up and work to prepare my food. . . It was very strange. Compared with this life, my life before had been like living in a locked box. Someone to do everything for me except think, and consequently I thought too much. But here the very fact of life was brought home to me. I spent weeks working about the house and grounds on the common necessities. By the time winter came on the place was fit to live in—and I was enjoying life. All the "brilliance" had faded away; I was as simple as a blade of grass. For a year I didn't write a word. I had the courage to wait for the real thing, nobody pestering me to be a "genius"! Some day you may read that first book. People said I had re-discovered the virtue of humility. I had.

THE BOY: I will read it! And how much more it will mean to me now!

THE MAN: I suppose you know the theory about vibrations—how if a little push is given a bridge, and repeated often enough at the right intervals, the bridge will fall?

THE BOY: Yes.

THE MAN: Well, that's the whole secret of what you have been looking for—what you found in my poems.

THE BOY: I don't understand.

THE MAN: A man's life is a rhythm. Eating, sleeping, working, playing, loving, thinking—everything. And when we live so that each activity comes at the right interval, we gain power. When one interrupts another, we lose. Weakness is merely the thrust of one impulse against another, instead of their combined thrust against the world. When I came here, feeling like a criminal, I was obeying the one right instinct in a welter of emotions. It was like the faintest of heart beats in a sick body. I listened to that. Then I learned physical hunger, then sleep, and so on. It's incredible how stupid I was about the elemental art of living! I had to begin all over from the beginning, as if no one had ever lived before.

THE BOY: That's what you meant in your poems about religion.

THE MAN: Exactly! I learned that "good" is the rhythm of the man's personal nature, and that "evil" is merely the confusion of the same impulses. As time went on it became instinctive to live for and by the rhythm. Everything about my life here was caught up and used in the vision of power—drawing water, cutting wood, digging in the garden, dawn. It was all marvelous—I couldn't help writing those poems. They are the natural joys and sorrows of ten years. As a matter of fact, though, I grew to care less and less about writing, as living became fuller and richer. People write too much. They would write less if they had to make the fire in the morning.

THE BOY: The first impulse . . . I see. Oh, life might be so simple!

THE MAN: Why not? The animals have it. Men have it at times, but we make each other forget. If we could only be each other's reminders instead of forgetters!

THE BOY: Yes! But I see the only thing to do is to go away, like you.

THE MAN: Not necessarily, I was merely a bad case, and required a desperate remedy, earth and air and freedom from others' will. I need the country, but the next man might require the city as passionately. Don't imagine that only the hermits, like me, live instinctively. It can be done in New York, too, only one mustn't be so sensitive to others. . . After all, friend, we were wrong in saying that this power lies outside the world of skyscrapers and business. It doesn't lie outside nor inside. It cuts across everything. Do you see? For it's all a matter of the man's own soul.

THE BOY: Then?

THE MAN: We can't live in a vacuum. The more you feel the force, the more you must act. The more you can act. And in the long run it doesn't matter what you do, if you do what your own instinct bids.

THE BOY: Then I could stay right in the midst of it?

THE MAN: Yes. And if you were thinking of writing poetry, it might even be better to stay in the midst of it. Drama, you know ... and it's time for a new drama.

THE BOY: It isn't that, with me. I can't write. . . I had one splendid teacher. He used to talk about things right in class. He said that most educated people think that intellect is a matter of making fine distinctions—of seeing as two separate points what the unintelligent would believe was one point; but that this idea was finicky. He wanted us to see that intelligence might also be a matter of seeing the connection between two things so far apart that most people would think they were always separate. I like that. It made education mean something, because it made it depend on imagination instead of grubbing. And then he told us about the history of our subject— grammar. How it began as poetry, when every word was an original creation; and then became philosophy, as people had to arrange speech with thought; and then science, with more or less exact, laws. I could see it—the thing became alive. And he said all knowledge passed through the same stages, and there isn't anything that can't eventually be made scientific. That made me think a good deal. I wondered if somebody couldn't work out a way of preventing anybody from being poor. It seems so unnecessary, with so much work being done. That's what I want to do. Thanks to you, I—

THE MAN: Here's Rex! Rex, know my good friend. I know you will like him. Rex always cares for the people I do, don't you, Rex?

THE BOY: Of course, I see one thing: it's the people nearest one that make the most difference. Mother, now, she will understand.... You don't believe in marrying, though, do you?

THE MAN: I certainly do!

THE BOY: But I thought—

THE MAN: You thought because I left one woman and hadn't found another that I didn't care for women? Others believe that, too, but it isn't so. On the contrary. You see, I didn't so much leave her as get away from my own failure. Of course, there is such a thing as the wrong woman. She makes a man a fraction. The better she is in herself, the less she leaves him to live by. One twentieth is less than one half. But the right woman! She multiplies a man. . .

THE BOY: Oh!

THE MAN: Why, you might have told from my poems how I believe in love.

THE BOY: I don't remember any love poems.

THE MAN: Bless your heart! Every one of them was a love poem. Not the old-fashioned kind, about fading roses and tender hearts.... I sent that book out as a cry for the mate. It is charged with the fullness of love. That's why I could write about trees and storms.

THE BOY: I suppose if I had been older....

THE MAN: It isn't one's age but one's need. She will understand. Look, the sun has gone round the corner of the house. Is that lunch you have in the parcel?

THE BOY: Yes.

THE MAN: Would you like to make it a picnic? I'll get something from the house, and then we can walk to the woods.

THE BOY: I'd love to!

THE MAN: All right, I'll be ready in no time. Come, Rex!

END OF PLAY

ASSIGNMENT *The Genius*   DATE:

Make notes of any three directions, settings, notes that the playwright gives at the beginning of the play.

Make a note of the time period for which the play was written.

Read the Character list. Write a feeling about each character based on your reading of the Character list. Why do you think the playwright used those particular names?

Who is the protagonist? Who is the antagonist?

What is the boy's objective?

What is the man's objective?

Was each character successful in achieving his objective?

What is the climax of the story? Write two lines that you designate as part of the climax.

Finish the sentence, "This play is about people who...."

How does the play end?

Tell the story in three sentences.

Cast famous people in the two roles.

The Boy will be played by

The Man will be played by

List any important props and stage business that the playwright indicates.

Visualize the colors each character is wearing. The colors should be contrasting to indicate the personality types. What is a shirt color for The Boy?

What is a shirt color for The Man?

What do you see as a set design?

What do you think the theme of the play is?

What lesson about life does The Man learn?

What lesson about life does The Boy learn?

Finish the sentence, "This play is about. . . " (try to phrase it without using any people's names)

This play is about

Character Biography for a Monologue from a Play

Constructing a monologue for a fully developed character requires that you have a thorough knowledge of the play's text and specifically the character's life in the script. One way to accomplish the latter is to create a biography for your chosen character. First, list all of the things you know about the character from your reading of the text. Be sure to look closely at what the character does, what the character says, what other characters say about the character, and stage directions. If no data is indicated in the script, you can create facts based on what you imagine. This will help you to "flesh out" the character more fully, to give the character depth and texture.

You may make changes as you continue to develop the character's monologue. You can use the character bio form to record any discoveries as you work on your monologue.

~~~~~~

ASSIGNMENT Character Bio for Harriet from *Overtones*
or The Boy from *The Genius*   DATE:
~~~~~~

Full Character Name:

Named After:

Age:

Place of Birth:

Residence:

Height:

Weight:

Hair Color:

Hair Length:

General Appearance:

Family / Relatives:

Friends:

Enemies:

Educational History:

Work History:

Skills:

Fears:

Good Habits:

Bad Habits:

Best Qualities:

Worst Qualities:

Childhood Memories:

Teenage Memories:

Adult Memories:

Favorites (food, clothing, art, music, TV show, movie, book, etc.)

Hobbies:

Personal Goals:

Professional Goals:

Ethics:

Values:

Style of Speech:

Commonly Used Words:

Lies He or She Tells:

Five Other Important Details:

A well-edited monologue communicates the character's story. The monologue does not give away the entire plot, but it does show the particular point of view of the character. The monologue tells the character's objective, thoughts, and feelings. It has a beginning, middle, a climax, an emotional arc, and a resolution.

ASSIGNMENT Telling the Character Story for Harriet from
          Overtones or for The Boy from *The Genius*   DATE:

Look over the lines of Harriet in *Overtone*s or The Boy in *The Genius* and tell the character's story in paragraph form. Choose either Harriet or The Boy. First summarize Harriet's or The Boy's story line. Now write the character's story that is shown in the play, here. Put in your own words.

ASSIGNMENT Creating a Monologue for Harriet from
          Overtones or for The Boy from *The Genius*   DATE:

Look through the script *Overtones* for Harriet or *The Genius* for The Boy and select a total of ten lines from the beginning, the middle, and the end of the script that are the keys to telling the character's story. Be sure to include the character's objective. A line can be considered more than one sentence. Copy the ten lines in the spaces below.

Character Name

Character's Objective

Line 1

Line 2

Line 3

Line 4

Line 5

Line 6

Line 7

Line 8

Line 9

End line

Scoring the Monologue with Intentions

In a monologue, the character has intentions and objectives that guide what he/she says. When you name your character's objective, you use active verbs. These verbs indicate what your character wants to accomplish. To form an objective, the word "to" can be inserted in front of an action verb. The verb is followed by a direct object. Example, "Judy wants Jim to give her a hug."

Below are some common active verbs to express the character's objective:

~ Achieve, acquire, activate, advise, analyze, apply, assess, avert, collaborate, communicate, compete, conclude, confirm, connect, convince, deal with, deduce, defer, demonstrate, describe, diagnose, discuss, earn, educate, elicit, emphasize, encourage, establish, evaluate, examine, explain, explore, foster, gather, identify, improve, increase, inform, inspire, instruct, involve, join, judge, justify, locate, manage, mediate, motivate, observe, organize, persuade, predict, prepare, prevent, promote, qualify, reinforce, relate, renew, reorganize, restore, restrict, reveal, scrutinize, solve, solicit, suggest, sustain, teach, terminate, unify, validate, visualize, want, widen, withdraw.

ASSIGNMENT Scoring the Monologue with Intentions and Harriet's or The Boy's Objective   DATE:

Look at the ten lines you have selected for your monologue. Assign a minimum of ten different active verbs to your monologue lines. Read each line and ask yourself what are you trying to do? What are you trying to accomplish? Next to each line, write your chosen active verbs.

Scoring the Emotional Beats

Scoring a role for a character's emotions means that you trace how the character feels throughout the play. It is the character's emotional arc and journey that makes for a strong monologue performance. The monologue lines you select also show the character's emotional changes or beats.

To score Harriet's or The Boy's monologue, choose from the emotions listed below. Happy or sad are the two basic emotions. You may also use any of the emotions listed below, if appropriate.

~ Angry, anxious, comfortable, confused, defensive, desiring, excited, fearful, happy, hopeless, indifferent, insecure, insulted, irritated, jealous, loved, mad, relieved, rejected, ridiculed, surprised.

ASSIGNMENT Scoring the Emotional Beats for Harriet from *Overtones* or The Boy from *The Genius*   DATE:

Reading the lines that you wrote above, decide the emotion the character is expressing in each line. Now chart the character's emotional arc and journey by writing down below each emotion that you identified.

Line   Emotion

Telegraming a Monologue

A telegram was a way of communicating beginning in the 1850s, and this was a method of communication until 2006 when Western Union discontinued this service. People sent telegrams when they wanted to communicate a brief message. The telegram contained a few words and short phrases with the word "stop" to indicate periods.

A sample telegram for Harriet might read:

To: Hetty

From: Harriet:

Am frustrated STOP Cannot marry who I want STOP Want riches STOP

Help me STOP Tell my true feelings

CREATIVE INQUIRY *CI*   DATE:

Think about the ten lines you chose for your monologue. Pick twenty-five words that express the thoughts and varied emotions of the character. The words should communicate the essence of the monologue. The word (stop) does not count as part of the twenty-five words. Write your twenty-five word telegram below.

Writing Your Edited Monologue
You know the complete story of your character as expressed in the script. You know the plot. You know the through line. You have determined your character's objective. You have located the emotional beats and changes.

You can now shape your monologue to ensure that there is a beginning, middle, a climatic build, and an end. The monologue cutting should tell a complete emotional story and convey the character's objective. It should be the appropriate length for a monologue, two minutes or shorter.

A tip to remember is that a double-spaced computer page with average sized font will run two minutes of oral presentation.

ASSIGNMENT Writing Your Edited Monologue for Harriet from *Overtones* or The Boy from *The Genius* DATE:

Looking at your selected lines for either Harriet or The Boy, decide on the opening lines and write them down below. The first lines need to express strong emotions and make a statement rather than ask a question.

Using Lines from Other Characters for Monologue for Harriet from *Overtones* or The Boy from *The Genius*
For Harriet or The Boy's monologues, you can use some of the other one or three characters' lines and turn them into your character's lines. In one script, the following exchange happens:

HARRIET: I am your subtle overtones.

HETTY: But together we are one woman, the wife of Charles Goodrich.

HARRIET: There I disagree with you, Hetty, I alone am his wife.

HETTY: *[indignantly]* Harriet, how can you say such a thing!

HARRIET: Certainly. I am the one who flatters him. I have to be the one who talks to him. If I gave you a chance you would tell him at once that you dislike him.

HETTY: *[moving away]* I don't love him, that's certain.

To construct a portion of a monologue for Harriet, using some of Hetty's lines, you might use the following idea:

HARRIET: I am your subtle overtones. But together we are one woman, the wife of Charles Goodrich. Hetty, there I disagree with you. I alone am his wife. You ask how I can say such a thing. I am the one who flatters him. I have to be the one who talks to him. If I gave you a chance you would tell him at once that you dislike him. I know you don't love him, that's certain.

ASSIGNMENT Editing Lines for Harriet from *Overtones* or The Boy from *The Genius* to Show the Climax   DATE:

Locate three lines for your character that are part of the climax of the conflict and story. The climax should be near the end of the script.

Write five lines that show the resolution of the character's story.

What is the tag or final line that your character will say?

ASSIGNMENT Writing Your Edited Script Monologue
for Harriet or The Boy   DATE:

Use your Harriet or The Boy's lines to write your monologue in paragraph form in the blank space below. Writing the monologue in your own handwriting or printing allows you to "own" the words as if you are creating the lines yourself, thinking about what to say.

ASSIGNMENT Record your Monologue for Harriet or The Boy DATE:

Record your monologue, letting your voice show the emotions that you identified in the previous experience. Use beats to indicate your transitions. Take a brief pause for each beat to show a shift in thought, emotion, or topic. Use your voice to build the climax of the monologue.

REFLECTIVE INQUIRY   DATE:

Revisit your monologue. See if you can hear the character's emotional beats and arc. Does your voice convey the character's essence and emotions?

Now make notes listing three vocal adjustments you want to make for future rehearsals with your constructed monologue.

Make sure you continue to work with your edited monologue from *Overtones* or *The Genius*. As you develop your character, you will gain new perspectives of the character. Feel free to examine your insights and make changes to the creative and reflective inquiries. This process of working a monologue is one that will be developed in the next section of this chapter.

Closure for Chapter Six: Acting and Script Analysis

ASSIGNMENT Closure   DATE:

It is important to review what you have studied by reflection on the topics presented in this chapter. Look back over your notes which you made as you studied the information in this chapter. The topics mentioned in Chapter Six are listed below. For each question, there are two spaces for answers. For answer number one, respond with something you remember about the topic. For answer number two, mention any idea in the topic that you found interesting and you would share with another emerging actor.

Introduction to Acting

1.

2.

History of Acting: Mechanical to Method

1.

2.

Master Acting Teachers

1.

2.

Acting Vocabulary

List five words and their definitions expressed in your own words.

1.

2.

3.

4.

5.

Reading and Analyzing a Script from an Actor's Point of View

1.

2.

Script Analysis of *Overtones*

1.

2.

Script Analysis of *The Genius*

1.

2.

Character Biography for a Monologue from a Play

1.

2.

Telling the Character Story for Harriet from *Overtones* or for The Boy from *The Genius*

~~~~~~

1.

2.

Creating a Monologue for Harriet from *Overtones* or for The Boy from *The Genius*

1.

2.

Scoring the Monologue with Intentions for Harriet's or The Boy's Objective

1.

2.

Scoring the Emotional Beats for Harriet from Overtones or The Boy from *The Genius*

1.

2.

Telegraming the Monologue for Harriet from *Overtones* or The Boy from *The Genius*

1.

2.

Writing your Edited Monologue for Harriet from *Overtones* or The Boy from *The Genius*

1.

2.

Using Lines from Other Characters for Monologue for Harriet from *Overtones* or The Boy from *The Genius*

1.

~~~~~~

2.

Editing Lines for Harriet from *Overtones* or The Boy from *The Genius* to Show the Climax and Resolution

1.

2.

Record your Monologue for Harriet or The Boy

1.

2.

In the next chapter you will learn the acting and staging of a monologue; you will experience various types of monologues and write original monologues. You are continuing your journey and nearing the final steps of your actor's basic study.

CHAPTER SEVEN: MONOLOGUES

Introduction to Monologues

Continuing your preparation to becoming an emerging actor, you have experienced: working with Theatre and acting vocabulary, reading scripts, forming positive attitudes, thinking creatively, relaxing your body, experimenting with movement and mime, practicing vocal exercises, rehearsing for improvisations, and learning script analysis. Now is the time to experience acting, staging, and writing various types of monologues for rehearsal.

Definition of a Monologue

In the Prologue of this book, you learned that a monologue is the lines for one character. The character can speak to him/herself, the audience, or to other characters without any other character interrupting his/her speech.

History of the Monologue

In ancient Greek Theatre, a single actor Thespis stepped out on stage; he was accompanied by the chorus, who spoke lines together. In Roman Theatre monologues were featured as a device to tell the passage of time, so that the scenes did not have to be acted on stage. From the Renaissance Theatre on, monologues focused on characters doing long speeches to think out loud about their objectives. Shakespeare's plays contained monologues called soliloquies, in which the character communicated thoughts directly to the audience. The character may have other characters on stage, but these other characters pretended not to hear. In modern acting, the monologue conveys thoughts and feelings; it can also be an actor's tool with which he/she auditions.

Monologue Vocabulary

In the Prologue and Chapter Seven of this book, you have read several terms that are used in monologue work. You might want to review the

following terms: genre, here and now, implied other, in the moment, indicating, moment before, and slate.

Types of Monologues

- ~ **Autobiographical Character Monologue**—A story based on a person's life.
- ~ **Reality-Based Monologue**—The real-life, exact words of people, based on real events.
- ~ **Contemporary Monologue**—The real-life day's events, which are part autobiographical and part opinion.
- ~ **Narrative Monologue**—A fictional story told in narrative form with the actor as storyteller.
- ~ **Dramatic Monologue**—A serious speech that involves one character speaking to another character without interruption.
- ~ **Soliloquy**—Thoughts and feelings expressed directly to the audience. The other characters on stage pretend not to hear what the character is saying to the audience.

In this chapter you will create an autobiographical character monologue. It can also have elements of the other types of monologues.

Why an Actor Studies Monologues

Like a musician who practices scales, a dancer who practices steps, an instrumentalist who masters his/her instrument, you are working on your actor's tool of monologue. Monologues are an ideal way to work out, explore and expand your character repertory. Monologues are short in length, and you can rehearse alone. Monologues are a valuable way for you to become proficient with different genres. You can experiment with different types of characters; some of whom you might not ever be cast to play. You can do monologues to challenge yourself by creating characters who are not like you in real life.

This chapter presents experiences in working with various types of monologues for rehearsals and creating original monologues. The monologue experiences in this chapter are for rehearsal only. The methods presented in this book can be used to work on future monologues.

The First Day: Monologue for Analysis and Staging

With your acquired skill of script analysis, you are ready to explore a short monologue and add staging. You will use the original monologue below. *The First Day* was written by playwright Mary Krell-Oishi. I have permission to incorporate this monologue for your work with analysis and staging.

Read the monologue silently.

The First Day
By Mary Krell-Oishi

Just breathe. Really, it isn't that hard. I do it every day. Just in and out. (breathing deeply, realizing it is loud, looks quickly around) Oh, good grief! Is everyone listening to me breathe? (scanning the room) Settle yourself. It's only school. I've been going to school since I was kid. I was a big deal in elementary school. Popular! Everybody loved me. (smiling at someone across the room, who has clearly looked away) What's his problem? (glancing at reflection in the window) A zit! He saw that zit on my nose! I've never had a zit before in my life. It was only a small bump last night. Now look at it. The first day of school, and my nose precedes me into the building by a foot because of this zit. Everyone is looking at me. I'll be known as the Human Zit for the rest of my school career. I should just go find my first class and hide out with the teacher. Those will probably be my new best friends. Teachers. Where's my schedule? I put it somewhere. (panic setting in) What if I can't find it? What do I do? Ask someone? Who? I don't see anyone I know. This school is big. I hate this school. I want to go back to sixth grade. I knew who I was there. Here I'll be the big loser who can't find my class and hangs out with the teachers. The Human Zit Loser who eats lunch in the library. Alone. There's got to be somebody here I know . . . (recognizing a friendly face, calling out) Chris? Hey! Over here. Chris! Yeah, Middle School! Totally ready. Hey, meet me for lunch? Yeah? Cool. (waving goodbye) Cool. (Confidence beginning to build) Now, where's my first period class? (heading off to find the new world)

ASSIGNMENT *The First Day:* Monologue Character Analysis   DATE:

The questions presented below can be used to analyze any monologue. After you read the monologue, you are ready to make artistic interpretations that prepare you to perform the character's story in a truthful, effective manner. Staging the character's thoughts and feelings is based on your monologue analysis.

Answer the questions in character, thinking like the character. Use "I am..." to answer the questions. Some answers may have to be created. To give inventive answers, you must find clues in the text. You can refer back to the text for ideas at any time.

What is your character's first, middle and last name?

How old are you?

What is your occupation?

To whom are you (the character) speaking?

Make a list all of the people including yourself to whom you speak.

What is your objective as indicated by the thoughts and feelings in this monologue?

What do you want? (Take your clues from the opening words.)

What action are you doing before the first line?

What is your exact location?

What are some things that you see in your location?

What is the time of day? Be specific.

 What is the story of your monologue in three sentences?

How does the title of your monologue relate to you as the character?

At the beginning of the monologue, how do you feel about the first day?

What and who do you see before you say the first line? Placing yourself in the situation "as if" you were experiencing the events allows you to imagine what you might see.

What do you hear?

What do you smell?

What do you taste?

Describe how you are dressed. Include colors, shoes, clothes, accessories.

What props are you carrying?

What is the moment before the first line? You will have to create the possible answers to this question.

What is your opening emotion? How do you as the character feel?

What is the last line, tag line of the monologue? Copy the tag line here.

What is your final emotion after the tag line?

What are the obstacles you face in the monologue? (Remember that obstacles are defined as the situations in a play that create conflict and delay or prevent the character's achieving an objective. Mention one internal obstacle, something inside yourself that holds you back, and one external obstacle, something outside of yourself which blocks you or causes you to hold back.)

Name four tactics that you use. Tactics are defined as part of your strategy used to achieve your objective.

What is your intention or objective? Use the word "to" plus an active verb . . . i.e. to obtain friends; to deny thoughts that hinder you; to talk yourself into being happy.

What good thing do you imagine will happen if you attain your objective? Use your imagination.

What bad thing do you imagine will happen if you fail to attain your objective?

What secret do you have? (This could be some feeling or fact that you know that you don't want known by others.)

At the beginning of the monologue what is your character's feeling?

In a well-written monologue, the main character changes emotionally. How do you change from the beginning to the end of the monologue?

What lesson does your character learn by experiencing the thoughts and emotions of this monologue?

What happens after the last line of the monologue? You can create what you think will happen.

ASSIGNMENT *The First Day*: Reading the Monologue backwards   DATE:

Read from the tag line to the first line. By knowing how the monologue ends, you can study the unveiling of the story from the end to the beginning. Add four new pieces of information that you discovered about your character by reading the monologue from the tag line to first line.

ASSIGNMENT *The First Day:* Scoring your Role—Marking
Your Emotional Beats for the Monologue   DATE:

Read the monologue a third time from the first line to the last line. Mark the beats, those moments at which a pause can be used to indicate the character's change of thought, change of mood, or change of emotion. A beat is over when the thought, mood, or emotion changes in some way. The end of the beat must have a transitional moment, in which you as the character show that you have a new thought, mood or emotion.

Use the beats as pauses in the monologue to show your character thinking. This technique makes your words sound more like real conversation with broken sentences, moments of reflection, or moments of embarrassment. Sometimes when you have a beat, you could end the monologue at that point. Something compels you to continue with a new thought, mood or emotion.

You can indicate the beats in your monologue by a slash. Marking your emotional beats might look like the example below.

Just breathe./ Really, it isn't that hard. I do it every day./ Just in and out. (breathing deeply, realizing it is loud, looks quickly around) / Oh, good grief! Is everyone listening to me breathe? (scanning the room)/ Settle yourself./ It's only school. I've been going to school since I was kid. / I was a big deal in elementary school. Popular! Everybody loved me.

Return to the monologue printed in this chapter and mark beats for the entire monologue. Mark the climax, the most intense part of the monologue.

ASSIGNMENT *The First Day:* Improvising your Monologue   DATE:

As an actor you create the soul and spirit of the character in *The First Day*. You live with the character's thoughts, his/her world point of view, and the feelings about being in this situation and life in general. You have read the monologue several times and have an understanding for the character. Now place the text aside and improvise the monologue out loud conveying in your own words as much of the content as you remember. Do not try to act the monologue. Just deliver the main message of the monologue. This exercise is not a memory test.

REFLECTIVE INQUIRY *RI*   DATE:

Revisit your monologue again. Make some notes on how you did. Did you remember the content? Did you leave out any sections?

ASSIGNMENT *The First Day*: Reading it again   DATE:

Now read the actual text again silently one more time. Put the text aside and improvise a second time. Pay attention to any sections that were not said in the first improvisation.

REFLECTIVE INQUIRY *RI*   DATE:

Revisit the text again. Make some notes on how it went this time. Did you convey any new parts that you did not portray in your previous improvisations of the monologue?

You are beginning to "own" the monologue's words, thoughts, and emotions. You are on your way to "becoming the character." You have read and worked on this monologue so much that you now are familiar with the words and do not have to read every word. You have memorized most of your monologue.

Warming Up

Warming up before acting is necessary, just like the required warm-up prior to any movement, mime, vocal rehearsal, and improvisational work. Engaging your five senses, your thinking process, and your emotional tools are essential for accessing the character's truth. In order to warm-up for rehearsing a monologue, get into the mood of the character, think about things from the character's perspective, feel like the character would if the character were to experience the thoughts and feelings expressed in the monologue.

ASSIGNMENT *The First Day*: Acting your Monologue Warm-Up   DATE:

Imagine yourself as the character in the situation. Using your answers from the above analysis, visualize what and whom you see. Look around as if you are the character. How do you feel about the people you see? What colors do you imagine? How do you feel about the colors? React to imagined sounds of the environment and the people. How do you feel about the sounds? Envision what smells are in the location. How do you feel about the smells? How does your mouth feel? Did you just have something to eat or drink? Imagine how your clothes feel on your skin. Do you have new clothes, shoes, and/or hair style? Take inventory of how you are feeling before the first line. Hear the imaginary prompt line or action that gives you a reason to speak.

In a quiet place, stand up. Think like the character and create a character stance and posture. Thinking as if you are the character helps you establish a physical attitude. Do you as the character have a straight or slumped posture; do you hold your head up straight or hold it down? As the character, establish the way you use your feet, hands, and face. How do you stand, use your hands, work your face?

ASSIGNMENT *The First Day*: Acting your Monologue Vocally   DATE:

Put into action all of the aspects of character development you have worked on. Create your character's vocal qualities using your voice to show emotions. Do you as the character use a loud or quiet voice, rapid or slow voice? Do you have a high or low pitch? Does your pitch vary? (You do not have to be concerned with staging at this time.)

Revisit your monologue. List three observations that you gained.

1.

2.

3.

Now note three vocal adjustments that you will implement in your future work on *The First Day*.

1.

2.

3.

 Periodically study *The First Day* monologue and add new insights for your analysis.

Keeping it Real and in the Moment—Not Indicating

You as an actor will devote part of your study to creating the deeper psychological workings of your character based on your script and your imagination. Your character's personality is a combination of physical, intellectual, psychological, and emotional qualities. You learn who the character is by what the playwright says about him/her, what the character says about him/herself, and what other characters say about him. In a play, you also can find out how other characters react to your character. To create depth and truth in acting, you turn the character into a living person, with unique individuality. You find as much in common with the character as possible. Finding shared qualities between you and your character adds complexity to your characterization. You can add depth to your character by tapping different parts of yourself that relate to the character and indulging your imagination on those aspects which differ. Investigating your character's personality allows you to shape the interpretation, which then affects your character's outward attributes. Making your character as complex as possible based on what the script says is one of your challenges to creating a multifaceted character.

"Indicating" is outwardly portraying to the audience what your character is thinking or feeling instead of the actor really thinking or feeling as if the thoughts and feelings were happening in the here and now of the character's life. Indicating is a traditional acting vocabulary word signifying "behaving or emoting without being connected to a truthful impulse" for doing the emoting or behavior. When you are indicating, you are pretending, rather than really feeling or thinking like the character would. Indicating is sometimes called fake acting. Using affected voices or behaving in an artificial way is indicating. When you push for a result, trying to cry, or trying to laugh, your acting becomes artificial. You are trying to "play" the emotion rather than thinking and feeling as the character. Acting that is indicating rather than real is sometimes the result of a lack of investigation or lack of attention to staying in the here and now for each rehearsal.

Working on any role over a period of time can lead to taking the words and emotions for granted. So keeping it truthful, new, and in the moment is the aim for each rehearsal and performance. You know how the piece ends; the character does not. So you must think like the character as he/she discovers, emotion to emotion, thought to thought, and moment to moment, until the surprise of the resolution takes place. So trusting yourself to find the objectives and strive for outcomes will help you develop an interesting character. To erase any tendency toward indicating, trust the moment instead of play-acting or playing the end of the monologue before the character arrives at the resolution.

The Theatre—acting, creating, interpreting—means total involvement, the totality of heart, mind, and spirit . . . the total development of a human being into the most he can be and in as many directions as he can possibly take.

Stella Adler, acting teacher

ASSIGNMENT Stella's quote   DATE:

Make some notes on why you think Stella Adler wanted her actors to be the most that they could be? What do you think the words "the total development of a human being into the most he can be and in as many directions as he can possibly take," mean?

ASSIGNMENT *The First Day*: Keeping It Real and In the Moment   DATE:

Read *The First Day* aloud, as if it is the first time you, as the character, have spoken the words. Also keep in mind what you as the actor know about the character and circumstances. It is the character who is experiencing the moment-to-moment beats. Read the monologue as if you are saying each word as you feel the emotion for the first time. You must convince yourself that you have never said the words before. You as the character are creating the words in the moment.

After you have read the monologue aloud, list one new insight about keeping it real and in the moment.

CREATIVE INQUIRY   DATE:

Think again about the monologue. List ten important words from the beginning, middle and end that can be considered as the text of your *The First Day* telegram from the character. This might help to circle the key words, and stage directions in the monologue.

1.

2.

3.

4.

5.

6.

7.

8.

9.

10.

Staging

You have analyzed, imagined, and experimented with the monologue *The First Day.* Now is the time to add action and staging to add some movement stimulated by the text and character's emotion. When staging your monologue, choose a performance space that is approximately six feet by six feet. This space is about the size of the typical audition space and works for the camera range for video work. You can adjust the size to smaller if your audition room is smaller. The square should be away from the walls of the room and not too close to the judges/camera. You might mark off the space with some kind of tape. Place the imaginary audience/camera downstage of the taped-off square.

To hold the audience's focus, make sure your face can be seen. On the opening slate, which includes the title, the playwright's name, and the role you are portraying, look directly at the audience, breaking the fourth wall. The slate establishes how professionally prepared you are. Many judges or casting directors decide if they want to listen and watch your performance based on how prepared and how professionally presented your slate is.

After performing your slate, establish your point of focus. For your focal point, the choices might include talking to yourself, to one other implied or invisible character, to two or more other characters, to a crowd, to the audience, to someone who is not there, or to God or the gods. Decide whether you will change your point of focus at some point during the monologue.

When you are speaking to yourself or to an implied other, you have some choices. If you are speaking to yourself, talk to "thinking land," which is full front toward the spectators, to the right or left and a bit above the audience's heads. Imagine how you would talk to yourself in real life. Your focus would probably move around, never resting on any one place for very long. It is recommended to never look down at the floor for too long a time. The audience loses a connection with your eyes. If you are talking to God or the gods, experiment with moving your eyes up, not your head, just your eyes.

If you are talking to one other character, place the implied other character toward the audience area, so your eyes can be seen. Place the other character just below your own eye line, to the right or left of the viewers. Do not establish eye contact with the judges while talking to the implied other character. Keep the other character in the same location. Looking at an immoveable object on the back wall of the performance room helps you keep the invisible acting partner in a fixed spot. Be sure the audience can see your eyes and mouth, so your body is full front, rather than profile.

The use of gestures needs selectivity. Unless the character's words, thoughts, or emotions guide you to gesture, the neutral stance with arms at your side is preferred. Arms behind your back or held tightly in front of your body restrict your movements. These constrained stances rarely help you create a character.

When staging and blocking your monologue, move only when you as the character have a reason to move. Choose transitions and beats during which you move. Limit your moves in a performance of your monologue. Every movement should be justified by the script. Let the character's emotion and thoughts guide the staging. Too much movement or too little movement is distracting and takes away from the character's story.

Unless the text requires you to sit, sitting while performing a monologue is not recommended. Even if there are instructions to sit, find a reason to stand at the beginning, soon after the monologue begins, and at the end, if the character is not chair bound.

In preparing your staging, consider the following options for variety in blocking. Downstage is used sparingly, because being too close to the audience is not comfortable for the spectators. Upstage center of the acting space is a strong position; center stage is a place of importance;

downstage center usually indicates confrontation. Upstage right or left indicates hesitancy; downstage right and left can be used to make strong statements.

If you choose to turn your back on the audience to walk upstage, make the movement brief, so you do not lose the audience's attention. Please be assured that turning your back to the audience can be effective, if the movement is motivated and does not take too long. When your back is turned, project your voice so you can be heard.

After your final line, give a tag look that communicates an emotion, then relax and smile.

ASSIGNMENT *The First Day:* Rehearsing the Staging for your Monologue   DATE:

Think about the following questions: Where on stage do you want to begin the monologue? At what part of the acting space do you want to be at the end of the monologue? Where do you want to be during the climax of the monologue? Based on the character's words, emotions, and thoughts, where and when do you want to move and when do you want to use gestures? What is your final tag emotional look?

Experiment with movement while reading your monologue. Video record your staging rehearsal.

REFLECTIVE INQUIRY   **RI**   DATE:

Recall how you felt when you performed in the video. Now answer the following questions:

Could you see your facial expressions at all times?

Did you have the balance of movement and stillness?

What five adjustments in staging will you make for the next rehearsal?

1.

2.

3.

4.

5.

Could you hear, understand and believe each word?

Make note of any changes in staging that affect projection, clarity and believability.

ASSIGNMENT *The First Day:* Rehearsing the Staging for your Monologue   DATE:

Rehearse your monologue again making adjustments. Rehearse until you have your staging completely integrated, and it feels natural. To keep each rehearsal truthful and in the moment, you must be fully engaged and make subtle adjustments. When adding action, remember your objective, recall what the character wants to do or to accomplish. Practice as if you were really in the situation. Experiment with your tactics. Let the subtext; that which your character really thinks or feels but does not say, guide you into truthful discoveries. Be sure to sustain the tag for an effective amount of time.

After you have rehearsed and made adjustments and rehearsed again and made more adjustments, you will feel comfortable and ready to memorize your words and staging.

Memorizing Monologues

Part of your actor's requirements for performance is memorization. If you are going to be an actor, you must be able to learn your lines accurately and within a time frame. Discipline and commitment are requirements for memorization.

Memorizing your monologue requires time and repetition. Once you have done all of your preparation work, which includes your script analysis, character analysis, and staging, memorization becomes easier. You know the character. You have created the physical and emotional character. Now comes the work of committing the words to memory. You memorize the lines so that you don't have to think about them. The key to remembering lines is to forget everything else except your monologue words, to think like your character, and place your character in the here and now.

There are a number of approaches to memorizing text, and each actor learns through experimentation what method works best for him/her.

- One approach is to record your lines in sections. Listen to the words and the feelings until you know the section by memory.
- Divide your monologue into beats and work on memorizing each set of words that occurs between the beats.
- Associate your lines with the movement you have added.
- Allow your sleeping state to work for you each night. Review your lines at night before you sleep. You may awake the next morning to discover that you know your lines.
- When you have moments, imagine yourself in the circumstances of the monologue and try saying the lines using an ordinary voice. Say them naturally as if you were creating them in the moment.

ASSIGNMENT *The First Day: Memorizing your Monologue 1*   DATE:

The first beat of your monologue is the slate. The slate is the title of your monologue, the title, the playwright's name and your character. In the monologue slate, it is recommended that you demonstrate professionalism and your preparation. Stand in neutral position and use your confident voice. Rehearsing your slate will help your security of the performance. Say your first and last names as if the two words are the most important words ever spoken. Be happy about the opportunity to perform and convey that feeling with your voice. Think of a clean, innocent joke that makes you smile. On the opening slate, be sure to establish eye contact with any listeners. Pronounce the title and playwright's name correctly. For *The First Day*, the author's name is pronounced Mary Krell (rhymes with Prell) Oishi (Oh-EE-she). Say the name of the character. Take a short silent beat. Do not bow your head. Move into your opening character position that you have chosen for the beginning of the monologue. Hear the silent sentence that prompts your character to speak. This moment before causes you to be active. Then speak the first lines.

Rehearse the opening slate, the transition from the slate into your character, and first two or three lines until you feel comfortable with memorization. Video the slate and then watch it.

REFLECTIVE INQUIRY **RI**   DATE:

Revisit your slate. Comment on the questions below.

How confident did you appear? How genuine did you appear?

How was your volume? Your articulation? Your energy?

How was your transition from the slate to the first lines of the monologue?

Was the silent transition the right length of time? Not too long? Not too short?

Was your character voice different from your neutral slate voice?

ASSIGNMENT *The First Day*: Memorizing your Monologue 2   **A**   DATE:

The second section to memorize is the end beat. Look at the end of the monologue. Remember how your character is feeling at the conclusion of the monologue. The final beat of your monologue contains a resolution for your character's objective. Practice the final lines and give a tag emotional look after the tag line. You might even walk a bit with the new attitude. Hold that look for a short beat, then relax, smile at the audience. Say "Thank you," expressing genuine appreciation as you exit the audition space. Rehearse the final beat and tag line and tag emotion until you feel ready to video.

Record and watch your rehearsal. Remember what has changed for your character emotionally from the first lines of the monologue to the final tag line. Change your voice and body to show emotional changes. Make sure that your tag look shows an emotion. At the end of your tag look, smile sincerely.

Locate the climax of your monologue. Rehearse this most intense section. Continue working on each section of your monologue until you have the monologue words and staging memorized

---

Rehearsing, rehearsing and more rehearsing enables you to integrate the character's words, emotions, thoughts, and staging into your muscle memory. You will arrive at the state of not having to think about memorization. Continue memorizing your monologue until it becomes natural for you to say. Try saying your monologue without holding the script in your hand, until you have the playwright's words memorized perfectly. Rehear, rehear, and rehear again building your memorization confidence.

The process that you used rehearsing with *The First Day* can be utilized in your monologue work for various other types of monologues.

Musical Theatre Lyrics as Monologues

Another type of well-written monologue that you can use for rehearsing solo work is in musical Theatre scripts. Each song in a musical is a character's emotional expression. A song by its very nature communicates passion. In a musical, the reason the character sings is that he or she is so full of emotion that words are not enough to convey the depth of feelings. The words to a song are called lyrics and contain a character's thoughts and feelings.

It is advisable to read the entire musical to see how the monologue fits into the story. Reading the script allows you to understand at what point of the character's journey the song appears.

Before you work on the vocal requirements of any musical Theatre song, you need to interpret the lyrics implementing the techniques used in preparing a monologue. When preparing for the performance of a song, you discover the given circumstances, CWOW—the who, what, when, where and why of the character; the reason for the song; how the song fits into the story, the objective, obstacles, and tactics within the song; the words, any repetitions of words or phrases, how the song ends, and how your character's feelings change from the beginning of the song to the end of the song. Your analysis is important, because it affects your character's choices.

Choosing a vital objective for why the character sings is necessary. By playing objectives in a song, your character communicates an objective. In songs, sometimes phrases or verses are repeated. Each repetition brings your character to a new discovery. Even though the words may be the same, the intention behind the words changes. How do the repeated words you sing move the story forward and build the emotion? It is essential that you use your actor's tools of movement, gesture, facial expression, and voice to express changes when the lyrics are repeated.

Questions to Answer for Interpreting the Lyrics of a Musical Theatre Song
~   What is the moment before the first line of the song?
~   What is the prompt line that causes you as the character to sing the first line?
~   What is the CWOW?
~   If you are onstage alone during the song, what are you trying to accomplish by vocalizing in this place and at this time?
~   What is the end feeling?

"Maybe": Musical Theatre Lyrics as Monologues

Below are the lyrics from a song called "Maybe" from the musical *Annie*, printed in the form of a poem. The first letter of each line is capitalized. Read the lyrics as if you are a young orphan who is dreaming of ideal parents.

> *Maybe far away*
> *Or maybe real nearby*
> *He may be pouring her coffee*
> *She may be straightening his tie!*
> *Maybe in a house*
> *All hidden by a hill*
> *She's sitting playing piano,*
> *He's sitting paying a bill!*
>
> *Betcha they're young*
> *Betcha they're smart*
> *Bet they collect things*
> *Like ashtrays, and art!*
> *Betcha they're good—*
> *(Why shouldn't they be?)*
> *Their one mistake*

Was giving up me!

So maybe now it's time,
And maybe when I wake
They'll be there calling me "Baby". . .
Maybe.

Betcha he reads
Betcha she sews
Maybe she's made me
A closet of clothes!
Maybe they're strict
As straight as a line. . .
Don't really care
As long as they're mine!

So maybe now this prayer's
The last one of its kind. . .
Won't you please come get your "Baby"

[ANNIE AND ORPHANS]
Maybe

ASSIGNMENT "Maybe": Analyzing Lyrics   DATE:

Look at "Maybe" again. Make some notes on what type of monologue do you think "Maybe" is. Re-read the beginning of Chapter Seven to help you decide what type of monologue "Maybe" is.

Next read the song as a monologue again and answer the questions below. You may have to create answers based on what you have imagined. Remember that as you work with the song as a monologue, you will make discoveries, and you will make adjustments. You will continue to make changes during your process until you are satisfied with your interpretation.

In the song, approximately how old is Annie?

What is Annie's first emotion?

What is Annie's objective?

What is the unheard prompt line to which Annie is responding?

When she says, "He may be pouring her coffee", who are the he and she that Annie is talking about?

Why is important for them to be doing simple things like pouring coffee and straightening a tie?

What image is created for Annie by the two lines, "Maybe in a house / All hidden by a hill"?

How does Annie imagine her parents?

What shift in emotion does Annie have on the two lines, "Their one mistake / Was giving up me!?"

Why does Annie want to be called "Baby"?

Why is it important for Annie to think that "he reads" and "she sews?"

If Annie is a young girl, why might she have a need for having parents who are "strict"?

What change in emotion does she have on these two lines, "Don't really care / As long as they're mine!"?

Her prayer is a different tactic she chooses to get her objective. What do you think the words "The last one of its kind..." means?

What does the tag line, "Maybe", tell about how Annie feels?

CREATIVE INQUIRY *CI*   DATE:

Think about the lyrics of "Maybe". Write them down in sentence form, so that they appear like a monologue, rather than like a poem. What new insights do you have now about the character by writing the lyrics in your handwriting in sentence form?

"Electricity": Musical Theatre Lyrics as Monologues

Below are the lyrics from a song called "Electricity" from the musical *Billy Elliot*. When you read the lyrics, imagine being a young boy with a desire to dance. In order to be allowed to dance, the boy must change his family's attitude to the idea of boys dancing.

I can't really explain it, I haven't got the words
It's a feeling that you can't control
I suppose it's like forgetting, losing who you are
And at the same time something makes you whole

It's like that there's music, playing in your ear
And I'm listening, and I'm listening, and then I disappear

And then I feel a change, like a fire deep inside
Something bursting me wide open, impossible to hide
And suddenly I'm flying, flying like a bird

Like Electricity, electricity
Sparks inside of me, and I'm free, I'm free

It's a bit like being angry; it's a bit like being scared
Confused and all mixed up and mad as hell
It's like when you've been crying
And you're empty and you're full
I don't know what it is, it's hard to tell

It's like that there's some music, playing in your ear
But the music is impossible, impossible to hear

But then I feel it move me
Like a burning deep inside
Something bursting me wide open
Impossible to hide
And suddenly I'm flying
Flying like a bird
Like Electricity, electricity

Sparks inside of me
And I'm free, I'm free.

Electricity, sparks inside of me
And I'm free, I'm free
I'm free. Free I'm free.

ASSIGNMENT "Electricity" 1   DATE:

Look at "Electricity" again. Make some notes on 1.) What type of monologue you think it is, 2.) The unheard line that prompts your speaking, and who says it to you, 3.) Your emotions throughout the song-monologue, and 4.) Your feelings.

ASSIGNMENT "Electricity" 2   DATE:

Write down the lyrics of "Electricity" in sentence form, so that they are in a monologue form, rather than in poem form. What new insights do you have now about the character by writing the lyrics in your handwriting in sentence form? Include beat marks to indicate changes in emotions or topics.

"Adelaide's Lament": Musical Theatre Lyrics as Monologues

Below are the lyrics from a song called "Adelaide's Lament" from the musical *Guys and Dolls*. In the song, Adelaide reads from a book and comments on what she reads. The book talks about psychosomatic illness; Adelaide thinks that her cold may be an emotional problem. Read the lyrics as if Adelaide is speaking her thoughts as she reads from a book.

It says here:
The average unmarried female
Basically insecure
Due to some long frustration may react
With psychosomatic symptoms
Difficult to endure
Affecting the upper respiratory tract.

In other words, just from waiting around for that plain little band of gold
A person can develop a cold.

You can spray her wherever you figure there's streptococci lurk
You can give her a shot for whatever's she's got, but it just won't work
If she's tired of getting the fish eye from the hotel clerk
A person can develop a cold.

It says here:
The female remaining single
Just in the legal sense
Shows a neurotic tendency, see note:
Chronic organic symptoms
Toxic or hyper tense
Involving the eye, the ear, the nose, and throat.

In other words, just from worrying if the wedding is on or off
A person can develop a cough.

You can feed her all day with the vitamin A and the bromofizz
But the medicine never gets anywhere near where the trouble is.
If she's getting a kind of name for herself, and the name ain't his
A person can develop a cough.

And further more, just from stalling, and stalling,
And stalling the wedding trip
A person can develop la grippe.
When they get on that train to Niagara
And she can hear church bells chime

The compartment is air conditioned

And the mood sublime
Then they get off at Saratoga for the fourteenth time!
A person can develop la grippe,
La grippe.
La post nasal drip.
With the wheezes
And the sneezes
And a sinus that's really a pip!
From a lack of community property
And a feeling she's getting too old
A person can develop a bad, bad cold!
[ADELAIDE sneezes]

ASSIGNMENT "Adelaide's Lament"   DATE:

What type of monologue is "Adelaide's Lament?"

What is the unheard line that prompts Adelaide's response?

How does Adelaide feel at the beginning of the song?

What is she talking about in the song?

What is her objective?

To whom is she speaking?

What tactic does she use to achieve her objective?

What kind of a character voice do you hear the character using?

At what point does she begin to figure out her problem?

What new realization does she come to by the end of the song?

How does she feel at the end of the song?

What does her tag look express?

_____

"Soliloquy": Musical Theatre Lyrics as Monologues

Below are the lyrics from a song called "Soliloquy", a song by Richard Rodgers and Oscar Hammerstein II written for the 1945 musical *Carousel.* In this song, Billy Bigelow expresses what he is thinking and feeling after he has learned that he is to become a father. He daydreams what it would be like to become a father to a boy, who would be named after him. Imagine yourself as a poor carnival barker standing alone in the carnival after hearing "You are going to be a father."

> *I wonder what he'll think of me*
> *I guess he'll call me the "old man"*
> *I guess he'll think I can lick*
> *Ev'ry other feller's father*
> *Well, I can!*
> *I bet that he'll turn out to be*

The spittin' image of his dad
But he'll have more common sense
Than his puddin-headed father ever had
I'll teach him to wrestle
And dive through a wave
When we go in the mornin's for our swim
His mother can teach him
The way to behave
But she won't make a sissy out o' him
Not him! Not my boy! Not Bill!

Bill... My boy Bill
I will see that he is named after me, I will.
My boy, Bill! He'll be tall
And tough as a tree, will Bill!
Like a tree he'll grow
With his head held high
And his feet planted firm on the ground
And you won't see nobody dare to try
To boss or toss him around!
No pot-bellied, baggy-eyed bully
Will boss him around.

I don't give a hang what he does
As long as he does what he likes!
He can sit on his tail
Or work on a rail
With a hammer, hammering spikes!
He can ferry a boat on a river
Or peddle a pack on his back
Or work up and down
The streets of a town
With a whip and a horse and a hack.

He can haul a scow along a canal
Run a cow around a corral
Or maybe bark for a carousel
Of course it takes talent to do that well.

Aha-ha-ha-ha!

He might be a champ of the heavyweights,
Or a feller that sells you glue,
Or President of the United States,
That'd be all right, too
His mother would like that
But he wouldn't be President if he didn't wanna be!
Not Bill!

My boy, Bill! He'll be tall
And as tough as a tree, will Bill
Like a tree he'll grow
With his head held high
And his feet planted firm on the ground
And you won't see nobody dare to try
To boss him or toss him around!
No fat-bottomed, flabby-faced,
Pot-bellied, baggy-eyed bully
Will boss him around.

And I'm hanged if he'll marry his boss' daughter
A skinny-lipped virgin with blood like water
Who'll give him a peck
And call it a kiss
And look in his eyes through a lorgnette. . .

Hey, why am I talkin' on like this?
My kid ain't even been born, yet!
I can see him when he's seventeen or so,
And startin' to go with a girl
I can give him lots of pointers, very sound
On the way to get 'round any girl
I can tell him . . .
Wait a minute!
Could it be?
What the hell!
What if he is a girl?
What would I do with her?
What could I do for her?
A bum with no money!
You can have fun with a son

But you gotta be a father to a girl
She mightn't be so bad at that
A kid with ribbons in her hair!
A kind o' sweet and petite
Little tin-type of her mother!
What a pair!

My little girl
Pink and white
As peaches and cream is she
My little girl
Is half again as bright
As girls are meant to be!
Dozens of boys pursue her
Many a likely lad does what he can to woo her
From her faithful dad
She has a few
Pink and white young fellers of two or three
But my little girl
Gets hungry ev'ry night and she comes home to me!

I-I got to get ready before she comes!
I got to make certain that she
Won't be dragged up in slums
With a lot o' bums like me
She's got to be sheltered
In a fair hand dressed
In the best that money can buy!
I never knew how to get money,
But, I'll try, I'll try! I'll try!
I'll go out and make it or steal it
Or take it or die!

ASSIGNMENT "Soliloquy"   DATE:

What insights do you have about the role of Billy? Is he a good guy or bad guy? How do you see him dressed?

What was the CWOW that you decided for Billy?

C

W

O

W

Write the lyrics in sentence form indicating emotions and marking beats. Mark each sentence using active verbs. Label the emotions that Billy experiences by writing them next to where they are revealed in the song.

What is Billy's final emotion? Did he achieve his objective?

"There's No Business Like Show Business": Musical Theatre Lyrics as Monologues

Below are the lyrics from a song called "There's No Business Like Show Business" from the musical, *Annie Get Your Gun.* As you read the lyrics, think about the questions below. After you read the lyrics, answer the questions, which are included at the end of the song. You may personalize the song, because the song relates to your acting occupation.

The costumes, the scenery, the makeup, the props
The audience that lifts you when you're down

The headaches, the heartaches, the backaches, the flops
The sheriff who escorts you out of town

The opening when your heart beats like a drum
The closing when the customers won't come

There's no business like show business
Like no business I know

Everything about it is appealing

Everything the traffic will allow
No where could you have that happy feeling

When you are stealing that extra bow
There's no people like show people
They smile when they are low

Yesterday they told you, you would not go far
That night you opened and there you are

Next day on your dressing room they've hung a star
Let's go on with the show

The cowboys, the wrestlers, the tumblers, the clowns
The roustabouts that move the show at dawn

The music, the spotlights, the people, the towns
Your baggage with the labels pasted on

The sawdust and the horses and the smell
The towel you've taken from the last hotel

There's no business like show business
If you tell me it's so
Traveling through the country is so thrilling
Standing out in front on opening nights
Smiling as you watch the benches filling
And see your billing up there in lights

There's no people like show people

They smile when they are low
Even with a turkey that you know will fold
You may be stranded out in the cold
Still you wouldn't trade it for a sack o' gold
Let's go on with the show
Let's go on with the show!
The show!
The show!

ASSIGNMENT "There's No Business like Show Business" 1 ⬥A⬥   DATE:

What is your CWOW?

C

W

O

W

As a musical Theatre character singing these words, what are you trying to accomplish? What is your goal?

What new ideas did you discover in the process of reading or speaking the song?

Where are you while singing the song? Choose a precise location.

Did you achieve your objective by the end of the monologue/song?

ASSIGNMENT "There's No Business like Show Business" 2 DATE:

Write the lyrics in sentence form. Mark the beats and label, next to the sentences, your active verbs and emotions.

You focused on the acting choices for the analysis of a song as a monologue. It is important that if you are singing for any audition, you must possess vocal abilities and skills. You need to master the musical aspects of a song before you audition with a musical Theatre number. You can study with a vocal instructor to work on the musical requirements. Working the acting aspects to add to your vocalization will help your song's interpretation.

Solo Actor as a Playwright

The next section deals with the solo actor as a playwright. A playwright is a person who writes plays; he/she can be referred to as a dramatist. The earliest playwrights were found among the Greeks, who wrote for contests in the fifth century BC. Playwrights study the art and craft of writing. Studying playwriting will benefit your acting career.

In this chapter there are experiences which encourage your past and present thoughts and feelings. Creating your own original monologue incorporates your thoughts and feelings into personal material. There will be exploration into happy and sad feelings from your past and present. During the personal reflections, if you experience disturbing feelings that seriously disrupt your daily life for two weeks or more, consider seeking professional help. Talk with an adult.

Writing an Original Monologue for the Solo Actor

The successful original monologue is a highly condensed emotional solo performance based on imaginative writings. The original monologue can be used in only auditions that ask for original works.

Why Write an Original Monologue

You have read plays and have original ideas about how characters are created. You are unique, with a distinctive point of view on life. You have a personal style. You are the expert on your life, and you have many past memories. You have something to say. You are passionate about many topics. You have a sense of lasting truths. You have a need to tell a story. You can get inside your character's head. You are an observer of life and human beings in action. You have private stories. You possess pictures and objects that remind you of some of your life's moments. You have many different emotions based on past experiences. You have dreams from waking life and from nighttime. You remember turning points in your life. You know everything about yourself, so you can relate to your personal stories better than anyone else.

You have relatives who are interesting characters. You might have an ancestor or neighbor on whom you want to base a character. You have read an interesting story about a person in a newspaper or social media or a character in a book and want to base a character on something that you have read. You have a lot of material which can be part of an original monologue.

Questions to Answer Before Writing an Original Monologue

- Why do I want to write an original monologue?
- Am I inspired?
- Do I have something to say?
- Do I think creatively?
- Do I feel comfortable sharing things about my life?
- Do I have any fears of writing?
- Can I suspend my judgment of my writing and my life?
- Am I willing to bend the truth for dramatic license?
- Am I willing to write and rewrite and rewrite?
- Can I continually ask myself, what happens next?
- Do I have a need to tell a story?
- Am I willing to write freely without editing at first?
- Am I comfortable working alone?
- Do I have feelings to express?
- Am I comfortable in having a work in progress as an ongoing project?
- Am I willing to accept that my ideas may be considered far- fetched and ridiculous by others?
- Will I be okay with thinking outside the box?

~ Can I doodle and write without staying within the box?
~ Can I eventually write a two to ten minute original monologue?

Writing original works allows you to inventory your past and present, to see yourself clearly, see others in a new light, to enhance creativity, to speculate about your future, and to provide a way for dramatic expression. The objective in this writing segment is to create an autobiographical monologue based on your memories and ideas for the future.

Warm-Ups for Writing Original Monologues

Warming up for an original writing process includes some of the same principles you used in improvisation preparation and creativity chapters. Trusting yourself that you have all of the creativity you need is important. Using spontaneous responses to prompts helps you tap into your creative inquiry. Responding in the moment with unconstrained ideas lets you generate thoughts and feelings. Thinking creatively allows you to experiment with text that you can later shape and mold into monologues.

ASSIGNMENT ABC Free Association at this Time in Your Life   DATE:

Look at the alphabet below and write down the first words that come to mind for each letter of the alphabet. Think freely without restricting or censoring your thoughts. Write the first words that you think of. Write one word for each letter of the alphabet. The alphabet is in random order.

D

O

M

Z

H

A

J

R

L

G

S

U

C

V

B

T

F

I

K

W

N

Q

E

X

P

Y

RI

REFLECTIVE INQUIRY   DATE:

Revisit your list of alphabet associations and circle the words that jump out at you.

List some of the circled words that make an impression on you.

The circled words may have particular meaning to you at this time in your life. Imagine a CWOW based on your words. Play yourself as the C. To whom are you talking? What is your objective? Where are you?

C

W

O

W

Creating Label Lines for Various Ages of a Character

Thinking like a character who experiences several ages is a situation that starts your creative writing and is an excellent way to warm-up. Use creative thinking as a way to create characters at various ages.

ASSIGNMENT Creating Label Lines for Various Ages of a Character   DATE:

Look at the following three prompts and write three to five label lines that show reactions, feelings, and thoughts about different objects and situations. Label lines establish CWOW in the first sentences of a monologue.

* You are a five-year-old child, and someone has handed you a double-dipped ice cream cone. Thinking as a five-year-old, what would you say? Write your reaction lines to the following situations as the designated ages. Use "What If…" What if you are that age and are receiving a double-dipped ice cream cone. What would be three to five sentences that you would say in response to the double-dipped ice cream cone?

*You are a fifteen-year-old person, wearing brand new clothes, and you are handed a double-dipped ice cream cone.

*You are a ninety-five-year-old person, and you are handed a double-dipped ice cream cone.

Characters Based on News Headlines

Headlines can be a source of inspiration as a warm-up for the creative writing practice.

ASSIGNMENT Characters Based on News Headlines   DATE:

Think of a character who might be telling the narrative story prompted by the following headline. Create CWOW that fits the news headlines. Add a label line to begin the original monologue. Have fun thinking outside the box.

News Headline	Character	Character's age	Occupation	To whom is the character speaking	Objective	Label line CWOW
An Example for the headline "Meeting for Open Meeting is Closed to Older People"	Herbert Finkle	Ninety Years old	Security Guard	Crowd of deaf, angry, senior citizens	To keep the seniors away from the meeting	(yelling) "Ok, you fellow oldsters, see my badge? Get out of the street. This meeting is closed, but I hear there is a sale on hearing aid batteries now across the street. Ten for $1.00"

"Eye Drops Off Shelf"						
"Enraged Cow Injures Farmer with Axe"						
"Two Sisters Reunited after 18 Years in Checkout Counter Line"						
"Man Struck by Lightning, Loses Sense of Taste"						
"Ice Cream Stores Closing Due to Lack of Ice"						

Comedy is simply a funny way of being serious.

Peter Ustinov, playwright, actor

Comic and Serious Perspectives

A monologue can be in the genre of comedy or in the genre of drama. It can also have elements of both styles. The end of the monologue determines the genre. If it ends happily, and the character overcomes the obstacles, it is comedy. If the character is overcome by the obstacles, and it ends seriously, it is considered a drama.

To create comedy, the writer thinks of a humorous character, the humorous implied other, a humorous objective, and a humorous location. The character in the monologue considers his/her objective as serious; the comedy resides in the treatment and how the audience views the journey. To write drama, think serious characters, serious other characters, serious objectives, and a serious location.

ASSIGNMENT Creating Comic and Serious Label Lines Based on Objects   DATE:

Read the following list of ideas for developing lines in comic and serious genres. Create a comic label line to the object. And then write a serious label line to the object. Use your imaginative thinking to create a character who might be involved with the object. Craft a comic and then a serious CWOW for each idea below.

Comic response to a cute puppy

Serious response to a cute puppy

Comic response to sitting on a piece of chewed gum

Serious response to sitting on a piece of chewed gum

Comic response to finding an envelope with a lot of money in it

Serious response to finding an envelope with a lot of money in it

Comic response to seeing a very famous person walk into the room where you are.

Serious response to seeing a very famous person walk into the room where you are.

ASSIGNMENT Memories   DATE:

Look at the list of topics below and respond with several memories from your personal history. Do a quick write response, without judgment. Write words, phrases, any notes based on your memories. Take approximately thirty seconds on each topic.

Happiness

Sadness

Anger

A Personal Belief

Death

Three Childhood Memories

Hopes for your Future

Think about the topics above. Which topics would you like to develop into a monologue?

Let the memory live again.

"Memory" from the musical *Cats*

Writing Your Creative Birth Announcement and Obituary

Personalizing your material gives you an opportunity to become invested in your writings. That is one of the ways to look at your early life and brainstorm about possible images and memories that could be the basis of an Autobiographical Original Monologue.

ASSIGNMENT Writing Your Creative Birth Announcement   DATE:

When you were born, someone else wrote your birth announcement. This exercise gives you an opportunity to be the writer of your birth announcement. If you know the facts of your birth, write your birth announcement in the space below. Include your name, the date, the location of birth, where your parents lived, their occupations, your weight, any siblings, and any unusual facts about your birth. If you do not know the facts of your birth, ask someone who might know.

ASSIGNMENT Writing Your Creative Obituary  DATE:

Write the details for your imagined death announcement. Include your name, date, the location of your death, the cause of death, your occupation, your hobbies, any personal life facts, family, and anything unusual about your passing. Include the created details of your memorial service or funeral, the date, the time, and the place.

Characters Based on Your Childhood

You can draw inspiration from your mementos, diaries, scrap books, and stories told to you by relatives. Taking time to find out about your past is very important for your writer's process. Engaging the five senses from your memory and asking yourself questions may stimulate feelings, images, or thoughts for characters based on your childhood. The ideas mentioned below are for you to do when you have time to locate the items and recall facts and emotions. Take your time looking at the pictures or objects.

ASSIGNMENT Your Childhood DATE:

Find a picture of yourself as a young child. It is important that you actually look at the picture for this experience, rather than merely remembering the picture. Recall the circumstances behind the picture. Now make some notes. What is behind the smile or frown? What were you thinking? How are you feeling?

Locate an object, a toy, or a book that brings up memories from your childhood. Where did you get the object? How did you feel about it when you were a child? How do you feel now looking at the object?

Uncover a letter, note, or card from someone in your past. How did you know the person who sent it? What was happening between the two of you at the time of the writing? How did you feel when you received the letter, note, or card? What would you say to the person today?

Look at picture of your family or a family member when you were younger. How are the people/person dressed? What was happening at the time of the photo? What do you imagine each person in the picture was thinking? What do you imagine each person in the picture is feeling?

Find a childhood award that you received. What was the title of your award? What were the circumstances of the award? What do you remember about receiving the award? How did you feel?

Locate a picture of a childhood pet, either yours of someone else's. What was the pet's name? What kind of personality did this pet have? Was it your pet or someone else's? What experiences do you remember about the pet? What happened to the pet?

Ask a relative about a story involving you as a child, in which you were old enough to remember the event. Record the story and then recall what you remember about the event.

Pivotal Moments

In recalling your childhood, noting the pivotal memories of your life helps you remember the moments that might stimulate an image, a feeling or a thought on which you can base your autobiographical monologue.

ASSIGNMENT Personal Timeline   DATE:

Fold a piece of blank, unlined paper lengthwise. The creased middle line represents a dividing line between contrasting emotions. This timeline represents your life's up and downs. Recall your childhood memories that are happy and sad and plot a graph. Below the line pinpoint a memory that is sad or serious. Above the line mark any happy, joyful or exciting memory. The depth of line below or the height above the neutral line indicates the intensity of emotional recall. Use phrases to label each event. For the experience you can go to a determined age, such as your present age or any other decisive time of life.

Example of the beginning of a personal timeline

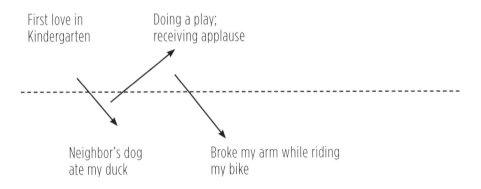

First love in
Kindergarten

Doing a play;
receiving applause

Neighbor's dog
ate my duck

Broke my arm while riding
my bike

Graph your personal timeline on this page. Include at least ten events.

Center line

- -

REFLECTIVE INQUIRY **RI**   DATE:

Revisit your personalized timeline again and answer the questions below.

What do you observe about your timeline?

What memories did you recall for this experience that you had not thought of recently?

Which memory has the happiest feelings attached to it?

Which memory has the saddest feelings attached to it?

What If...

Thinking about your life from a somewhat objective view allows you to see the overview of events. For writing it is interesting to think creatively about your memories as follows: what if the event had not happened, or what if something different had happened. To stimulate inventive ideas for your writing, think of some "what ifs" from your personal timeline.

ASSIGNMENT What If...   DATE:

Select three key events from your timeline; write some ideas of what you imagine might have happened if...the event had not happened in that particular way, but instead had happened in some other way. You create the "If" . . .

Event   What If. . .

1.

2.

3.

For the second part of your timeline, imagine the years ahead of you and create a timeline based on how you think your life will go.

Future Timeline

Your age today   A future age

Writing a Letter to Someone from your Past

Writing a letter to someone from your past is an experience that allows you to express your thoughts and feelings freely. You can express feelings without the fear of being censored or rejected, because the letter will not be sent. An important aspect of drafting a letter to someone from your past is that you need not send it, so the content will be known only to you. Once you compose your letter, you can decide to keep or destroy the letter. It is the process of putting your thoughts and feelings in writing that is important. Recording your feelings in this way may generate an image, a thought, or an additional feeling on which you can base your autobiographical monologue.

ASSIGNMENT Writing a Letter to Someone from your Past  DATE:

Think of someone from your childhood life to whom you want to express yourself in writing. The message can be written from the age you are now and addressing thoughts and feelings that you felt in the past. Do it as a quick write without concerns for grammar, spelling, or punctuation.

Dear_____

REFLECTIVE INQUIRY **RI** DATE:

Revisit how it felt to write a letter to someone from your past. Make some notes on this below.

_____

_____

Acting is the ability to dream on cue.

Ralph Richardson, actor

Nighttime Dreams: Childhood Dream Recall

Your dreams are intense sources of rich, creative imaginative material for your autobiographical writings. Tapping into your nighttime dreams allows you to share a creative part of you. Dreams may connect you to your unconscious world of hopes, fantasies, fears, concerns, and imagination. Paying attention to your dreams builds your collection of images.

ASSIGNMENT Nighttime Dreams   DATE:

Review the information in Chapter Two: Creativity about remembering your dreams. Remembering a childhood dream may allow you to get in touch with memories to inspire your autobiographical writings. Now answer the following questions when writing your Childhood Dream.

Are you in the dream?

If so, how old are you?

In what location/s does the dream take place?

Who are the other people, if any, in the dream?

What things do you see?

What sounds do you hear?

What smells are in the dream?

What tastes do you remember?

How did the objects feel through your sense of touch?

What are the colors in the dream?

What is the temperature in the dream?

Do you watch yourself in the dream?

What is your character's emotional arc, if any?

What conflict or problem do you encounter?

What is the final feeling at the end of the dream?

What title would you give your dream?

List any image, thought, or feeling from the childhood dream that might be the basis for your autobiographical character monologue.

Writing a Monologue: Creating a Character
Now is the time to create a character to use as the subject of your autobiographical monologue. Look over your inspirations: pictures,

awards, objects, letters, birth and obituary, timeline, and nighttime dream. Identify a total of one or two images that stimulate strong emotional responses in you.

Decide if you will be using yourself as narrator through the journey of your own past images. This narrative monologue will feature you as the narrator. You as the narrator might be working on a problem you are trying to solve by revealing images from your past. Your narrator can represent you, the author, and thereby act as a character who ties all of the memories together. Your narrator may speak directly to the audience and express a definite point of view. You have something to express and have thoughts and feelings that deeply concern you. You do not have to come to a resolution. You can end with a thought-provoking idea, feeling, or question. You may leave the conflict or issue unresolved.

In your monologue, you may want to play yourself at different ages. Your character wants to achieve a goal and has a need to speak. You may talk to implied others, to the audience, or to yourself. You may place your character in more than one setting and in different time frames.

ASSIGNMENT Creating a Character Biography DATE:

Create a biography of your character. The biographical answers may be based on fact, or they may be fictional.

Character's age

Location of the memory monologue

Date of the memory monologue

Memory details

Memory character's objective in the monologue

Talking to whom

Five senses details

Emotions

Climax of your memory monologue

End of your memory monologue

Tag line and tag emotion of your memory monologue

_____

Writing a Monologue: First Draft

Soon you will write a first draft of your autobiographical monologue. This first draft is a rough draft. Do it as a quick write. Write freely without concern. Allow ideas to lead you. Write quickly. Do not stop to censor or revise. Do not analyze. Do not pay attention to proper grammar or punctuation. Do not allow yourself to edit any information at this point. Do not cross anything out. Go with the flow. Trust your stream of consciousness. Keep writing until the entire story is told.

ASSIGNMENT Assessment of Your First Draft of Your
Autobiographical Memory Monologue   DATE:

Read the first draft as if you did not write it. Read it from an objective point of view. Does the story engage you? Is it interesting? Is it easy to follow? Does your character seem believable? Does your character grow or change? Do you need to say more? Does your character have a character arc? Does the character develop as the story unfolds? Make some notes on these questions below.

Now write down three revisions you intend to make to your first draft of your autobiographical memory monologue.

1.

2.

3.

Now write your revised monologue.

ASSIGNMENT Revisions to your Autobiographical Memory Monologue   DATE:

Continue the rewriting process for the text. Do not be concerned with grammar or punctuation. Once you feel that the autobiographical monologue is complete, give it a title, stage it, and memorize it using the techniques outlined in this chapter. Your creative monologue can be used for any audition that requests original material.

Character Monologue from the play Our Town

If you read lots of monologues to see how they are written, you will become accustomed to how a well-written monologue is constructed. Below is an example of a well-written monologue from the classic play written by Thornton Wilder. The character of Emily has passed away while giving birth to her child. She leaves her grave to visit her mother in Grover's Corners one last time. Her mother does not see Emily or hear Emily's thoughts. Think about how this monologue compares to your own.

> *Oh, Mama, just look at me one minute as though you really saw me. Mama! Fourteen years have gone by! – I'm dead! – You're a grandmother, Mama – I married George Gibbs, Mama! - Wally's dead too. – Mama! His appendix burst on a camping trip to Crawford Notch. We felt just terrible about it, don't you remember? – But, just for a moment now we're all together – Mama, just for a moment let's be happy – Let's look at one another! I can't! I can't go on! It goes so fast. We don't have time to look at one another. I didn't realize. So all that was going on and we*

never noticed! Take me back – up the hill – to my grave. But first: Wait! One more look! Oh, earth you're too wonderful for anyone to realize you! Do any human beings ever realize life while they live it – every, every minute?

Closure for Chapter Seven: Monologues

You have studied acting and staging a monologue, and worked with and written an original monologue. The first part of closure for Chapter Seven involves your reflecting on facts presented in this chapter. In your mind, condense all of the information under each topic and make a note of the most valuable fact for your monologue study below.

ASSIGNMENT Closure   DATE:

Introduction to Monologues

Definition of Monologue

History of the Monologue

Monologue Vocabulary

Types of Monologues

Why an Actor Studies Monologues

Monologue for Analysis and Staging *The First Day*

Monologue Character Analysis for *The First Day*

Reading the Monologue backwards

Scoring your Role—Marking Your Emotional Beats for the Monologue *The First Day*

Improvising your Monologue *The First Day*

Acting your Monologue Warm-Up *The First Day*

Acting your Monologue Vocally *The First Day*

Keeping it Real and in the Moment—Not Indicating

Keeping it Real and in the Moment, *The First Day*

Telegramming your Monologue *The First Day*

Staging your Monologue *The First Day*

Rehearsing the Staging for Your Monologue *The First Day*

Memorizing your Monologue *The First Day*

Musical Theatre Lyrics as Monologues

Questions To Answer for Interpreting the Lyrics of a Musical Theatre Song

Lyrics as Monologue for a young girl, from the musical *Annie* "Maybe"

Song-Monologue for a young boy, from the musical *Billy Elliot* "Electricity"

Song-Monologue for an adult female, from the musical *Guys and Dolls* "Adelaide's Lament"

Song-Monologue for an adult male, from the musical *Carousel* "Soliloquy"

Personalizing the Song "There's No Business Like Show Business," from the musical *Annie Get Your Gun*

Solo Actor as a Playwright

Writing an Original Monologue for the Solo Actor

Why Write an Original Monologue

Questions to Answer Before Writing an Original Monologue

Warm-Ups for Writing Original Monologues

ABC Free Association at This Time in Your Life

Creating Label Lines for Various Ages of a Character

Characters Based on News Headlines

Comic and Serious Perspectives

Memories

Writing your Creative Birth Announcement and Obituary

Characters Based on Your Childhood

Pivotal Moments

What if. . .

Writing a Letter to Someone from your Past

Nighttime Dreams: Childhood Dream Recall

Writing your Childhood Dream as a Narrative

Creating a Character from your Memories for your Autobiographical Monologue

Writing your First Draft of your Autobiographical Monologue

A Character Monologue from the play *Our Town*

You are nearing your goal of acquiring skills and techniques that make you a knowledgeable actor. You have analyzed scripts, constructed a monologue from a script, gained more information about being an actor, staged a monologue, tapped into your memories and composed an original monologue. You now have abilities that you can use in auditions.

You are approaching the end of *The Student Actor Prepares: Acting for Life.* You have acquired the basic resources to achieve your goal of becoming an actor.

The final chapter addresses auditions and professionalism. It is followed by the epilogue, which includes advice that you can use in your future study.

CHAPTER EIGHT: AUDITIONS

Introduction to Auditions

By participating in this book's assignments and inquiries, you have the basic actor's tools needed to prepare for audition study. You are ready with the knowledge of how to analyze scripts, how to prepare, and how to present a monologue. Being an actor equipped for auditions requires a positive attitude, knowledge of the audition process, and professionalism. This book is entitled *The Student Actor Prepares: Acting for Life*; many of the audition tips will help with your life full of auditions, whether on stage, or offstage in any job interview. Auditioning for the Theatre requires skills that will also help you in your offstage life.

Being on time, prepared, confident, and positive are admirable life skills. These traits are valuable in any audition as well. With job interviews you hope that you will get the job; in auditions you hope to achieve your objective of getting the role. You are considered a success if you get the role.

Success is defined as an achievement, the accomplishment of goals. Your success can be measured by being true to who you are, being motivated, being responsible, being goal-oriented, and being happy about your choices.

Sometimes success in the Theatre is thought of as being paid to act, achieving fame, and/or appearing on Broadway. A more helpful definition of success may be evaluating your goals as you proceed in life's journey, making adjustments as you progress toward your goals, and making decisions for your personal happiness. This is like a character achieving his/her objective by using tactics, assessing, and restructuring his/her strategies. You can be an actor and use acting skills and/or apply to other careers. As an actor, you can achieve appearances in regional Theatre, or perhaps by working in the educational Theatre world of schools. You can choose to work in fields related to the stage, such as radio, film, television, and other digital media.

One truism about success in auditions is that if you do not show up to audition, chances are that you will not be cast.

Showing up for an audition is the usual requirement for casting.

Eighty percent of success is showing up.

Woody Allen, director, actor

Definition of an Audition

An audition is a demonstration of your actor's skills. It is the process that includes the trying out for a role in a play. The audition is a short performance seen by a casting director who will decide if you are capable to act in a project. In this chapter you learn the various types of Theatre auditions. Tips are given on how to prepare for an audition, what to do after an audition, and how to be an audience member.

You need to have preparation that includes: how to cultivate a confident and positive attitude about the audition process; how to find a suitable monologue; how to dress; and how to format resumés and obtain headshots. Part of being prepared is being knowledgeable about the different types of auditions, and what to do and not to do in an audition, and learning how to be a professional.

This chapter contains tips for successful auditions. Periodically there are Reflective and Creative Inquiries.

Positive Attitude about the Audition Process

Auditions can be thought of as stressful. You care; you are nervous; there might be many others who want to be cast in addition to you. If you are cast, then you have succeeded in achieving your objective. The flip side of not getting cast may add stress to the audition. Dealing with audition stress and managing the fright of the audition will be less a factor if you have positive, coping skills. Periodically review the information in Chapter One: Acting.

A tactic for developing your positive attitude about the audition process is: Think of your audition as a doorway to possibly working in a certain role, with a certain director, or in a certain theater. Enjoy the exciting prospect of the audition to show your joy of acting, your preparedness, your talent, and your professionalism.

In developing your positive attitude toward auditions, it will help if you focus on the benefits to you of the audition process. The audition gives you the opportunity to display your talents, at a place where your abilities will be appreciated. You have a chance to meet people who love acting and the Theatre. You will work with creative people in a collaborative project.

It helps if you remember that the casting director wants you to succeed. The director has a challenge: he/she has a role to cast. You could be the solution to the director's problem. The director is hoping that his/her version of a specific character will walk in. You may be that person.

Tips to Build your Positive Attitude about the Audition Process

~ Have joy about an opportunity to show your skills.
~ Avoid focusing on the negatives or rejections.
~ Enjoy the newness of each audition.
~ Think of the performance of any audition as a performance in a really small room for your new best friend, the director.
~ Being professional is important in any audition.
~ Develop a code of ethics that includes discipline in all working circumstances.
~ Keep your code of morals intact.
~ Read books about acting.
~ Be able to discuss acting teachers and styles.
~ Study acting theories. Know about trends in your acting profession.
~ Practice daily to be ready for any audition.
~ Enjoy meeting actors and directors.
~ Think of each actor/director/casting aide as a potential partner in acting.
~ Observe people in various situations. "People watch."
~ Be yourself.
~ Laugh at appropriate times.
~ Be pleasant to work with.
~ Delight in discoveries.
~ Applaud yourself and others each day.

REFLECTIVE INQUIRY **RI**   DATE:

Revisit the tips above. Pick out the three tips that you think might work for you.

1.

2.

3.

Before you go to Auditions

It is important to contact the company producing the play to find out the title of the play, the theater, the director, the roles, the rehearsal schedule, and production dates. Before you go to auditions, be certain that you are available for all of the rehearsals and productions. If you get cast and then tell the director that you have conflicts, you will cause problems for the director and cast. Be sure to know the audition times, the location of the auditions, and what type of audition the director is expecting.

Read the play; study the play; understand its genre. Look up any historical information about the play and playwright. Search who has played the roles before. Read about the time period of the play. Research any reviews about any productions in the past.

Look at the age ranges of the characters. Choose ones close to your own age, unless you are in an academic or educational setting where you get to play older and younger than your actual age.

If you really want to be a part of the play, consider more than one role, if that is possible. You limit your chances of being cast if you choose only one role. Be honest; you must really want the roles for which you audition and be happy if you are cast in any of your chosen roles. Prepare a different audition for each of the roles that you would consider playing.

If you only want one role, be up front with that commitment. Be prepared that there might be many actors who want that one role that you selected.

Prepare your resumé and headshot. Even at a middle or high school audition, it is a good practice to have your resumé formatted correctly and have a separate picture of your face that you can leave with the director.

Preparing your Resumé

While you are preparing to become an actor, you can collect information needed for your resumé. Your resumé has several purposes: to let the prospective director know about your training and skills; to get your productions, training, and skills organized; to have something to leave with the production company for future audition notifications; to have a listing of all of your past directors and teachers, so that others can see with whom you have worked.

Prepare your conflated resumé, your all-inclusive resumé, and add to it each time you take a workshop, add a new skill, and take each role and/or technical position you did. A conflated resumé is one that includes everything in regard to your productions, training, and skills. This comprehensive resumé is one that you leave at home, so that you can edit what you need to create a one-page resumé to take to auditions. List the following information in your conflated resumé:

- The title, year, location, role/crew and director for every Theatre performance from your earliest age to the present. This includes each monologue and scene that you have ever performed.
- The title, brief description, location, teacher, and length of time for every Theatre/Dance or Vocal workshop/class/camp/course of study.
- Titles, location, any rating, ranking, or award for every festival, Theatre conference, or competition that you ever attended.
- Title, location, sponsor, and placement or award, for every dance/ vocal performance.
- All awards/honors you ever received in school, community. Begin with your youngest age to present.
- References who know your work. List the names, titles, and their contact information. Be sure to get permission of any reference before you list them on your resumé.
- Skills and, for each, your level of expertise, such as beginning, intermediate, advanced, or expert. Includes talents.

Once you have collected the information for your conflated resumé, you can edit the material to suit various types of auditions. The resumé for a Theatre audition will list your productions, your workshops, your dance, vocal, and acting training, and talents and skills that might be used in the Theatre.

Keep your edited resumé to one page in length. Make it visually appealing, using plain font. Electronically create your resumé. Make it easy to read.

Your resumé should have your name in bold letters at the top, with all contact information directly beneath, where it is easy to find. See "Example of a Resumé" below. Any performer's union affiliation that appears under your name and contact information should be abbreviated. There will be more about union affiliation in the last chapter of this book.

Include your name, contact information, and the age range that you feel you can play. Your age range includes the youngest age you could play, to the oldest age you could play. List your productions in reverse chronological order, starting with your most recent job first and working backwards. List your work experience, education, and technical skills.

List workshops and with whom you have studied. Many times in Theatre, directors and teachers know one another. It is advantageous to mention names of your teachers. Casting directors are impressed with quality instruction. Tell the truth. Do not add untrue listings to your resumé. Theatre people know other Theatre people; they will check your information.

Last, include Theatre skills and talents. You never know when things, such as accents, roller skating, acrobatics, juggling or being able to balance a ball on your nose will come in handy!

Print your resumé on white paper.

Example of a Resumé

GAI JONES   (Name of agent)

(actor's website)   (phone number of agent)

SAG/AFTRA

CELL PHONE_____

E-MAIL _____

HR: hair color   EYES: eye color   AGE RANGE: _____

HT: height   WT: weight

FILM

OCW HOUR	HOST	OCW STUDIOS

Theatre

MIRACLE WORKER	ANNIE SULLIVAN	OCW THEATER
AS YOU LIKE IT	ADAM	OCW THEATER
PETER PAN	LOST BOY	OCW THEATER
BUS STOP	CHERIE	CSUF THEATER
THE HEIRESS	CATHERINE	CSUF THEATER
SUMMER AND SMOKE FOOTLIGHTERS	ALMA	FULLERTON
READERS Theatre	PERFORMER/DIRECTOR VENTURA	SR. Theatre
38 YEARS OF PRODUCTIONS	DIRECTOR	GAI JONES Theatre
10 YEARS OF PRODUCTIONS	DIRECTOR/ACTOR	OJAI ART CENTER Theatre ELITE Theatre, OYES Theatre

TRAINING

COMMERCIAL WORKSHOPS	CAROLYNE BARRY	CAROLYNE BARRY STUDIO
COMMERCIAL INTENSIVE	MICHAEL DONOVAN	DONOVAN STUDIOS
VOICE-OVER WORKSHOPS	BILL ACKERMAN	KALMENSON & KAL
THE ACTOR'S BOOTCAMP	PATRICK FEREN	THE ACTOR'S BOOTCAMP
COMEDYSPORTZLA	JAMES BAILEY	NATIONAL COMEDY THEATER.
BA SPEECH/DRAMA	OCWMA Theatre	CSUF
EXPERIENTIAL PSYCHODRAMA	UCI	
ACTING	NYU, A.C.T.,	ROOSEVELT UNIVERSITY

SPECIAL SKILLS

IMPROVISATION, Theatre EDUCATOR, TEXT BOOK AUTHOR, CA YOUTH IN Theatre FOUNDER, VIRTUAL Theatre TEACHER, SAGE TO STAGE CREATOR, NATIONAL WORKSHIP LEADER FOR ENSEMBLE BUILDING, READING FOR THE BLIND, CERTIFIED PET THERAPY, SR. READERS Theatre, LEGISLATIVE ACTION COMMITTEE, AFTRA SENIOR CAUCUS, DREAM INTERPRETION, SEWING, STORY LADY, MIME, GIBBERISH, ACCENTS: BRITISH, SOUTHERN, OKLAHOMA, VOICE-OVER ACTOR, EDTA HALL OF FAME, CA SENATE HONOREE; THE WORLD WHO'S WHO OF WOMEN, WOMEN IN Theatre (W.I.T) HONOREE, UNIVERSITY/COMMUNITY COLLEGE ASSOCIATE PROFESSOR.

REFLECTIVE INQUIRY **RI**   DATE:

Revisit your list of unique skills that you prepared in Chapter One: Approaching Acting with a Positive Attitude for Who You Are and How to Deal with Inhibitors. Create an updated list of your skills and talents; list ten things that you could include on your resumé for a Theatre audition.

1.

2.

3.

4.

5.

6.

7.

8.

9.

10.

Headshots

One of the supplies that you need when you become a professional actor is your 8x10 glossy—a color headshot that shows a close-up of your face—stapled to your resumé. If you are younger than eighteen and not involved in professional Theatre, you do not need expensive head shots. Your looks change rapidly until you are an adult. You can have a picture of your face and shoulders taken and printed at less expense than professional headshots. Be sure what you wear as a top is a solid vivid color, and that your shirt does not have writing or logos on it.

The picture should be of the real you without too much makeup. Be sure your hair style is what you will wear to the audition. The director will look at your picture after you complete your audition and after you leave the audition space. The director needs to remember you by looking at your headshot.

Your headshot and resumé should be stapled together back to back, blank side against blank side. Never tape, glue or paper clip your picture and resumé together. Always staple all four corners of your picture and resumé together.

Guidelines for Auditions

The general tips for all auditions include showing up on time with resumés and headshots, and dressed appropriately. Bring a small dictionary in your audition bag to look up any unfamiliar words, and your own pencil or pen. Arrive at least one hour before your call time. Enter the audition waiting room at least thirty minutes before your audition time. You need to sign in in advance of your audition time, printing your required contact information on the sign-in list. Listen and follow directions exactly. Put any food, phone, and make-up away before entering the audition room. Leave plenty of time to stay later than your audition time. Be nice to any production assistant. Be quiet while waiting to audition. Know about the production, including dates, director, etc. Have your audition monologue prepared. Enter with confidence. Make no excuses. Make the room your own. Ask questions when you truly need answers and at an appropriate time. Take direction if it is given. Make bold choices. Keep staging simple. End confidently. Wait to be excused. Really mean it when you say thank you. Know when call backs are. If you are called back, wear the same outfit you wore to the first audition.

Types of Auditions
There are several types of Theatre auditions that you might be asked to do.

Cattle Call

You might be requested to stand on stage, while the casting director and staff look at you. This is referred to as a cattle call. Basically the auditors are looking at you to see if you physically fit the role.

Tips for a Cattle Call
~   Be sure to find out what you are to wear to the cattle call.
~   Have your resumé ready. Bring multiple copies.
~   Arrive with a positive attitude.

- Keep a genuine smile.
- Remember there are certain things that you cannot change; your height, your weight.
- Be who you are without any apologies.
- Wait to be called.
- Approach the stage with a positive attitude.
- Stand still, facing the auditors unless or until told differently.
- Follow directions.
- Keep emotionally centered no matter what others do or say while you are standing there.
- Respond when you are asked to move or say something.
- Be sure to schedule plenty of time to attend the cattle call.
- Wait to be asked to stay or to be excused.

Interview Audition

You might be asked questions as part of an interview audition. The secret to an interview is to be excited about who you are. When you answer questions and talk with the casting director, be moderately exuberant without being obnoxious. The interview usually takes place as the casting director reads your resumé. So practice talking briefly about each item on your resumé. Stay away from answering with just the words, "Yes" or "No" without explaining more about the topic. Also time your answers, so the answers are not too long-winded. Practice speaking without using filler words, such as, "Umm," "Uh," or "And . . . " Be sure to look the interviewer in the eye, making him/her a new friend with whom you really want to share your interview information.

Tips for an Interview Audition

Rehearse answering the questions that were presented in Chapter One as part of the Actor's Personal Autobiography. Record your answers.

Listen to your recording. Ask yourself how interesting, genuine, and happy you sound about who you are.

Think about your thoughts and views about various topics. Complete the following sentences:

- I see myself as . . .
- The thing I like best about me is . . .
- My dream is to . . .
- The most important thing in life is . . .
- If I could one change one thing about the world, it would be . . .

- I hope . . .
- I wish . . .
- I fear . . .
- I want . . .
- Five years from now . . .
- Ten years from now . . .
- By the time I am older I want to have accomplished some of the following things . . .

Periodically complete the sentences with other answers and additional ideas.

Improvised Audition

The improvised audition includes the director giving the actor some prompts to see how the actor reacts and thinks on his/her feet within a limited time frame. There is no script for an improvisation. An improvised audition may be the entire tryout, or may be added to any other type of audition. If you practice using all of the tips from the chapter on improvisation, you will be ready if a character is given to you at the time of audition. Remember CWOW and beginning with label lines, calling the implied other by name and ending your improvisation, once it has built and comes to a resolution.

Tips for an Improvised Audition
- Once you are given a prompt, use what brief time you may be allowed to plan CWOW.
- Plan a story line for the character who wants the objective and what might happen.
- Plan a climax to the improvised story.
- Plan a potential tag line and tag look that displays an emotion.
- Plan a title.
- Deliver your slate.
- Face the auditors, so they can see your face.
- Move your improvisation with energy.
- Keep within the time limit, if given. Otherwise it's best to be brief. Auditors sometimes ask for more.
- End with a tag look.
- Approach the casting director and say "Thank you."
- Exit with energy.

Cold Reading Audition

Another audition type is the cold reading audition. This involves reading from a monologue or script not provided in advance by the auditors. When you arrive, you will be given a script to read. Ask for time at the location to study the script. If it is a monologue, determine the CWOW (Character—who is the personality you will be playing? Who—to whom are you talking [it could be an implied character; it could be yourself]. Objective—what does your character want? Where—where does this monologue take place?) Choose some simple stage business that your character might be doing during the monologue. Identify various emotions based on the text, and use vocal variety to show the emotions. Be sure to have in mind how the character changes from the opening line to the tag line. Determine some emotional beats of silence. Use your dictionary, which you packed in your audition bag. Mark your script indicating the climax; circle some words that you would use to telegram this monologue. Determine your character's final tag look and emotion.

Tips for a Cold Reading Audition
- Memorize your name.
- Memorize the title of the play, the playwright, the name of the character, and the first line of the script.
- Memorize the final line of the monologue.
- Take the stage area with energy, showing that you are healthy, hearty, and happy to be at the audition.
- Set any chair that you might use in the audition. Position your chair before you begin your slate.
- Deliver your slate while standing.
- Make eye contact with the auditors while delivering your slate.
- Smile when you say your name; pretend that you are greeting the director as a new friend.
- Take a short beat to establish your character with a physical stance.
- Establish a beat before the opening line.
- Begin your monologue with a bold emotion that is based on the first line.
- Play the room, backing up from the casting director if the room is small.
- Establish the fourth wall when you go into character and place the implied other to the right or the left of the auditor. Do not make direct eye contact with the auditor after you establish the fourth wall.

~ Continue the monologue until the end. Hold the tag look for a beat, then relax your body and make eye contact with the auditors and smile.

~ Do not say "Thank you" until after you have finished the final beat of the monologue, relaxed, and smiled; then you can move toward the casting director or start toward the door.

Prepared Audition

A prepared audition means that you have had the monologue or script before arriving for the audition, and have been able to work with the material, work on the staging, and have memorized a monologue— something chosen by you or by the casting director. All of the tips for cold reading apply for the prepared audition. You practice greeting the auditors, introducing yourself, giving the play title, playwright's name, and character's name. The way you conduct yourself in the moments before your performance will work in your favor or detract from your audition. Looking over the Chapter on Monologues helps you review tips for monologue performance.

Entering, auditioning, and leaving the room with confidence—no matter how you think you did—shows assurance. Even if something goes wrong in your audition, end positively. Make bold mistakes. Do not make excuses; give a genuine "Thank you," and leave with a smile.

Establishing confidence without appearing cocky is something to rehearse. It helps to record various slates and end thank yous. Coming in with desperation takes away from the successful audition process. You want to be well trained, prepared, energetic, easy to work with, respectful, reliable, committed, confident, and able to take directions and make adjustments.

Tips for a Prepared Audition
~ Read the play/s from which the monologue(s) is selected.
~ Study the play, playwright, historical eras, and any other information about productions.
~ Think of the audition process as working toward an objective: you want to convince your friend, the casting director, to accept you as a reliable co-worker, based on your prepared work.
~ Rehearse, rehearse, and rehearse more.
~ Record your rehearsals.
~ Make adjustments.
~ Rehearse your entrance.

- ~ Breathe.
- ~ Make the room your own.
- ~ Make eye contact with the auditors.
- ~ Slate yourself, your monologue, and your character.
- ~ Transition into your monologue with a character stance.
- ~ React to the unheard line that stimulates your monologue.
- ~ Play the emotions truthfully.
- ~ Use physical, vocal, and emotional variety.
- ~ Build your monologue to a climax.
- ~ Establish your final tag line emotion.
- ~ Hold the tag look for a moment.
- ~ Take a beat.
- ~ Relax.
- ~ Smile.
- ~ Approach the auditors to say "Thank you."
- ~ Make a positive exit.

Musical Theatre Auditions

Be sure to read the audition notice to see what the musical is; whether the casting director wants a song from the musical for which you are auditioning; if contrasting songs are required; if there will be an accompanist who will use your sheet music at the audition, or if you have to bring your own audio equipment; if there is a dance and acting audition in addition to the vocal audition.

Tips for a Musical Theatre Audition

- ~ Have at least two prepared songs ready to sing.
- ~ Have sixteen bars of an up-tempo or fast song prepared.
- ~ Have sixteen bars of a ballad or slow song ready to sing.
- ~ Have the entire pieces of your two chosen sixteen-bar songs ready to sing, if the auditors ask you to perform them.
- ~ Analyze the characters in the songs.
- ~ Rehearse the songs with physical, vocal, and emotional variety.
- ~ Bring your sheet music or a recording with orchestration only on the recording.
- ~ Walk confidently into the room and hand your picture and resumé to the members of the auditioning panel, when your name is called.
- ~ Smile and introduce your audition.

~ Walk to the pianist, and hand him/her your sheet music. Make sure the music is marked clearly to indicate the sixteen bars that you will sing.

~ Make sure to show your sheet music to the accompanist and to show him/her where you will begin and end the number. You will sing the number in the same key as on your sheet music.

~ Step to the center of the audition space, announce your selection, and sing.

~ Do not look directly into the eyes of the panel. Pick a point directly above the heads of the panelists, and play the song or scene to it.

~ Smile at the end.

~ Wait to be excused.

~ Thank the auditors on the way out.

The Perfect Audition Monologues

There are many monologues from which you can choose for an audition monologue. In picking the perfect audition monologues, you may have some questions. Should you: perform a Shakespeare monologue or no Shakespeare; have one, two, four or how many monologues; perform a monologue with dialects or no dialects; do two minutes of performance or less than two minutes; sit or not sit; include a musical Theatre song or not sing at all; dress like the character, or professional attire; begin with a comedy or end with a comedy; begin with classical humorous and classical serious or contemporary humorous and contemporary serious; pick a monologue from the play for which you are auditioning or no monologue from the play; do a monologue from a monologue book, internet, movies, poetry, or other sources or monologue edited from a published play; pick a monologue from a familiar play or new play; do only characters in my age range or do extreme ages; pick anything with controversial subject matter and language or not?

Choosing the perfect monologue(s) for your prepared audition involves reading the requirements of the audition to see what is asked for. Those printed requirements will answer many of your questions. Otherwise the guidelines below are good for a prepared audition.

~ Most auditors encourage you to do something other than perform a Shakespearean monologue, unless you are auditioning for a Shakespearean play.

- Have a minimum of two rehearsed and memorized monologues that show variety of genres and characters.
- Have at least two more ready in case the director asks if you have anything else. You should have four prepared monologues ready for any audition. One speech is a two-minute contemporary, humorous monologue, and one is contemporary, serious monologue. You should also have one classical, humorous monologue and one classical, serious monologue. By reading the list of plays included in an earlier chapter, you have a wealth of well-written scripts with complex characters from which to choose monologues.
- Do not do dialects unless you are performing a monologue in which you can use your natural dialect.
- Have two minutes maximum for each monologue, including the slate, emotional changes, and staging.
- Do not sit while presenting the slate, the monologue's beginning and end, unless the character requires that you are chair bound.
- Only include a musical Theatre song if you have rehearsed the song.
- Dress in professional attire. Do not dress like a character.
- Make sure all selections are equal in strength.
- Perform your comedy first if you are auditioning for a comedy, and your serious monologue first if you are auditioning for a serious role.
- Decide which monologues are the strongest and show the most variety: classical humorous and classical serious or contemporary humorous and contemporary serious. If you are auditioning for a classical humorous play, you want to perform your classical humorous monologue. When working on a classical monologue, study the era. Look back at the list of plays in the Prologue. Choose some of the listed plays to read for good monologues.
- Choose a monologue from a play. Unless you are instructed to, you need not audition using a monologue taken from the play for which you are auditioning. You can find anthologies of monologues edited from play scripts. You might find monologues from other plays by the playwright of the play for which you are auditioning.
- Find plays that have a character with enough lines to edit a monologue. Do not use monologue books or other non-play sources.
- Find familiar plays but not overused monologues. New plays are great if the monologue is well written.

- ~ Choose monologues that are age appropriate and within your age capabilities.
- ~ Stay away from subject matter that is controversial and avoid controversial language.

Royalties

As you learned in the Prologue of this book, royalties are the monies paid to the playwright for permission to perform his/her play. Payment of a royalty fee and receiving performance rights means that you have permission to use and perform the playwright's property. This includes full-length plays, scenes, and monologues. You should acquire rights before including a playwright's monologue in your auditions.

The playwright is entitled to be paid. Even if you want to perform a published work for a non-paying audience, you need to apply for rights and pay the minimal cost if there is one. Playwrights need to make a living, and royalties are a way that playwrights make their money for the use of their published works. Check with the publishing company to see if you need to pay royalties for your monologue audition. Sometimes publishing companies give permission to perform a monologue for auditions at no cost.

Audition Professionalism

Professionalism is the skill, judgment, and appropriate behavior that is expected from a person who is trained to do a job. If you are a professional in acting, you need to conduct yourself in order to convey your behavior as well trained.

When you think of acting as a business as well as an art and a craft, you will make choices that advance you in the acting profession. You are an actor and the primary manager of your career, so it is to your advantage to be professional to advance your career.

There are some important qualities that identify you as a professional actor: competence, reliability, honesty, integrity, respect, being positive, supporting others, staying on task, and listening carefully. The more you put into practice the ideas above, the better you feel about your contributions to your profession.

You may have heard the advice that says if you show up on time, it means that you are late; if you are late, you are fired.

Show up fifteen minutes early. Know your lines cold. Choose a good, fun physical objective. Bring to rehearsal and to performance those things you will need and leave the rest behind . . . Rehearsal is the time for work. Home is the time for reflection. The stage is the time for action. Compartmentalize and cultivate that habit and you will find your performances incline to take on the tinge of action.

David Mamet, playwright, acting teacher

CREATIVE INQUIRY   DATE:

Think about the quote above. Make some notes about your ideas about what David Mamet is saying.

Unprofessionalism at an Audition

Some of the best ways to develop guidelines for being professional is to see what other actors have done and think of a better choice.

CREATIVE INQUIRY *CI*   DATE:

Think about the following audition mistakes and write down a better choice beneath it.

Be rude to the assistant, director, or any actor at the audition. Be demanding and needy with anyone involved at the audition site.

Show up late and talk loudly or text inside the audition room on your phone. Be in a hurry.

Enter yawning, and sleep while sitting in the audition waiting room.

Wear revealing shorts and/or tops to an audition. Wear dangling jewelry.

Bring your lunch with you to eat in the audition waiting room. Chew gum.

Do warm-up exercises in the audition waiting room.

Write your name messily and misspell acting vocabulary words.

Create workshops and productions to pad your resumé.

Be unprepared, leaving your resumé and headshot elsewhere.

Mispronounce the title of the script and/or playwright's name.

Present an unrehearsed monologue.

Give personal excuses for a poor audition.

Complain loudly if you are made to wait. Leave early if you have to wait.

Talk badly about the other actors who are waiting to audition.

Show irritation if the casting director does not let you finish your monologue.

Yell all of your lines in your monologue.

End the monologue with the word "Scene" and "Thank You" as if they were the final lines of your monologue.

Refuse to follow directions or take adjustments that the director wants you to try.

Be bitter and bad mouth the production, actors, and the director, if you are not cast.

After an Audition

Probably the most difficult part of the audition process is after the audition. You have to wait. You have no control over when, how, or if you will be notified about the casting. Do not expect to receive any message if you are not cast.

Keep yourself stress free after you leave the audition. Be kind to yourself. After each audition compliment yourself. Give yourself an inexpensive, healthy treat.

As you think about your audition, remember the aspects that you felt good about. Think about the parts when you felt less sure. Vow that for the next audition, you will rehearse any points that felt weak.

If there is a call back, consider it a compliment. Wear exactly the same outfit that you wore to the first audition. Sometimes the auditors need to be reminded what you looked like at the first audition.

If you are cast, you deserve congratulations. Your work in the play now begins. If you are not cast, decide if you want to contact the director for two reasons: one to find out how you can improve for your next audition, and/or to volunteer, if appropriate, to take on an understudy role or participate in some other way with the production.

CREATIVE INQUIRY *CI*   DATE:

Think about your next audition. Make a list of positive things you will remember to do in your next audition.

Audiences

Audiences are the people for whom you perform. As actors, you ask spectators to suspend disbelief when the house lights go down, and the curtain goes up, and to believe that what you have created is play's reality. Most audience members want you to do well. If they are polite, listening and responding in proper ways, you, the director, and technical staff members love them. If the audience is not responsive, the company members tend to blame the audience.

The lack of responsiveness could be for any one of several reasons: the time of the performance, the date, the weather, the temperature in the auditorium, the poor timing of the technical cues or an off performance by the ensemble. Sometimes the mood of an individual audience member can affect the atmosphere.

Performances are usually scheduled for the weekends. The general perception of Friday audiences is: they are wide awake, having finished their work and feeling buoyant at the prospect of the weekend. On Saturday, the reality of the weekend has sunk in, and the people have spent time shopping or working at home, and sometimes are tired. Sunday matinees and evening productions often find the audience thinking about going back to work.

If the audience is unresponsive, the actors need to challenge themselves to bring the viewers along for the journey. If the audience is rude or does not know Theatre etiquette, the actors need to find new energy to take the focus from anyone being rude.

You should remember that each audience might contain at least one member who has never seen a play before. Your performance will entice him or her to see another play, or not.

What the audience is not, is the director. So when audience members give critiques to you after the show, perhaps your best response is to say that you will discuss their evaluations with the director. You can say "Thank you for your thoughts. I am glad you were able to attend the production."

Your objective is to have the audience understand each word and action, to hear each word, and to understand the character's journey and the story of the play. If you engage, educate, and entertain, you have done your job.

Being an Appreciative Audience Member

There is a professional obligation that should be part of any actor's toolkit: that of being a good audience member. It is beneficial to any actor to be an exemplary audience member. As an actor you prefer audience members who are attentive and appreciative. Being an appreciative audience member for other actors is a good way to show your professionalism.

An important part of being an actor is viewing live Theatre. Attending elementary school plays, community Theatre, educational or school productions, and professional performances brings depth to your play knowledge and appreciation of the talents it takes to achieve an excellent production. Being an appreciative audience member gives other actors the attention they deserve. Being quiet and listening are important; laughing at appropriate moments, and applauding at the end of musical numbers, a scene, an act, the final line, and at the curtain call lets the actors know that you are an appreciative audience member.

Appreciating other artists requires Theatre etiquette. The opening song from the musical *The Frogs* is entitled "Invocation and Instructions to the Audience." The song details what to do and what not to do while viewing a play.

...some do's and don'ts. Mostly don'ts.
Please don't cough,
It tends to throw the actors off.
Have some respect for Aristophanes
And please,

Don't cough.
Don't say "What?"
To every line you think you haven't got.
And if you're in a snit
Because you've missed the plot
(Of which I must admit
There's not an awful lot).
Still, don't
Say–
What?
If you see flaws, please,
Don't drop your jaws, please
No loud guffaws, please,
When actors enter late.
Where there's a pause, please.
Lots of applause, please.
And we'd appreciate
You turning off your cell phones while we wait . . .
(A cell phone rings.)
Unbelievable.
Unbelievable.
I think it's you.
(answering)
Hello? This really isn't a good time.
I said, this really isn't—can you hear me now? Can you hear me now??

Don't go "oh,"
Each time you see an actor that you know.
And if you have to use the lounge below,
Don't wait until we're halfway through the show,
Especially if you're sitting in the middle of a row.
No smokes, no chow—
Unwrap the candy wrappers now.
When we are waxing humorous,
Please don't wane.
The jokes are obscure, but numerous—
We'll explain.
When we are waxing serious,
Try not to laugh.
It starts when we get imperious,

And if you're in doubt, don't query us,
We'll signal you when we're serious—
It's in the second half.
Do not intrude, please,
When someone's nude, please.
She's there for mood, please,
And mustn't be embraced.
. . . When everything's up-ended,
We can all depart.
And now. . .
But first—
We start.

As an actor it will serve you well to become an appreciative, well-mannered, Theatre audience member. You are helping the actors do their jobs. The actors have an unwritten contract with the audience. The performers will do their best to be heard, understood and convey believable moment-to-moment work; the audience is to listen without distractions, and be appreciative.

The actors should care for the audience and treat them with respect; the audience should care for the actors and treat them and other audience members with respect. The audience can hear the actors. The actors can hear the audience.

When the lights dim, it is the time to willingly suspend disbelief and enter into the world of the playwright's creation. It is the quality of the performance, matched by the quality of audience attention that creates excellent Theatre.

Being an Unappreciative Audience Member

In the Theater,

~ Eat.
~ Unwrap candy.
~ Take pictures with or without flash or video record.
~ Cough.
~ Applaud at inappropriate moments.
~ Sing along with the vocalists.
~ Hoot and holler, particularly during kissing scenes.
~ Use a cell phone (There is a story of a well-known actor performing Shakespeare when a cell phone rang from the first row. This actor without losing a beat, took the phone away from the audience member and said, "She's busy watching me in a play and will not take your call.").
~ Text.
~ Bring a child to an adult play.
~ Put your feet on the backs of seats.
~ Chew gum.
~ Get up in the middle of the play to use the restroom.
~ Wear overwhelming perfume or cologne.
~ Talk during the play including the overture.
~ Keep your headphones in your ears.
~ Lean your heads together with your loved one.
~ Arrive late so you have to disrupt people and actors.
~ Sleep during the performance.
~ Snore or mumble.

There may be at least one person in the audience who has never seen a play. It is up to you, the actor who is in the audience, to exhibit exemplary audience behavior.

Closure for Chapter Eight: Auditions

ASSIGNMENT Closure   DATE:

Re-read the information presented in this chapter. Create a telegram similar to the telegram that you have created when working on monologues. Think of five words about each topic that represent the essence of the topic. Write those five key words on the line below the topic.

Introductions to Auditions

1.

2.

3.

4.

5.

Definition of an Audition

1.

2.

3.

4.

5.

Positive Attitude about the Audition Process

1.

2.

3.

4.

5.

Tips to Build your Positive Attitude about the Audition Process

1.

2.

3.

4.

5.

Before you go to Auditions

1.

2.

3.

4.

5.

Preparing your Resumés

1.

2.

3.

4.

5.

 Example of a Resumé

1.

2.

3.

4.

5.

Headshots

1.

2.

3.

4.

5.

Guidelines for Auditions

1.

2.

3.

4.

5.

Tips for a Cattle Call

1.

2.

3.

4.

5.

Tips for an Interview Audition

1.

2.

3.

4.

5.

Tips for an Improvised Audition

1.

2.

3.

4.

5.

Tips for a Cold Reading

1.

2.

3.

4.

5.

Tips for a Prepared Audition

1.

2.

3.

4.

5.

Tips for a Musical Theatre Audition

1.

2.

3.

4.

5.

The Perfect Audition Monologues

1.

2.

3.

4.

5.

Royalties

1.

2.

3.

4.

5.

Audition Professionalism

1.

2.

3.

4.

5.

Guidelines for Unprofessionalism at an Audition

1.

2.

3.

4.

5.

After an Audition

1.

2.

3.

4.

5.

Audiences

1.

2.

3.

4.

5.

Being an Appreciative Audience Member

1.

 2.

3.

4.

5.

Being an Unappreciative Audience Member

1.

2.

3.

4.

5.

You have information to help you succeed in auditions. You are nearing the end of *The Student Actor Prepares: Acting for Life*, so the final chapter is an epilogue or afterword that contains advice for your future.

The final chapter is the completion of my letter which began in the Preface and continued through all eight chapters.

EPILOGUE: AFTERWORD

Introduction to the Epilogue

An epilogue or epilog is a piece of writing at the end of a book or play, which brings closure to the work. If the author speaks directly to the audience, the epilogue is considered an afterword. The epilogue in a play is the final scene of the play that comments and/or summarizes the events. It provides an overview of key advice. Final bits of guidance are disseminated so that you can apply the lessons to your next steps in your future in acting and in life.

Think of yourself sitting with me having a cup of coffee or lemonade and talking for hours about your future. This is Grand drama mama Gai, a sage of Theatre education, sharing vital tips. This epilogue is my sharing of a wealth of experiences.

Thus we begin. I will be direct with advice.

Advice for your Future

Leave the Drama Onstage
Be dramatic onstage. Use theatricality onstage, not offstage. Need I say more?

Values
Stay true to your values.

If someone is asking you to do anything that feels uncomfortable, walk away. Protect your values in all of your work. Your principles are important throughout all of your life's journeys, no matter what your age. Do not do something that you think feels wrong.

Theatre attracts many unique, free-thinking talented people who are diverse, and sometimes appear outrageous. The artistic young person today may be the next well-known director of tomorrow. So working with visionaries can offer you a unique learning opportunity, a chance to expand both your skills and your understanding of Theatre. Embrace their creativity.

You can tell the difference between someone asking you to take a risk artistically and someone asking you to do something that would require you to give up your values. Compromising your values is the time for you to say "No."

Imagination, industry, and intelligence—"the three I's"—are all indispensable to the actress (actor).

Ellen Terry, actor

Use your intelligence along with your intuition to evaluate any situation that seems wrong. Walk away. It is the other person's loss.

Fame
Work for success, rather than fame.

Fame is a vapor, popularity an accident, and riches take wings. Only one thing endures and that is character.

Horace Greeley, American Newspaper Editor, 1850s

Achieving fame in Theatre sometimes depends on luck—being in the right place at the right time. Fame is defined as widespread reputation, especially of a favorable character. It is only the few who achieve fame in acting. Work for success instead of fame. Be the best actor you can be.

The talent of success is nothing more than doing what you can do well, and doing well whatever you do without thought of fame. If it comes at all, it will come because it is deserved, not because it is sought after.

Henry Wadsworth Longfellow, American Poet

Scams
Beware of scams.

There are many opportunists who are eager to take advantage of you as an aspiring actor. These scammers prey on the inexperienced, and their only goal is to make money without giving you anything in return. The following is a list of guidelines that will help keep you from becoming a victim.

~   Never pay anything up front for management or agent representation.
~   Be wary of any person or company who wants you to take classes with them for which you have to pay, or to pay for head shots from an unreliable photographer.
~   Check out references. Ask around for experienced workshop teachers.
~   Be careful of any company who says they can relocate you and thereby get you in front of any agents. Companies that claim to connect New York to LA actors, promising an agent each day of your stay often charge high fees and offer you readings with less than reputable agents. If it feels like a scam, it may be.
~   Never pay to audition, no matter what you read or are told. Paying to audition is usually a scam.
~   Do not pay for a workshop until you have audited the workshop, and consulted with those you respect in the acting business.

The Next Steps
Strive for excellence.

You are ready to think about your future in the study of acting. In the process of working with this book: You have reflected. . . You have created. . . You have observed. . . You have imagined . . . You have recalled. . . You have described. . . You have documented . . . You have organized . . . You have communicated . . . You have applied. . . You have examined . . . You have concluded. . . You have analyzed. . . You have brainstormed. . . You have thought outside the box. . . You have assessed . . . You have evaluated.

As you progress through your future in acting, strive for excellence.

If you are a student in middle school or high school, take a Theatre class, if it is offered. In many middle schools and high schools, today educational Theatre is included in the Visual and Performing Arts Departments, as a part of the core curriculum. Visual and Performing Arts has a framework and standards. The study also has assessment principles. The Twenty-first Century Life Skills Map is integrated into the Theatre study.

Excel in the study of acting. Become a part of the International Thespian Society, an honor society for students, which recognizes excellence in Theatre Arts.

If your middle school or high school does not offer Theatre classes or Thespian Society, study at good community Theatres, nearby college or universities, or private acting coaches.

If you are in college, study acting. Seek out the best acting training, working hard and learning from professors.

Live a balanced life—learn some and think some and draw and paint and sing and dance and play and work every day some.
Robert Fulgham, American author, primarily of short essays

Balance

Balance your work and occupation.

Sometimes actors become very involved in the acting world and forget life outside the Theatre. You will need to balance your acting and your work, whether your work is student or some other occupation. You need to maintain your family life, your unstructured time, and your goal of staying fit and healthy. Take inventory of your physical being. Are you exercising, eating healthily, and having energy?

Take care of your intellectual assets. Do you maintain a sense of humor, exercise your creativity, and challenge yourself at school and with life-long learning? Care for your spiritual side. Do you maintain a firm belief system, silent times, strong values? Pay attention to your emotional wealth. Are you self-confident, express feelings in a responsible way, comfortable with yourself? Maintain your social life. Do you value friends, family, play time, getting along with others? Take caution with your lifestyle. Do you have hobbies, good habits, relaxation opportunities?

Acting Goals Reassessment

First, have a definite, clear practical idea; a goal, an objective. Second, have the necessary means to achieve your ends.
Aristotle, Greek philosopher

Imagine that you are explaining to me what you acting goals are from this day on. List three goals.

1.

2.

3.

Periodically throughout the rest of your life, edit your goals, adding and subtracting ideas.

ABCD of Goal Setting
Life is to be taken one step at a time, progressing through studies, moving toward an occupation and evaluating your life's choices. Achievable, believable, concrete, and desirable are the classifications for identifying your goals.

Think of an *achievable personal* goal. This means you can reach this goal, you are certain you can achieve it. Examples, I want to work on my relations with person x. I will exercise more often.

Beginning with short-term goals helps you focus on reachable goals that can be accomplished in the near future. Then you can celebrate your realized goals and strive to reach long term goals.

Think of the first letter of each word: A, B, C, D: Achievable, Believable, Concrete, and Desirable

~~~~~~

CREATIVE INQUIRY **CI**   DATE:

~~~~~~

Think about the questions below and answer them carefully. It is advisable for you as an actor to establish a short-term acting goal. What do you want to accomplish in acting in the very near future? You may make it as short term as this week.

Write one *achievable* short-term personal goal.

What is your deadline for your *achievable* short-term personal goal?

Write a short-term personal *believable* goal. This can be defined as a goal that you believe is achievable.

How convinced are you that this short-term personal goal is *believable*?

Write a short-term personal *concrete* goal. This means you will see a noticeable result or outcome if your goal is achieved.

What will be the *concrete* result if your short-term personal concrete goal is achieved?

Write a short-term personal *desirable* goal. A short-term, *desirable* goal indicates that you wish for the result to happen. If it occurs, it will prove beneficial.

How *desirable* is this short-term personal goal?

It is worth developing a long-term acting goal too. What do you want to accomplish in acting in approximately ten years? What do you want to be doing? What is your eventual objective?

You know yourself. You have goals. You are ready to work on advocacy.

Advocacy

Be an advocate in life.

Advocating means to speak or write in favor of; to recommend publicly. You need to be an advocate, sharing what skills you have acquired with everyone you know. You can use your talents to "lobby" for worthy causes. You know how to organize and prepare presentations for audience approval. Whether advocating for legislative action to support the arts, raising awareness for your school's Theatre department, or helping humanitarian causes, you can achieve success using your acting talents. Much of acting is about communicating, performing, presenting, responding, and connecting. You know how to analyze, evaluate, and refine your work to achieve a goal. You adapt your work in response to audiences, and you use established ideas and create new ones to pursue an objective. Being an advocate for a worthy cause and allows you to use your acting skills.

Actor's Advocacy Tool Kit

The definition of advocacy is the act of pleading for, supporting, or recommending; active espousal. As you achieve success in feeling good about who you are, you are ready to develop your advocacy tool kit. The tool kit contains all of the positive things about you, which you can access quickly to share with others. Include your resources, updates on the facts about the acting profession, and a short statement outlining the mission and goals of your chosen profession or avocation.

An important focus of your advocacy tool kit includes knowing your audience. Each audience has different expectations of you and your plan. You will speak differently with changed language to your peers than you do to your family, adults, older people, or younger people. Identify your audience. Adapt accordingly when presenting to: parents, the business community, administrators, school boards, legislators.

Be prepared to talk about the positive things that you get out of acting study. Be prepared to put forth a wide range of beliefs that support the value of your choice. Explain your thoughts rationally. Keep your emotions under control. Make your statements clear, concise, and objective. Do not badger or get defensive. Talk eloquently without tears but really mean it.

You may or may not talk someone into supporting you, but you hopefully will feel integrated and passionate about your efforts. Convince your audience that you will continually evaluate your choices, make changes, and keep loved ones informed about your choices.

As an actor you are a business owner; the business is you. You are your own advocate, manager, and business partner. You need to understand contracts and percentages that agents and managers are eligible to receive and when. You need to know that no one can require you to pay for headshots or pay for classes before representing you. It is essential to develop standards and communicate what you will and will not do to get a role. Sacrificing your standards for so-called instant fame is not who you are. Anyone with less than honorable intentions deserves to lose the opportunity to work with you. There will be others who are above reproach who will cast you. Keep the integrity of yourself in the business.

ASSIGNMENT Actor's Advocacy Took Kit   DATE:

Imagine that an older person whom you respect expresses concern about your study of acting and your future acting occupation. What is your label line to explain your mission and passion in a controlled, logical disciplined way?

CREATIVE INQUIRY   DATE:

Think about what your opening lines to that older person might be. Explain your mission and passion about the study of acting and your future acting occupation.

Advocacy Elevator Speech

Maximizing your unique qualities and abilities will help you promote yourself. Your elevator speech is a short speech that you can deliver succinctly between floors one and five, or five and one during an elevator ride.

My own elevator speech to legislators is, "I am a professional Theatre educator. I believe in sequential standards-based Theatre education taught by credentialed Theatre teachers. I support awards for Theatre educators and students. Theatre is sometimes the reason students attend school. The study of Theatre Arts helps with the twenty-first century skills of collaboration, communication, and creative and critical thinking. I hope you will support Theatre arts initiatives in our schools."

CREATIVE INQUIRY   DATE:

Think about some of the major ideas that you want to include in your elevator statement. Make some notes below.

You may have read bumper stickers that espouse beliefs and mission statements. Here is your chance for you to develop a bumper sticker. It is a challenge to condense your principles to a succinct, short phrase with a limited number of words.

ASSIGNMENT Bumper sticker   DATE:

Design a bumper sticker that encapsulates your acting mission statement into ten words or less.

Brainstorm with some ideas below.

Print your final bumper sticker below.

Ensemble Acting Member

Be an exemplary ensemble member.

In your work as an emerging actor, you are developing practices that can be an asset to you when you become a member of an ensemble of actors. When you rehearse individually, you are able to experiment with practices that you find work or don't work for you. Once you have refined some confident habits, you will feel comfortable moving into any ensemble with a high level of expectations for yourself and others. Communicating your ideals to your ensemble members tells them how you prefer to proceed in the collaborative process.

> *As you navigate through the rest of your life, be open to collaboration. Other people and other people's ideas are often better than your own. Find a group of people who challenge and inspire you, spend a lot of time with them, and it will change your life.*
>
> Amy Poehler, actor

One of the objectives of working in an ensemble is to create an atmosphere where your partner and you feel good about the collaboration. You want to be an actor with whom other actors and directors look forward to working.

You are an imaginative, emerging solo actor. Most of the work in this book presents experiences for the individual student actor. When you begin to work with scene partners and directors, it is important to be a positive member of the Theatre ensemble. Enter into the collaborative work with your affirmative attitude. Be a creative, confident co-worker in your acting craft. Listen to your fellow actors and director. Watch and observe. Network, network, network. The person you work with today may be able to hire you in the future, no matter what job they hold today.

Compliment other actors. Say thank you at the end of each workshop. Make up awards for fellow actors.

> *Be nice to people on your way up because you meet them on your way down.*
>
> Jimmy Durante, singer, pianist, comedian, actor

Here is a list of guidelines to help you achieve that goal of being the best ensemble acting member.

- Set an example of arriving early and being prepared.
- Support your partner to build an ensemble.
- Respect each other.
- If you have a director, let the director direct. Do not direct each other, unless you are requested to do so.
- Laugh with each member of the ensemble.
- Set goals for each rehearsal.
- Decide on rehearsal schedules and stick to them.
- Demand, in a professional way, quality work from yourself and your scene partner(s).
- Create a safe environment in which to take risks.
- Be willing to discuss your characters. Really listen to your partner(s).
- Discover new things about your scene together.
- Memorize your lines early.
- Be patient with each other when working on memorization.
- Make your partner(s) feel good.
- Thank each ensemble member at the end of each rehearsal.

> *The one great thing about a continuing collaboration is that they know you. And if you're really lucky, they really believe in you and think that your talent has some unending bounds to it.*
>
> Mark Ruffalo, actor

Continuing your Acting Study

Be a student of acting all of your life.

Enroll in an acting course and/or voice and dance lessons. Even the most seasoned professionals keep studying their craft. The performer's body is an instrument, and the more finely tuned it is kept, the better able it is to play roles. When choosing an acting or singing course, make sure the teacher is a trained professional with a background in Theatre or music. You are never too old to learn a new acting skill. Take a tap dance class; take vocal music lessons. Study a new acting trend.

College/University/Conservatory/Degrees

Plan carefully about attending an institution of higher learning. When you are ready to think about attending an institution of higher learning for an undergraduate or graduate degree, there are things to consider. It is advisable to talk with those who will support you financially while you attend a post-secondary institution.

The following is a list of questions you must explore while choosing the schools to which you will apply.

- In what environment, do you want to live? Urban? Rural? Dormitory? Off-campus?
- Have you studied college guides for Theatre colleges and universities?
- What is the history of the school?
- Who are the graduates of the college/university, and where are they working in the profession?
- Do you know if the college or university has regional auditions near your home?
- Can you audition at state and national festivals?
- Does the college/university allow its undergraduates to perform?
- Does the college/university offer an AA, BA, BFA, MA, and/or MFA?
- What course titles are included in their curriculum?
- What previous grades do you need for admission?
- What are your chances of getting into the school?
- Does the school offer career preparation for after you graduate?
- What type of audition do you need?
- How much weight is put on the audition?
- What acting technique does the school endorse?
- Do they have opportunities for study abroad?

- ~ Can you visit and sit in classes while in session?
- ~ What is the title of the acting degree you will receive if you finish the acting program?
- ~ Does the Theatre Department provide showcases for their students so that professional agents can view them?
- ~ What is the cost of tuition?
- ~ Have you completed all financial aid applications?
- ~ Have you contacted local civic and business organizations to see if they offer scholarships for which you can apply?
- ~ Are there scholarships available through the institutions Financial Aid Office?
- ~ What amount and type of financial aid is available from all sources put together?
- ~ Will you be allowed to work in the Theatre Department and audition if you are not a Theatre major?
- ~ Will you be allowed to work in Theatre and audition outside of school while attending?

Apply to a minimum total of eight community colleges, colleges, universities, and/or post-high-school conservatories. One of these should be an institution for which you would need no financial aid to attend; another of these should be your ideal school, the one for which you might need a full financial ride to attend. Others would fall between these two financial extremes. You should apply to a wide range of colleges and universities, including your dream college.

Be aware that some non-public institutions set their own criteria for giving financial aid; however, a large dollar amount may still leave you a large sum to pay because a non-public institution gets no tax monies, so must charge you for more of its costs. Also do not make the mistake of thinking that if an institution charges more it must be a better place.

If the financial aid that is offered, plus your own financial resources if any, is not sufficient, you may contact an institution's Financial Aid Office and respectfully try to negotiate more. If you try to envision paying for the entire several years of study, that can be daunting; perhaps if you can pay somehow for the first year or first semester, more financial aid will come through. If you obtain financial aid, but find that you must put off entering, ask the college's Financial Aid Offices if they will hold that financial aid for you until you can begin. This is sometimes possible, as post-secondary institutions like to attract older students. Once enrolled be sure to complete any needed financial aid forms each year.

Do you want a liberal arts degree? Many knowledgeable people advise that you begin at a two-year community college or a small liberal arts college for an undergraduate degree. You will take part in a variety of opportunities and study a widespread, exploratory view of what college offers, and then you can specialize in Theatre for a Bachelor of Arts (BA) or a Bachelor of Fine Arts (BFA). After that, but not necessarily immediately after that, you may want to decide it is to your advantage to earn an additional degree called a graduate-school degree, such as a Master's degree.

Do you want a conservatory degree? Look at the school's alumnae to see what they doing in Theatre or film. Visit the campus; ask to sit in on a class. Study what credentials the faculty have. Ask what performance and showcase opportunities the conservatory offers for underclasspersons.

There are many factors to consider when you are choosing a college, university, or conservatory.

Majoring in Theatre as an undergraduate with an Emphasis in Acting
Think carefully before you decide to major in Theatre with an emphasis in acting.

The Theatre degree often appears on the Worst-Paying College Degrees List. It is said to have the lowest paying starting salary along with Fine Arts, Hospitality and Tourism, Education, Horticulture, Music, Theology, and Social Work. So why would you major in Theatre in college? You study Theatre not to become rich; you study Theatre, because you love the Theatre.

> *You need to be aware of the many skills you learn as a Theatre major. Really. You're a better candidate for employment than perhaps you know.*
>
> Louis E. Catron, playwright, professor

Majoring in college in Theatre will give you skills to become a professional actor. Majoring in Theatre in college will also benefit you in numerous occupations. Skills that are developed by majoring in Theatre include:

- ~ Organization.
- ~ Discipline.
- ~ Dependability.
- ~ Loyalty.
- ~ Leadership.
- ~ Workability.
- ~ Energy.
- ~ Enthusiasm.
- ~ Ability to work under pressure.
- ~ "Can-do confidence."
- ~ Hands-on experience.
- ~ Learn-by-doing.
- ~ Communication skills.
- ~ Imagination.
- ~ Reasoning.
- ~ Sound judgment.
- ~ Motivation.
- ~ Commitment.
- ~ Cooperation.
- ~ Independent working ability.
- ~ Time management.
- ~ Initiative.
- ~ Respect for deadlines, structure, authority.
- ~ Adaptability.
- ~ Flexibility.
- ~ Work under pressure.
- ~ Ability to take rejection.
- ~ Goal-orientation.
- ~ Concentration.
- ~ Dedication.
- ~ Responsibility.
- ~ Improvisation skills.
- ~ Ability to work within a limited budget.
- ~ Stick-to-it qualities.
- ~ Listening ability.
- ~ Empathy.
- ~ Problem-solving skills.
- ~ Capability to communicate emotions.
- ~ Management abilities.
- ~ Collaborative expertise.

- ~ Composure.
- ~ Honor and respect for diverse views.
- ~ Memorization expertise.
- ~ Language skills.
- ~ Creativity.
- ~ Innovation.
- ~ Capacity to assess and improve.

Let them (employers) know that a theater major has had far more excellent experience than any other major could have accumulated.

Louis Catron, playwright, professor

Careers

Dream about your future career. Make plans for achieving your future career. Assess your career goals. Be open to where your future career may lead you.

Only dreams keep us going. . . When you are acting, don't settle for anything less than the biggest dream for your. . . future.

Michael Shurtleff, acting teacher

Broadway or Other Performance Possibilities

You may want to star on Broadway. To appear in a production in New York City's Broadway area is the epitome of success for many actors. This goal is an exciting aspiration for which you can choose to aim. Sometimes saying that you want to star in a Broadway show indicates that you would be happy to achieve professional work in quality locations.

Making career choices that help you advance toward the Broadway goal starts with the study of what it takes to get to Broadway. Being a triple threat with acting, singing, and dancing skills is the first step toward achieving professional musical Theatre work. Attending a college, university, or conservatory, that offers showcases with Broadway casting directors is essential. Moving to New York or other Theatre cities and taking temporary jobs that leave your days open for auditions is another step. Continue to network with other actors. Sometimes doing acting jobs with young companies for free will provide networking opportunities. Each planned step moves you closer to your Broadway goal.

Another way to succeed in professional Theatre is to think about opportunities outside of New York City. There are many regional Theatres around the United States and other countries with which you can sign on as an apprentice and study with company directors and teachers. Many times, making a living doing Theatre is possible living in various regional Theatre areas.

What a young actor needs is to play a number of various parts in quickest possible succession, under experienced direction with an experienced company and before the public.

Anonymous

Theatre Educator

Think about being a professional Theatre educator. One of the best professions is that of Theatre educator.

Theatre teachers:

~ Make lifelong impressions on their students.
~ Experience joy when their students succeed.
~ Have passion for their work.
~ Care about their students.
~ Challenge themselves and their students.
~ Are lifelong learners.
~ Are unique.
~ Love working with unique, creative students.
~ Are willing to say, "I don't know; let's work on it together."
~ Teach life skills, by stimulating creative thinking and problem solving.
~ Are mentors; sometimes they are thought of as a "Drama Mama" or "Drama Dad."
~ Help their students grow and develop into well-adjusted, productive adults.
~ Incorporate many other school subjects: science, math, history, physical education, language arts, business, technology, psychology, economics, and art.

Remember that not all actors can be excellent Theatre teachers. Teaching Theatre is a unique art form that takes study and experience in order to educate students. Do not assume that if you have a Theatre degree, that you will be allowed to teach Theatre in a public school.

Teaching might even be the greatest of the arts since the medium is the human mind and spirit.

John Steinbeck, author

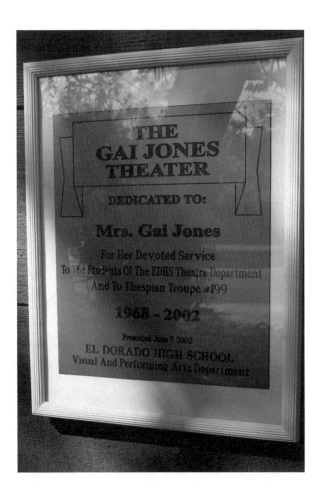

Other Careers in which Acting is a Valued Skill

Be open to careers in which you can use your acting talents and skills.

There are additional careers in which you can use acting skills. The following list includes careers in the arts and occupations in which actors might be employed. The jobs are listed in alphabetical order.

~ **Actor**—Theme parks, television, radio, movies.
~ **Arts administrator**—Community arts councils, schools, studios, galleries, businesses, museums.
~ **Camp owner**—Theatre after-school programs, summer camps.
~ **Casting director**—Person who views auditions and helps in the selection.
~ **Children's Theatre performer**—An actor who specializes in entertaining children.
~ **Community arts activist**—A person who helps professional artists work with people who do not normally engage in the arts.
~ **Company manager**—A person whose job is to manage the people who will do the work.
~ **Consultant**—A person who gives professional or expert advice.
~ **Critic**—Judge, newspaper television, internet critic.
~ **Director**—Community Theatre, theme parks, education, professional Theatre.
~ **Drama therapist**—A person who is skilled in using dramatic arts and psychotherapy to help clients.
~ **Dramaturge**—Researcher who studies the play from a social, political, cultural, and historical perspective and works with actors, directors and technical designers.
~ **Events planner**—A coordinator who works with aspects of an event or meeting.
~ **Government services**—Legislative aides, legislator, arts council members, cultural arts commissioner.
~ **Life coach**—A person who helps with goal setting, positive thinking, relationships, career choices.
~ **Parks and recreation director**—Director of neighborhood or city programs.
~ **Producer**—Organizer for plays, television, movies, events.
~ **Psychodrama therapist**—A person who works with clients using role playing and dramatic techniques to gain insight into problems.
~ **Teacher**—Theatre, English, and History teachers for all levels of education.

- ~ **Technical Theatre Professional**—Designer, builder and/or operator of all of the Theatre aspects of a production.
- ~ **Television**—Staff for production, production and location management, camera, lighting, grip, sound, make-up and hair, wardrobe, set construction, dressing, special effects, props.
- ~ **Theatre supply business**—Provider of the tangible technical items for a production.
- ~ **Voice actor**—A person who performs, using the voice only, in a variety of media.
- ~ **Voice coach**—A professional who works with someone who wants to improve their voice.
- ~ **Writer**—A person who writes for plays, television, movies, and webisodes.

Understudying a Role

Consider taking an understudy role.

Understudying is a paid job in equity productions. You learn from the actor for whom you are the understudy. Do not compete. Work collaboratively. Ask if the understudy will be able to perform. Be professional, be memorized, and be ready to go. If networking with the actors, director, and techincal staff and what you might learn by understudying the role will advance your acting study and career, consider the understudy role.

Volunteer

Share your acting knowledge with youth and senior citizens.

Directors

You are the director of your own life.

Lee Childress, Founder of the M.A.C.Y. Awards

Study how to direct plays.

Many times actors become directors. The director is thought of as the all-knowing person behind the curtain. If you can be the constructive guide to actors and technical staff then you possess important qualities to become a director.

To direct a full production requires lengthy study about directing, including academic and practical experience. Nonetheless, limited directing of short scenes can be experienced by high school students and even some advanced middle school students, with guidance.

If you are curious, like to read scripts, relish studying directing theories, love going to all kinds of Theatre, have time to learn how to direct different genres, can be positive no matter how the production looks, can live with uncertainty until the final curtain call and the strike of the set and technical aspects of the play are finished, and you like to work with diverse, artistic, sometimes overly emotional people, then you possess even more of the qualities of a director.

As an excellent director, you must be able to:

- Share the knowledge from your formal training and work experiences.
- Communicate directing theories and techniques.
- Know all aspects of a production.
- Use leadership skills.
- Understand that not all excellent actors are good directors, and not all directors are good actors.
- Direct in a variety of venues.
- Read many plays.
- Talk about different types and genres of plays.
- Discuss new plays.
- Understand and articulate the playwright's vision.
- Realize the genre of the play.
- Create a vision for the play that is based on the playwright's theme.
- Understand the collaboration process.
- Remember how important the process is.
- Enjoy the process.
- Take part in every aspect of the production.
- Be organized, creative, and willing to work long hours.
- Share your vision with all of the technical designers and staff.
- Talk with designers in technical Theatre terms.
- Work well with an assistant director and the stage manager.
- Listen to your actors and the production team.
- Encourage all of your colleagues to take concerns to designated individuals, rather than letting dissatisfactions simmer.
- Trust your intuition.

~ Listen to suggestions. Evaluate each suggestion if it supports your vision.
~ Work with all kinds of talent.
~ Employ positive psychology.
~ Network and know what people's strengths are.
~ Remember all of the people you have met, to be able to contact them when their talents are needed.
~ Work with new playwrights who are developing their scripts.
~ Facilitate quality rehearsals.
~ Observe closely every actor and know how to work with him/her.
~ Audition and select a cast.
~ Tell an actor why he/she did not make the cast.
~ Understand budgets and be able to work within them.
~ Work with low budgets. Do not lose money on a production.
~ Work as an acting coach for each actor in the cast.
~ Show patience while working work with actors who do not understand.
~ Think of a variety of ways to get actors to work as an ensemble.
~ Keep the morale up. Deal with conflicts in a professional, productive way.
~ Be constructive in all comments and notes that you share with colleagues.
~ Keep rehearsal notes short.
~ End rehearsals at a reasonable time.
~ Avoid having some actors doing nothing during a rehearsal.
~ Keep the public performance moving at a proper pace.
~ Keep your personal life separate from your directing life.
~ Grab a broom and sweep when needed; do what is needed to help the play.

The only way to learn how to direct a play is to get a play, get a group of actors who are simple enough to allow you to direct them, and direct.

Tyrone Guthrie, director and teacher

Acronyms for Unions and Associations

Know unions and associations, how to achieve your professional acting status, and what the union and association can do for your profession.

Theatre people love acronyms. Knowing the following initials helps in communicating with others and understanding what the unions and associations can do for your career.

Professional Theatre Unions (cited from Stage Managers' Association)
Join professional unions. They benefit you by providing protection and services for your career.

Actors' Equity Association
AEA was founded in 1913 and is the labor union representing actors and stage managers in the legitimate Theatre in the United States.

American Federation of Television and Radio Artists
AFTRA represents its members in four major areas: 1) news and broadcasting; 2) entertainment programming; 3) the recording business; and 4) commercials and non-broadcast, industrial, educational media. In 2012, SAG and AFTRA became a joint union: SAG/AFTRA.

American Guild of Musical Artists
AGMA is the labor organization that represents the men and women who create America's operatic and dance heritage.

American Guild of Variety Artists
AGVA is a labor union founded in 1939 to represent performing artists and stage managers for live performances in the variety field. The variety area of performance includes singers and dancers in touring shows and in theatrical revues (non-book shows; book revues may be under Actors' Equity jurisdiction), theme park performers, skaters, circus performers, comedians and stand-up comics, cabaret and club artists, lecturers/poets/monologists/spokespersons, and variety performers working at private parties & special events.

Association of Theatrical Press Agents and Managers
ATPAM members are press agents, publicity and marketing specialists, company managers, and house and facilities managers, who are devoted to the health, vitality and success of staged entertainment of all types.

Directors' Guild of America
DGA represents Film and Television Directors, Unit Production Managers, First Assistant Directors, Second Assistant Directors, Technical

Coordinators and Associate Directors, Stage Managers, and Production Associates.

International Alliance of Theatrical and Stage Employees

IATSE is the labor union representing technicians, artisans and crafts persons in the entertainment industry, including live Theatre, film and television production, and trade shows.

Screen Actors Guild

SAG represents and coordinates the activities of the various persons engaged or employed as performers in the motion picture industry. Since 2012, it is part of the AFTRA/SAG union.

Stage Directors and Choreographers Society

SDC is a national independent labor union representing members throughout the United States and abroad.

Associations

Join associations. The networking within formal groups provides you a safe place to share with people who understand your work and passion, no matter what your future occupation. Often, by participating in association work, you will make positive contacts that benefit you in your future.

American Alliance for Theatre and Education (AATE)

The American Alliance for Theatre & Education connects and inspires a growing collective of Theatre artists, educators, and scholars committed to transforming young people and communities through the Theatre arts.

Educational Theatre Association

The Educational Theatre Association (EdTA) is a national nonprofit organization with approximately 90,000 student and professional members. EdTA's mission is shaping lives through Theatre education by: honoring student achievement in Theatre and enriching their Theatre education experience; supporting teachers by providing professional development, networking opportunities, resources, and recognition; and influencing public opinion that Theatre education is essential and builds life skills. EdTA operates the International Thespian Society (ITS), an honorary organization that has inducted more than two million Theatre students since its founding in 1929. EdTA also publishes *Dramatics,* a monthly magazine for high school Theatre students, and *Teaching Theatre*, a quarterly journal for Theatre education professionals.

Association for Theater in Higher Education (ATHE)

Association for Theater in Higher Education (ATHE) is a comprehensive nonprofit professional membership organization. Founded in 1986, ATHE serves the interests of its diverse individual and organizational members, including college and university Theatre departments and administrators, educators, graduate students, and Theatre practitioners. The Association's web site is www.athe.org. Vision: An advocate for the field of Theatre and performance in higher education, ATHE serves as an intellectual and artistic center for producing new knowledge about Theatre and performance-related disciplines, cultivating vital alliances with other scholarly and creative disciplines, linking with professional and community-based Theatres, and promoting access and equity. Mission: To support and advance the study and practice of Theatre and performance in higher education.

American Association of Community Theatre (AACT)

The American Association of Community Theatre provides networking, resources and support to suit the needs of all those involved in community Theatre.

Acting in Later Life

Community Theatre

Involvement in community Theatre is a viable opportunity to experience a variety of roles. Attending the productions that are offered is a way to check out the quality of work the community Theatre provides. Working in intergenerational productions with actors of various ages, and in the education branch of the community Theatre provides chances to experience a range of plays with numerous directors.

Workshops
Develop a workshop.

Take Theatre workshops. If you want to be certain that a particular teacher of a class is well-suited to your needs, ask to audit the workshop. Auditing allows you to watch a workshop in session without paying.

Think of something about which you are an expert and develop your own workshop to teach.

~ What is a skill you have? You can teach how to face the fear
   of public speaking with a title such as "Butterflies to Bravos:
   Overcoming the Fear of Public Presentations."
~ Are you good in improvisation? You can teach an improv workshop
   on "Time to Have Some Fun: Improv for Quick Thinking."
~ Are you a positive person who does well in public speaking?
   You can teach "They Really Like Me! How to Shine in a Public
   Performance: Tapping into Positivity and Creativity for Public
   Performances."
~ Are you organized? You can teach a workshop on "How to Organize
   your Life."
~ Do you have the ability to make people laugh? You can teach a
   workshop on "How to Spread Joy in the World."

CREATIVE INQUIRY **CI** DATE:

Think about five ideas you can use to develop workshops.

1.

2.

3.

4.

5.

Theatre has no categories; it is about life. This is the only starting point, and there is nothing else truly fundamental. Theatre is life.

Peter Brook, Director

Acting for Life: A Story about a Life-long Acting Learner

Gai Jones, Theatre educator, director, actress, author

Recently I have discovered an expanded understanding of arts efforts through instructing older actors, in Sage to Stage, an acting workshop that I created for senior citizens. Students who are fifty-five years and older are workshop participants. With more leisure time, retired and older active people take part in meaningful experiences. Geriatric students find that the arts is a natural place for their expansion into another dimension. I have expanded my life's views by being with these wonderful human beings, some seasoned performers, other newbies to the stage and to the thrill of achieving "the natural high of performing."

By dramatically shaping their stories, I experience life through the eyes of older actors. I have helped format a life story of a retired colonel into an original dramatic monologue about his memory of Pearl Harbor as a seven-year-old and how he heard enemy planes on December 7, 1941. I have vicariously glimpsed an older woman's memory of playing with a girl named Anne in Amsterdam. I have provided an opportunity for a vocalist who last auditioned in England as a boy for a role in *Oliver* and was rejected, and recently played the Bill Sykes role in our community Theatre production. My neighbor, a ninety-one year old retiree, who was a homemaker even as a young child after her mother died, signed up for Sage to Stage. She wrote a monologue recreating her life as a caretaker for her dad, her husband, and her children. She revealed in a workshop session a dream to sing in front of an audience. She worked on the song, "I Am Woman, Hear Me Roar." She performed. She did it. The audience applauded. I as a teacher could not be more proud for her.

A shy, insecure older lady, Miriam (not her real name) took the workshop on her daughter's recommendation. The elderly student's husband had just died after years with Alzheimer's. Miriam apologized to her fellow senior students for her inexperience and her fear of performing. After weeks of our reassuring, she succeeded in making us laugh. The acting assignment was to create a list of "Great Things about Getting Older." Her thoughts included that as a senior, she no longer needed a fake ID to buy beer, that she was not afraid to tempt fate by breaking the chain of luck-bringing letters and emails, and that finally she could throw away pictures of people she does not remember or did not like. We laughed with her. She smiled with the recognition that she had engaged us. She relaxed.

After our workshop sessions ended, our group went to see a professional production of the one-man show *Simon Wiesenthal*. Miriam sat in the first row; she was the recipient of a flower handed to her by the actor onstage. In the Talk Back with the actor, Miriam revealed that she had lost numerous family members in the Holocaust. On the way home Miriam expressed her joy of being able to share in Theatre experiences as a part of our workshop. She glowed about the experience of taking part in Sage to Stage and attending the Theatre with fellow student actors.

The day after our Theatre production attendance, I received a call from her daughter. Miriam returned home that night. She suffered a massive heart attack, which ended her life.

Miriam is evidence that art enhanced her later life's experiences. I as a teacher of Theatre Arts am a provider of the creative experiences. I invest in students who want to enrich their lives even though it may be unknown territory. My vision of the fragility of life and honoring the individual's story is expanded by working with Theatre arts students, particularly the elderly sages of the stage. I feel that I unwrap myself as a gift to people who want an opportunity to celebrate. I feel enriched.

I feel privileged that working with Sage to Stage actors has pushed my teaching beyond the traditional curricular study to a rich field of untapped creativity.

Leading the list of human fears is public speaking. It can be part of a list to take charge of one's present by facing the fear of performing before a public. My gift is to give actors of any age the opportunity to succeed in creating the magic that comes from a presentation. I give them the confidence to develop their acting abilities.

The audience's smile or sound of appreciation sparked by a well-executed line or a bold character choice is the greatest pay-off from my gift for teaching acting.

It is part of my expanded vision to continue to be enthralled and surprised by my students and the power of teaching acting.

My hope for you is that you look at the journey recounted above and see how you can create your own successful Theatre journey.

My Final Words of Advice—Discover Ways to Compliment Others and Say Thank You

Complimenting Others

The custom of applauding at the end of a workshop is recognized by the teacher as a thank you. It is a compliment to the workshop leader. The habit of giving sincere compliments to fellow ensemble members and crew members at the end of each rehearsal can be beneficial to your working relationships. In addition to direct compliments for their work, some of the most valuable compliments to a fellow actor or staff member are that you enjoyed working with him or her, or that you learned something positive by working with him or her.

Saying Thank You

In my years of teaching and directing, I have received numerous thank yous, which I cherish.

Below are some ideas of how to say thank you, as you journey through life.

"Thanks for the great performance. Sometimes I feel alone and get scared. Now, by seeing your play, I know I'm not alone. I can talk to someone else and feel better. Thanks."

"I just wanted to express my thanks for four years of wonderful memories in the Theatre. I used my experiences to apply for a college scholarship. I received the scholarship."

"Over the years I've grown up with you in Theatre. You're a great inspiration, and I feel very honored to be a part of your life."

"So this is the last time we will dance with the audience. Thank you for all of the lessons and strength you have given to all of us."

"When I first started high school, I was lost among a sea of people. However, you found an individual in me and helped me recognize that I do have a voice in this world."

"Thanks for all of your support and love. I will always treasure what you taught me.

"You have created something that can never be destroyed. You believe in us and in Theatre. And you let us create the magic.

"I have so much respect for you as a teacher and a friend. Of all the classes I have taken in high school, Drama has been the most beneficial.

"Thank you for teaching me so much about Theatre, respect, and life."

"Your passion for Theatre and love of the art form has inspired me to be my best."

"Thanks for supporting the Mime Club!"

"Thank you for four of the best years of my life. I have overcome my obstacles because you were behind me with encouraging words and wanting the best for me. The theater is like a second home for me."

"Thank you for letting me do improvisation. I am not a good reader, so I feel like a rock star when I can improvise."

"I love you being my director. You make everything in Theatre an adventure."

"All the world's a stage, and you're the star!"

"The past years have prepared me for a wondrous stage of life that I'm about to enter. Thanks for the confidence."

"Now as I go along I take what you have taught me and share my thoughts with others. I want to teach."

"Thank you for casting me as a Researcher. I love how history and Theatre interact."

"You're there when we need you, and your love for us is true. You never make a big fuss, and I hope you know your message does reach us. You are a rock in a storm. You'll lend a hand and make us feel important. Words just cannot seem to express the feelings we have when we were distressed. You loved us all, and we feel needed. And through all the greatness we ever received, you never take credit. You smile. So this note is for you, our teacher, our friend, our mentor, our director."

Most recently I received a thank you from a fifth grade student who performed in my direction of *Annie, Jr.* She said, "Thank you for teaching me to make brave choices."

Perhaps the most amusing thank you was given to me after the El Dorado High School Theatre was named for me. A young student whom I had not formerly met burst out, "You're . . . you're. . . the Theater building, where I have my Drama class. Thank you. You're not dead."

If you ever have a chance to thank someone who helped you on your road to success in Theatre, I hope you will find imaginative ways to say Thanks. Mention your mentors in *Playbill*; tell your friends and students about your teachers; thank them on the Red Carpet.

- ~ Keep your passion. It will serve you well wherever life's road takes you.
- ~ Keep your dreams alive, making adjustments as you enjoy the journey.
- ~ Keep creating and reflecting.
- ~ Keep your resolution to be the best in whatever occupations you choose.
- ~ Keep working toward your dream.

At first, dreams seem impossible, then improbable, and eventually inevitable.

Christopher Reeve, actor

Thus my letter *The Student Actor Prepares: Acting for Life* ends with best wishes in the future and Break a Leg. It is just the beginning for your Acting for Life.

Gai Jones

Go confidently in the direction of your dreams. Live the life you've imagined.

Henry David Thoreau, author

ASSIGNMENT Your Journey   DATE:

Now is the time for you to tell your journey to the present date. Recall the first time you knew acting was in your future. Describe the event, the feelings, and any details. Continue your journey throughout your life to today's date. Periodically add to your journey.

All dreams can come true, if we have the courage to pursue them.
Walt Disney, film producer, director, animator, entrepreneur

INDEX